Revised 2nd Edition

FLAGSTAFF HIKES

and MOUNTAIN BIKE RIDES

by
Richard K. Mangum
and Sherry G. Mangum

HEXAGON
PRESS

Flagstaff, Arizona

NONLIABILITY STATEMENT:
While we have expended considerable effort to guarantee accuracy and have personally taken every one of these hikes, errors in field notes, transcription and typesetting can occur. Changes also occur on the land and some descriptions that were accurate when written may be inaccurate at press time. One storm, for example, can block a trail or road. In addition to the problems of accuracy, there is the problem of injury. It is always possible that hikers may sustain harm while on a hike. The authors, publishers and all those associated with this book, directly or indirectly, disclaim any liability for accidents, injuries, damages or losses that may occur to anyone using this book. The responsibility for good health and safety while hiking is that of the user.

*You may order copies of this book
from the publisher*

*Hexagon Press
300 E. Bennett Drive
Flagstaff, AZ 86001*

$17.00 each
Includes Tax and Shipping

Printed on recycled paper

TABLE OF CONTENTS

Nonliability Statement 2

Table of Contents 3

About the Authors 4

Tips on Flagstaff Hiking 5

How to Use This Book 6

Location Map 7

The Hikes, A-Z 8-217

Index 218-221

Mountain Biking, Trails Suitable For 222-224

Rules of the Trail 224

New For This Edition

Altitude	7200
7000	
Feet: 200	Easy
Miles: 1.0	

Mountain Bike Trails   Hike-In-A-Box   Improved Maps

Type entirely reset in a new, easier-to-read typeface.

ABOUT THE AUTHORS

RICHARD K. (DICK) MANGUM

Dick was born in Flagstaff. From childhood he has enjoyed getting out into the woods, canyons, hills and mountains surrounding his birthplace.

After graduating from Flagstaff High School, he attended the University of Arizona, where he obtained his BS and law degrees. He returned to Flagstaff and engaged in the general practice of law for fifteen years, then became a Superior Court Judge in Flagstaff in 1976, a position he still holds.

This book combines two of his favorite hobbies, hiking and writing. He wrote the articles, drew the maps and typeset the book.

SHERRY G. MANGUM

Although Sherry was not born in Flagstaff, she has lived there since she was seven years old. Like Dick, she enjoyed getting into the outdoors from the time she was a toddler.

Inheriting her love of photography from her parents, both professionals, she has refined her skills to produce the photographs used in this book.

Adept at all aspects of photography, she prefers landscapes. Her work has been published in books and periodicals since 1978. Sherry's camera of choice is a Nikon F4.

TIPS ON FLAGSTAFF HIKING

WATER

Don't count on finding water anywhere. Take your water with you.

HIGH ALTITUDE

Hikes in Flagstaff start at 7000 feet and go all the way up to 12, 643 feet, the highest point in Arizona. High altitudes mean:

1. You won't have the energy you are used to.
2. Hiking will be a lot harder on your heart.
3. You will be drier than usual.
4. You will sunburn more easily.
5. It will be much colder than normal, especially at night.
6. Alcohol is much more intoxicating.

THE TERRAIN

Flagstaff country is generally benign. You can get lost in the woods, but you won't if you stay on the hikes described in this book.

ROCK CLIMBING

We do not provide any rock climbing information. If you want to go rock climbing, you are on your own.

VARMINTS

Because Flagstaff is cool and has long winters, you won't find many mosquitoes. Pests like chiggers are absent. Ticks are rare in the high country. There are a few black widow spiders around, but no scorpions. Rattlesnakes are not entirely out of their range, but they are not plentiful. Even so, don't do anything stupid like reaching blindly under a rock or brush pile.

WEATHER

Flagstaff's regular snow season is anytime between Halloween and Easter. Don't count on hiking in the high country then. Summers are perfection, though rain is common between the Fourth of July and Labor Day.

ACCESS

Some of these hikes are totally unavailable in winter. Hikes in the high mountains are impossible then because of snow. The average snowfall in Flagstaff is 110 inches, and the mountains get even more. In addition to the obvious road problems caused by snow, some of the back roads are barred by locked gates during the winter. Call the Forest Service for road data.

HOW TO USE THIS BOOK

Alphabetical arrangement. The 105 hikes in this book are arranged from A-Z starting on page 8 and running to page 217.

Index. The index starts at page 218. It groups the hikes by geographical areas and by special features.

Layout. The text describing a hike and the map of the hike are on facing pages so that you can take in everything at once. You don't have to hunt to find maps.

Maps. The maps are not to scale but their proportions are generally correct except for a few that are schematic. **The main purpose of the maps is to get you to the trailhead.** The maps show mileage point-to-point, while the text gives cumulative totals, so you have both.

Larger scale maps. The maps in this book show each hike. For the big picture buy a Forest Service map.

Map Symbols. Shields and striped lines indicate paved roads. Boxes and solid lines indicate unpaved roads.

Bold type. When you see a trail name in **bold** type it means that the hike is described in this book.

Ratings. We show hikes rated as easy, moderate and hard. These ratings are based on our own reactions. We are middle-aged deskbound types, not highly conditioned athletes who never tire.

Adjust our ratings for your own fitness level. The altitude profile included with each map may be the best indicator of how hard a hike is.

Mileage. Driving distance was measured from Flagstaff City Hall located at the corner of Route 66 (Santa Fe) and Humphreys Street. All hikes start from this point and were clocked in our 1986 Toyota Tercel. Milepost locations are also shown on the maps (By MP) on highways that have them. Hike mileage was measured by a pedometer.

Altitude. We measured altitude with a pocket altimeter. These are not perfectly accurate, but the span of distance between the high and low points on a hike should be accurate.

Access roads. To reach many of these hikes you will have to travel unpaved roads, some of them rough. Our Tercel has 4-wheel drive but not much clearance. Our access ratings were based on how well the Tercel handled the roads. Some drives required a high clearance vehicle.

Safety. We avoid taking risks on hikes. None of these hikes requires risky climbing.

Grand Canyon. We have three hikes outside the boundary of Grand Canyon National Park but none inside because there are already several good books on the market describing hikes inside the Grand Canyon.

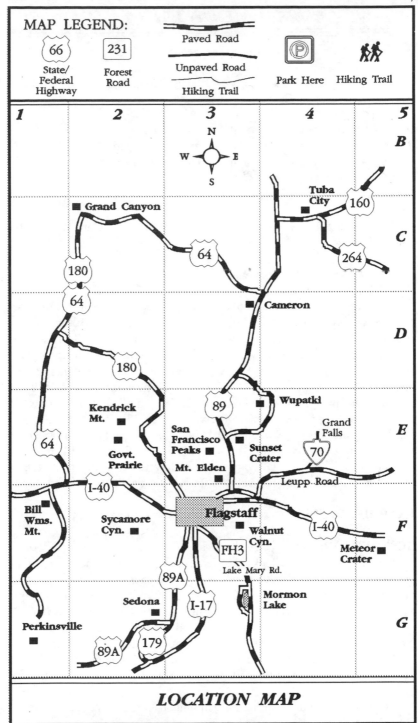

MAP LEGEND:

66 State/ Federal Highway

231 Forest Road

Paved Road

Unpaved Road

Hiking Trail

P Park Here

Hiking Trail

LOCATION MAP

A-1 MOUNTAIN

General Information
Location Map E2
Bellemont and Flagstaff West USGS Maps
Coconino Forest Service Map

Driving Distance One Way: 9.9 miles (Time 30 minutes)
Access Road: All cars, Last 4.9 miles good gravel road
Hiking Distance One Way: 1.0 miles (Time 40 minutes)
How Strenuous: Hard
Features: Landmark hill north of Flagstaff

NUTSHELL: This hike takes you to the top of a prominent landmark on the Flagstaff horizon.

DIRECTIONS:
From Flagstaff City Hall Go:
      West a block on Route 66 (Santa Fe), then south, beneath the railroad overpass on Sitgreaves Street. The street name will change to Milton Road as you go farther. At 0.50 miles you will reach a Y intersection. The right fork is named West Old US Highway 66. Take it. You will soon leave town, driving on a stretch of fabled Highway 66. At the 4.8 mile point you will merge onto Interstate-40 West. Look for Exit 190 at the 5.3 mile point, and take it. Turn right at the stop sign and take gravel road FR 506. Follow it to the 7.5 mile point, where you will be on top of Observatory Mesa. Here you will meet FR 515 forking to the right. Go left here, staying on the main road. It will curl around toward A-1 Mountain. At 8.2 miles there is a fork. Go left, again on the main road. At 9.7 you will come to a radio tower. Go beyond it on a rocky road to the 9.9 mile point, just before a fenced stock tank. Park at this point.

TRAILHEAD: There is a road going uphill to your left. Walk the road.

DESCRIPTION: Before you walk up the mountain, take a minute to look at the tank. You will see what looks like a large corrugated metal shed roof resting on the ground. It slopes downward. A gutter catches all the rain water that runs off and channels it into a pipe that flows into a large round metal tank from where it feeds out into a trough. This is an upscale version of the old rain barrel.
      As you walk this road uphill, you will wonder who made it and why. It goes as straight up a mountain as a road can, with impossibly steep grades for driving. Was it a fire break? The area around A-1 Mountain was the subject of one of the largest forest fires in Flagstaff's history in 1951. Dick remembers it well.
      A-1 Mountain is one of those mountains that does not have a single

top. You will reach the first knob at 0.20 miles. You can see a higher knob ahead of you. Here the road really gets steep. You climb it to the half mile point, where you are in the basin of a volcano. There is a right fork in the road at 0.6 miles. Take it. The road straight ahead dwindles down to nothing. The right fork takes you to a higher knob and ends on the north face of the mountain at about one mile. One of the main reasons for climbing a mountain is to have the views. Unfortunately, the forest on this top is so heavy that you only get glimpses of the countryside. Too bad, as this mountain is well located.

The Forest Service has done a massive thinning of the young pine trees around A-1, an example of its extensive silviculture program in the woods of northern Arizona.

This mountain was named after the Arizona Cattle Company, which had a huge ranch in the rangelands around the mountain in the 1880s. Its brand was the A-1.

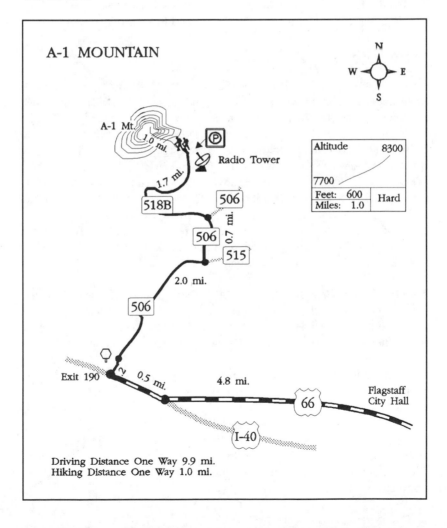

A. B. YOUNG TRAIL

General Information
Location Map F3
Munds Park and Wilson Mt. USGS Maps
Coconino Forest Service Map

Driving Distance One Way: 21.0 miles (Time 30 minutes)
Access Road: All cars, Paved all the way
Hiking Distance One Way: 1.6 miles (Time 80 minutes)
How Strenuous: Hard
Features: Views

NUTSHELL: This is a steep trail up the west wall of Upper Oak Creek Canyon near Bootlegger Campground, 21 miles south of Flagstaff.

DIRECTIONS:
From Flagstaff City Hall Go:
    West one block on Route 66 (Santa Fe) then left (south) on Sitgreaves Street under the railroad overpass. As you continue south you will see the street signs calling the street Milton Road, as Sitgreaves Street blends into Milton. At 1.7 miles you reach the intersection of Forest Meadows, where there is a traffic light. Here you turn right. You will see a sign for Highway 89A, which is the road you want. At the next corner turn left on Beulah and follow it out of town. Beulah will connect onto Highway 89A which is the road to Oak Creek Canyon and Sedona. At 13.8 miles (MP 390) you will reach the canyon rim and begin the winding descent. After you have completed the switchbacks and are on the canyon floor, drive to the 21.0 mile point (MP 383), the Bootlegger Campground. Parking is scarce in the campground and you will probably have to park on the shoulder of the highway.

TRAILHEAD: Walk through Bootlegger Campground, where you will see a trail going down to the creek. You must wade the creek or try to hop across it on boulders. There is a marked trailhead on the other shore. This is a maintained trail. You will see a rusty sign reading, "A B Young #100."

DESCRIPTION: Once you get across the creek you will see an old road running parallel to the creek. This old road was formerly the main road through Oak Creek Canyon and it is not what you want. Your trail goes uphill.
    The trail is a broad one at the beginning. It started its life as a cattle trail, but it was improved during the 1930s with CCC labor, so it is better engineered than many of the old cattle trails that are now hiking trails. It was widened and the grades were moderated so it is not as vertical as it was originally.

An interesting thing about the hike is that you experience three conspicuous life zones. Down at the creek, there is the lush riparian habitat. As you begin to climb, you get into a high desert life zone. At the top, you are in a pine forest. Once you rise above the trees at creekside, you are on an exposed face with no shade. This can be a very hot hike in the summer though it is in the cool upper canyon.

The hike is steep, so although the trail is a good one, it is a hard climb. You get some fine views as you go. At the top, you will notice that the trail continues. For the purposes of this book, we have ended the trail at the top, but you can continue southwest about 1.25 miles to a fire lookout tower. If this tower is occupied, the ranger probably will be very glad to have your company and share the tremendous views. The tower is the East Pocket Fire Lookout Tower, as this part of the rim is called East Pocket.

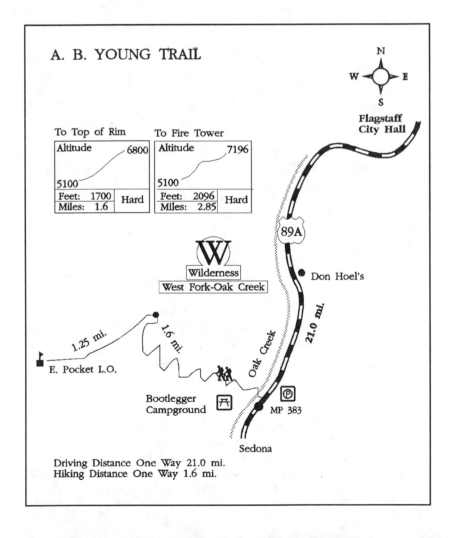

ANTELOPE HILLS

General Information
Location Map E2
Wing Mountain USGS Map
Coconino Forest Service Map

Driving Distance One Way: 18.5 miles (Time 40 minutes)
Access Road: All cars, Last 4.0 miles good gravel road
Hiking Distance One Way: 0.8 miles (Time 45 minutes)
How Strenuous: Moderate
Features: Views

NUTSHELL: This mountain 18.5 miles north of Flagstaff is located at the northeast end of Government Prairie and gives tremendous views of the prairie to the south.

DIRECTIONS:
From Flagstaff City Hall Go:
     North on Humphreys Street for 0.60 miles. Turn left at the stoplight onto Columbus Avenue and follow it around a big curve to the north. You will see the street signs call this road Columbus at first, then Ft. Valley Road and then Highway 180. Stay on Highway 180 to the 14.5 mile point (MP 230), where an unpaved road takes off to the left. Turn left onto this road, FR 245, and follow it to the 17.6 mile point where it intersects FR 171. Turn left onto FR 171 and follow it to the 18.25 mile point, where FR 812 goes off to the right. Turn right on FR 812 and take it to the 18.5 mile point. Park there.

TRAILHEAD: You will see the Antelope Hills to your right (north). You will also see a primitive road going to it and then going straight up the side of the mountain. Hike this road.

DESCRIPTION: We have included several of the hills surrounding Government Prairie in this book. While they all have features in common, each has its own distinct characteristics and personality. The Antelope Hills are the farthest north of the group, being situated at the north end of the prairie and close to Kendrick Peak.

     The trail was not made for hiking. It looks like kamikaze four-wheelers created it by charging straight up the mountain in a *falter-and-die* test of their machines. It is easy to follow, but it is not pleasant, as it goes straight up. An engineered trail would zigzag so as to moderate the grade.

     The Antelope Hills have two knobs. The southern knob that you climb first is bare. As a result it provides some great views. You can see particularly well to the south, where the whole sweep of the Government Prairie is in view, although your ability to see beyond the midpoint is restricted to the opening between Klostermeyer Hill and Rain Tank Hill. The views east are also fine, as you look onto the western side of the San Francisco Peaks. We were here in October and saw a great display of yellow and red aspen leaves on the slopes of the peaks.

Once you reach the top you will find that there is only a small drop in elevation to the saddle between the knobs and that it is easy to walk down to the saddle and then up to the end of the north knob. Sad to say, the views to the north are not good because of the heavy timber that grows on the north knob.

On your way up or down, check out the ruins of an old cabin and outbuildings at the foot of the hill to the east of the trail about thirty yards. You will also see a couple of platforms about eight feet high. These are part of a research project into the life of the prairie dog. There is a large prairie dog colony surrounding the platforms.

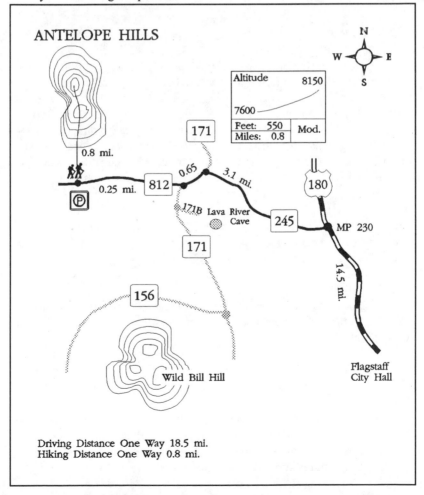

ANTELOPE HILLS

Altitude 8150
7600
Feet: 550 | Mod.
Miles: 0.8

0.8 mi.
0.25 mi. 812 0.65 3.1 mi. 171 180
171B Lava River Cave 245 MP 230
171
14.5 mi.
156
Wild Bill Hill
Flagstaff City Hall

Driving Distance One Way 18.5 mi.
Hiking Distance One Way 0.8 mi.

A(U)BINEAU CANYON

General Information
Location Map E3
Humphreys Peak and White Horse Hills USGS Maps
Coconino Forest Service Map

Driving Distance One Way: 24.9 miles (Time 50 minutes)
Access Road: All cars, Last 5.3 miles gravel, in medium condition
Hiking Distance One Way: 2.4 miles (Time 2 hours)
How Strenuous: Hard, Steep trail, High altitudes
Features: Alpine scenery, Vast views

NUTSHELL: This is a killer hike up the north face of the San Francisco Peaks about 25 miles north of Flagstaff.

DIRECTIONS:
From Flagstaff City Hall Go:
　　　　North on Humphreys Street, 0.60 miles to the stoplight. Turn left on Columbus Avenue and follow it north around a curve, where the road changes its name to Ft. Valley Road, and later is posted as Highway 180. At 19.6 miles (MP 235.1) turn right on Hart Prairie Road, FR 151. At 21.2 miles, turn left on FR 418 and continue on it to the 24.3 miles point, where you will see a sign for the Bear Jaw and Abineau Trails. The access road to the trailhead is marked FR 9123J. Turn right onto it and follow it to the 24.7 mile point, where you fork left, then to 24.9 miles, where you will reach the parking area. Park at the parking lot

TRAILHEAD: The cinder road on which you drove in is blocked by a row of boulders at the parking lot. Walk past the boulders and go on down to the end of the road. The trail takes off to your right, uphill.

DESCRIPTION:
　　　　You actually start this hike on a new connecting trail that climbs about 0.4 miles from the parking lot and then meets the Abineau Trail. Here you turn right and go uphill.
　　　　The Abineau Trail was used by sheepherders years ago as a means of taking their sheep to high summer pastures. The first mile of the trail was a road from Reese Tank. The Reese Tank part of the trail is now bypassed by the new routing.
　　　　The present trail starts rather mildly, moving through a nice forest, then the pitch changes to a steeper grade. Soon it will become obvious to you that you are in a canyon. Just above the 9000 foot level, the forest is entirely spruce and the trail is very rocky and steep.

Near the top, you break out into a small park, treeless in spots. The view is quite breathtaking. Ahead of you (south), is the towering top of Mt. Humphreys, highest point in Arizona at 12,643 feet. Behind you (north), you can see forever. From this spot it's a hard haul up to FR 146, the end of the trail, at 2.4 miles from the parking area. The portion of FR 146 from Jack Smith Spring to the east is also known as the Abineau Pipeline Trail.

If you want to do the loop, walk along east on FR 146 for a distance of 2.0 miles to the Bear Jaw Trail (signed) and go down it. This will add 2.0 miles to this hike, for a loop total of 7.05 miles, compared to a total of 4.8 miles going up and down the Abineau Trail only.

You will find alternative spellings for this trail. Most of the old sources show it as "Aubineau." A couple of decades ago the name began to appear as "Abineau." We show the alternative spelling so people will know it is the same trail.

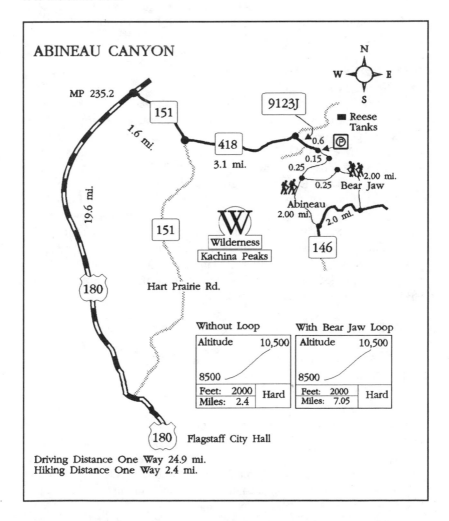

BABE'S HOLE

General Information
Location Map F2
Sycamore Point USGS Map
Coconino Forest Service Map

Personal Favorite

Driving Distance One Way: 24.1 miles (Time 1 hour)
Access Road: High clearance needed for last 1.8 miles
Hiking Distance One Way: 1.2 miles (Time 1 hour)
How Strenuous: Moderate
Features: Remote hidden spring, Virgin forests

NUTSHELL: Located 24.1 miles southwest of Flagstaff, this trail takes you to a remote and beautiful spring hidden away on the east side of Sycamore Canyon. **A personal favorite.**

DIRECTIONS:
From Flagstaff City Hall Go:
 West one block on Route 66 (Santa Fe), then left (south) beneath the railroad overpass on Sitgreaves Street. The street name will change to Milton Road as you go farther. At 0.50 miles you will reach a Y intersection. The right fork is named West Old US Highway 66. Take it. You will soon leave town. At 2.6 miles you will reach a road going to the left. This is the Woody Mountain Road, FR 231. Take it. It is paved about a mile and then turns into a cinder road. At 16.6 miles you will intersect FR 538. Turn right onto FR 538 and follow it to the 22.3 mile point, where it intersects the Kelsey Spring Road, FR 538G. Take 538G. This road is very rough. At 22.7 miles you hit another intersection where a road forks to the left. This is FR 538E, the Dorsey Spring Road. Stay on FR 538G and follow it to its end at 23.7 miles, where it meets FR 527A. Turn left onto the Kelsey Trail road to the 24.1 mile point, the parking area. This last 0.4 mile stretch is terrible, a real tire-eater.

TRAILHEAD: You will see a big sign at the parking area.

DESCRIPTION: This trail shares the same right of way with the **Kelsey Spring Trail**, and you have to pass through Kelsey Spring to reach Babe's Hole. The comments about the Kelsey Spring hike apply here.
 The parking lot is located right on the edge of the rim, so the trail immediately plunges down into the canyon. It is steep but not slippery. It passes through a beautiful forest, which gets more beautiful and interesting as you go.
 Kelsey Spring is easily reached in 0.5 miles. It is located on a shelf of level land. Enjoy it and then continue down the canyon on the same path

until you reach Babe's Hole.

As you leave Kelsey Spring, you enter an unusual life zone where the prevailing pines disappear, to be replaced with oaks and other deciduous trees. The area seems to get a lot of moisture, so the vegetation is heavy.

At Babe's hole several hill folds come together to make a small protected pocket of land. You can see why it got the name "hole" as it really is a small and enclosed area, but "hole" is a word that is used disparagingly and in this sense it does not fit at all, for Babe's Hole is one of the most beautiful places we have seen in Arizona. It looks otherwordly, with many bent trees overarching and protecting the spring, which is lined with a small circle of rocks and roofed over with poles. It is very quiet. A fantastic place.

From Babe's Hole you can continue downhill another 0.15 miles, where there is a trail junction. The **Kelsey-Winter Trail** takes off to the left, to **Dorsey Spring** and then **Winter Cabin Spring**, while the trail to Geronimo Spring goes down to the bottom of the canyon.

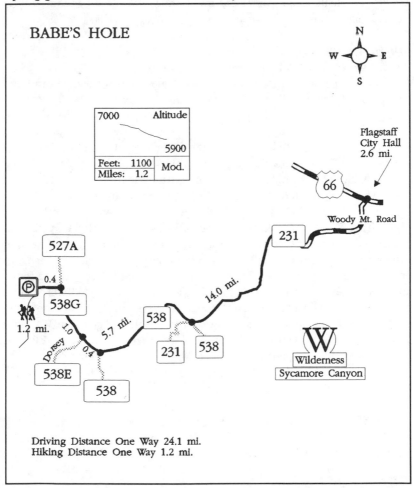

BABE'S HOLE

BEALE ROAD, GOVERNMENT MT., WEST

General Information
Location Map E2
Parks, Moritz Ridge and Williams USGS Maps
Kaibab (Williams) Forest Service Map

Driving Distance One Way: 34.7 miles (Time 1.5 hours)
Access Road: All cars, Last 17.0 miles medium gravel road
Hiking Distance One Way: 2.5 miles (Time 1.5 hours)
How Strenuous: Easy
Features: Auto tour and hike over historic road to spring with petroglyphs

NUTSHELL: This is a combination auto tour and hike following portions of the historic Beale Road, ending at Laws Spring, where there are interesting petroglyphs.

DIRECTIONS:
From Flagstaff City Hall Go:
        West a block on Route 66 (Santa Fe), then south, beneath the railroad overpass on Sitgreaves Street. The street name will change to Milton Road as you go farther. At 0.50 miles you will reach a Y intersection. The right fork is named West Old US Highway 66. Take it. You will soon leave town, driving on a stretch of fabled Highway 66. At the 4.8 mile point you will merge onto Interstate-40 West. Look for Exit 185, "Transwestern Rd., Bellemont" and take it. It is at the 10.8 mile point. From the exit turn right and go to the frontage road, where you turn left onto FR 146. You are now following another stretch of U.S. 66. Stay on this to the 18 mile point, where you will see FR 107 fork right. Take FR 107 and follow it to the 24.3 mile point, across Government Prairie, where you will see a post with a metal camel symbol at the intersection with FR 100. These posts will now guide you and you will find them at every intersection. They mark the Beale Road. Turn left on FR 107 and go to the 26.8 mile point, where you meet FR 141. Turn right and go to the 27.1 mile point, where you turn left and go to the 27.7 mile point. Turn right here and go to the 28.5 mile point. Here you turn left on FR 97 and go to the 30.9 mile point. Take a left and go to the 31.8 mile point, where you will meet FR 713. Turn right on FR 713 and drive it to the 34.5 mile point. Here you will turn left on FR 730 and drive to the 34.7 mile point, where you will see a camel post with the symbol burned on. Park here.

TRAILHEAD: The Beale Road markers with the camel burned on (rather than metal signs) indicate foot trails. The post where you parked marks the beginning of the hike.

DESCRIPTION: The Forest Service, with the help of Jack Smith, who has devoted years to locating the Beale Road, has done a marvelous job of marking the road. Both the auto tour and the foot trail are easy to follow.

You will hike through woods where you sometimes see the Beale Road and sometimes don't. The way is clearly shown with cairns, blazes and posts. You will cross FR 136 in about two thirds of a mile and eventually emerge onto an open flat where the **Beale Road—Laws Spring** hike starts, at 1.5 miles. If you have not seen Laws Spring, then by all means keep following the markers for another mile.

We think it is great fun to follow this old road and put ourselves in the places of the pioneers. What hardships they endured! To have gone through here in 1857 and laid out a route that had water, grass and terrain passable by wagons was a great feat and Beale carried it off nobly.

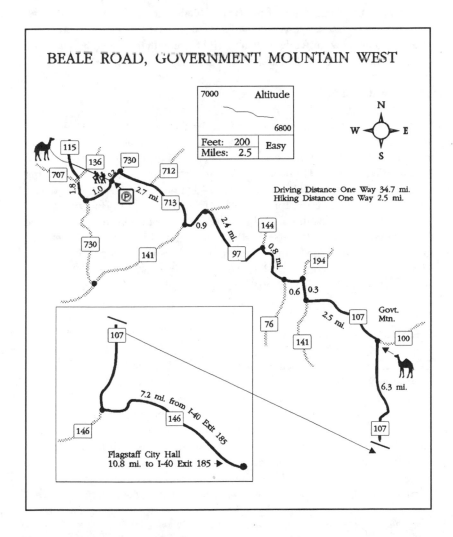

BEALE ROAD ON GOVT. PRAIRIE

General Information
Location Map E2
Parks and Wing Mt. USGS Maps
Kaibab (Williams) Forest Service Map

Driving Distance One Way: 24.3 miles (Time 40 minutes)
Access Road: All cars, Last 11 miles good gravel road
Hiking Distance One Way: 2.3 miles (Time 1.5 hours))
How Strenuous: Easy
Features: Historic road, Views

NUTSHELL: This stretch of the Beale Road crosses Government Prairie. The old wagon tracks are visible and have been marked. A hike across the prairie would be worthwhile in its own right, but with the added bonus of the wagon road, it becomes a fascinating experience.

DIRECTIONS:
From Flagstaff City Hall Go:
West a block on Route 66 (Santa Fe), then south, beneath the railroad overpass on Sitgreaves Street. The street name will change to Milton Road as you go farther. At 0.50 miles you will reach a Y intersection. The right fork is named West Old US Highway 66. Take it. You will soon leave town, driving on a stretch of fabled Highway 66. At the 4.8 mile point you will merge onto Interstate-40 West. Look for Exit 185, "Transwestern Rd., Bellemont" and take it. It is at the 10.8 mile point. From the exit turn right and go to the frontage road, where you turn left onto FR 146. You are now following another stretch of U.S. 66. Stay on this to the 18 mile point, where you will see FR 107 fork right. Take FR 107 and follow it to the 24.3 mile point, where FR 107 and FR 100 join. Park off FR 107 on the right (east) just below the intersection.

TRAILHEAD: At the gate.

DESCRIPTION: The Beale Road was scouted in 1857 by a government sponsored party led by Lt. Edward Beale. It was this *government* sponsorship leading to the establishment of a *government* road that gave the name Government Prairie. Beale returned with a work party in 1858 and 1859 to develop the road. Thereafter it was used as a major transcontinental highway until the coming of the railroad in 1882. On the first expedition Beale used twenty camels, an experiment designed to see how well they could handle American deserts. This explains why a camel is used as a symbol for the road. You will see the camel burned onto the posts that mark the trail. Beale loved the camels but the cowboys (camelboys?) hated them and they never caught on.

At the junction of FR 107 and FR 100 you will see a fence to your right with a gate. Go through the gate to begin walking the Beale Road. You will pick up markers there. The right of way is marked with posts, rock cairns, blazes and brass caps. In 0.15 miles you will come upon an old homestead to your left. There isn't much left , but you can make out the outlines of stones that were used as footings.

At 0.3 miles you will leave the road you are walking and go across country. This takes you from open land, then through woods. At 1.3 you break out onto the main part of the prairie where you will see the wagon tracks very clearly and follow them the rest of the way. You cross FR 793 at the 1.4 mile point. When you reach the 2.3 mile point the road leaves the prairie and enters a wooded area in front of **Wild Bill Hill**. We end the hike here (the road continues) as crossing the prairie makes a good day hike.

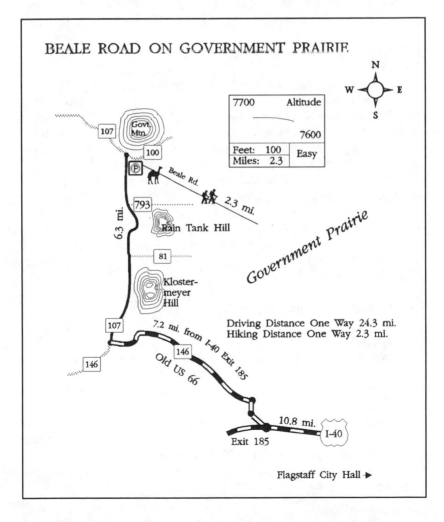

BEALE ROAD ON GOVERNMENT PRAIRIE

7700	Altitude
	7600
Feet: 100	Easy
Miles: 2.3	

Govt. Mtn.

Beale Rd.

2.3 mi.

6.3 mi.

Rain Tank Hill

Kloster-meyer Hill

Driving Distance One Way 24.3 mi.
Hiking Distance One Way 2.3 mi.

7.2 mi. from I-40 Exit 185

Old US 66

Government Prairie

10.8 mi.

I-40

Exit 185

Flagstaff City Hall ➤

BEALE ROAD–LAWS SPRING

General Information
Location Map E2
Squaw Mountain and Williams, USGS Maps
Kaibab (Williams) Forest Service Map

Driving Distance One Way: 36.25 miles (Time 1 hour)
Access Road: All cars, Last 9 miles good gravel
Hiking Distance One Way: 1.0 miles (Time 40 minutes)
How Strenuous: Easy
Features: Historical 1850s wagon route, Spring with petroglyphs

NUTSHELL: This hike takes you over a mile of the historical Beale Road and stops at Laws Spring, where you will see rock art.

DIRECTIONS:
From Flagstaff City Hall Go:
　　　　West a block on Route 66 (Santa Fe), then south, beneath the railroad overpass on Sitgreaves Street. The street name will change to Milton Road as you go farther. At 0.50 miles you will reach a Y intersection. The right fork is named West Old US Highway 66. Take it. You will soon leave town, driving on a stretch of fabled Highway 66. At the 4.8 mile point you will merge onto Interstate-40 West. Drive I-40 West to the 24.1 miles point (MP 172), where you will take Exit 171 for Pittman Valley. Turn left at the stop sign and take paved road FR 74, toward the Compressor Station. The paving will end at 27.3 miles. At 31.8 miles you will intersect FR 141 and go right on it. At 32.3 miles you will see a sign for Boulin Tank and intersect FR 730. Turn left on FR 730 and follow it to the 34.5 mile point where you join FR 115. Turn left onto FR 115 and follow it to the 36.25 miles point. There you will see a 4 x 4 post with a camel symbol. Park nearby.

TRAILHEAD: The camel post is the trailhead.

DESCRIPTION: The Beale Road was an heroic undertaking. The United States acquired this part of Arizona in 1848 after the Mexican War and Congress sent Beale to explore it and find a travel route across northern Arizona to California in 1857. Beale's party included camels to deal with deserts. Beale located a good route roughly following the thirty-fifth parallel. In 1858 and 1859 he returned under a Congressional grant and developed the road for travel. About seventy-five percent of the old road has been located, thanks largely to the efforts of Flagstaff's Jack Beale Smith. The Forest Service joined with Smith in the project of marking the road and their efforts made this hike possible.

As you begin the hike, look across the field to the west and imagine you were Beale in 1857. Your first task, as always, was to wind up the day's march at a water hole. Where would it be in this landscape? Begin hiking and you will find out. The way is well marked with posts, cairns, brass caps, blazes and ribbons. The country is flat and open, surrounded by mountains and hills.

At about a half mile you will cross a little drainage with a show of green, but this has no available water. Keep going. You leave the field and enter a forested area. As you near the one mile mark, you will see tall trees and a small canyon. Then you see basalt rocks forming a basin. Keep going, and *voila*, there it is, a rock tank with a pond in the bottom. The water is muddy but it is dependable. Mission accomplished.

The words, "Laws Spring" were chiseled into a rock in 1859 by a member of Beale's crew. Laws was a officer in the party. Look carefully and you will see other rock art, both ancient Indian and modern. The Forest Service has placed a nice explanatory plaque on the face of a boulder at the spring.

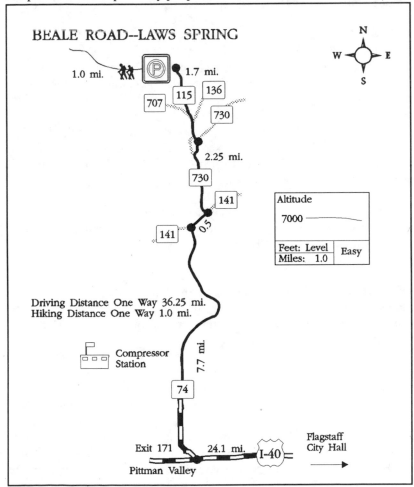

BEAR JAW CANYON

General Information
Location Map E3
Humphreys Peak and White Horse Hills USGS Maps
Coconino Forest Service Map

Driving Distance One Way: 24.9 miles (Time 50 minutes)
Access Road: All cars, Last 5.3 miles gravel, in medium condition
Hiking Distance One Way: 2.65 miles (Time 2 hours)
How Strenuous: Hard, Steep trail, High altitudes
Features: Alpine scenery, Vast views

NUTSHELL: This is a killer hike up the north face of the San Francisco Peaks about 25 miles north of Flagstaff.

DIRECTIONS:
From Flagstaff City Hall Go:
　　　　North on Humphreys Street, 0.60 miles to the stoplight. Turn left on Columbus Avenue and follow it north around a curve, where it changes name to Ft. Valley Road, and then to Highway 180. At 19.6 miles (MP 235.1) turn right on Hart Prairie Road, FR 151. At 21.2 miles, turn left on FR 418 and continue on it to the 24.3 mile point, where you will see a sign for the Bear Jaw Trail. The road to the trailhead is marked FR 9123J. Turn right on it and follow it to 24.7 miles and fork left, then to the parking area, at 24.9 miles. You will see a parking area to your left.

TRAILHEAD: The cinder road on which you drove in is blocked by a row of boulders at the parking place. Walk past the boulders and continue 0.15 miles to the end of the road. The trailhead takes off to the right (south) uphill there.

DESCRIPTION: The Forest Service recently changed the trailhead from its old location at Reese Tanks to this new location. The information in the first printing of this book was for the former trail layout. The new alignment shortens the hike and makes it less demanding.
　　　　From the end of the road, you will hike up a trail segment, newly built, which meets the Abineau Trail in about 0.25 miles. From here you walk a 0.25 mile leg of the old Abineau Trail to the left.
　　　　At the end, 0.65 miles from the parking area, you are at the old Bear Jaw-Abineau trailhead. Go right, uphill. From here the trail moves through some beautiful woods, featuring heavy stands of aspens. You will pass through some old sheepherder camps, complete with herders' names (mostly Spanish and Basque) carved on the aspens. The trail is quite steep and just goes up and

up without respite.

You will climb through these woods for about 2.0 miles, to the end of the trail at the 10,500 foot point, where it terminates at Forest Road FR 146, and you will see a sign there showing the Abineau Trail 2.0 miles to your right (west). You can return the way you came for a 5.3 mile total hike or you can make the hike a 7.05 mile loop using FR 146 as a connector to the Abineau Trail.

To use the Abineau loop, walk west (your right) on FR 146 a distance of 2.0 miles, a beautiful and fairly level walk through a magnificent forest.

The Abineau Trail intersects FR 146 in a treeless park, a great view platform. You will see that FR 146 continues beyond the Abineau connection and ends against the side of Mt. Humphreys where some digging has taken place, probably the City trying to capture a spring.

The Abineau Trail is 2.4 miles to the parking lot, the upper portion being very steep and rocky.

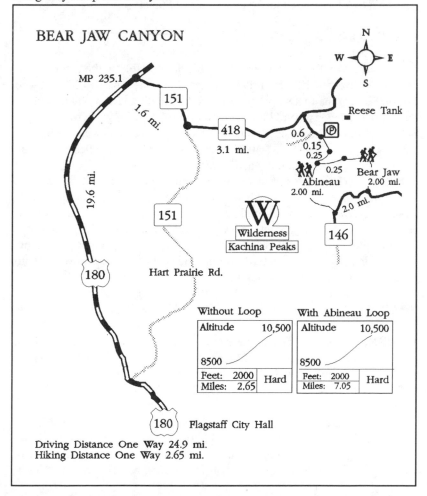

BENHAM TRAIL

General Information
Location Map F1
Bill Williams Mountain USGS Map
Kaibab (Williams District) Forest Service Map

Driving Distance One Way: 38.4 miles (Time 60 minutes)
Access Road: All cars, All paved except last 0.20 miles
Hiking Distance One Way: 4.5 miles (Time 2.75 hours)
How Strenuous: Hard
Features: Beautiful forest, High mountain, Views

NUTSHELL: This hike takes you to the top of Bill Williams Mountain outside the Town of Williams, about 30 miles west of Flagstaff.

DIRECTIONS:
From Flagstaff City Hall Go:
       West on Route 66 (Santa Fe) a block, then follow the curve left on Sitgreaves Street under the railroad overpass. The street name will change to Milton Road at the first stoplight. Keep going south on Milton until you are out of town, headed toward Phoenix on I-17. At 2.0 miles you will reach Exit 340B, which is an access ramp onto I-40 West. The sign will say, "Williams and Los Angeles." Get onto I-40 West and stay on it for 31.6 miles, where you will see the Williams Exit, #165. Get off on that and at the stop sign, go left to Williams. Go into downtown Williams and turn left at Fourth Street at the 34.5 miles point, where you will see a sign reading, "Ski Area, White Horse Lake." Follow Fourth Street south, which takes you out of town into a valley. Here the road is still paved and is designated FR 173, the Perkinsville Road. At 38.2 miles turn right onto the trail access road. You will see a sign reading, "H.L. Benham Ranch 0.5" here. Take this road about 0.20 miles to a fork. Turn right and park in the trail parking area.

TRAILHEAD: You will see a sign marking the trailhead at the parking area.

DESCRIPTION: The sign at the trailhead indicates that this trail was built in 1920. It was abandoned in 1951 when the nearby FR 111 (the present road to the top) was built. It was reopened as a recreational trail in 1976. The trail was named after H. L. Benham, who was the Ranger for the Williams District in 1910-1911.
       It is hard to tell whether this trail was built as a road or as a pack trail. There are places where it is wide enough for a road, but the upper half looks only wide enough to have been a pack or foot trail. In any event, the trail was well engineered so that it climbs 2000 feet gradually. This means a lot of

zigging and zagging.

The trail goes up the east and south faces of the mountain. It does not get as much moisture as the **Bill Williams Mountain Trail** on the north side. Consequently, the forest is mostly pine with a lot of oak, until you reach aspen groves in the last mile. You will encounter a point in the first mile where logging has taken place, an ugly shock, and a poignant contrast to the unspoiled forest on either side.

At about the 1.5 mile point you will enter into a gorgeous grove of oaks, really special. Mile posts have been inserted along the trail to mark your way. According to Dick's pedometer, they are accurate. You will cross the road, FR 111, five times. The fifth time is at the 4.0 mile point, where the trail ends. You then walk the road the final half mile to get to the lookout tower. Until you reach the 3.5 mile point, views are scarce because the forest is so heavy. At the top, however, the views are glorious.

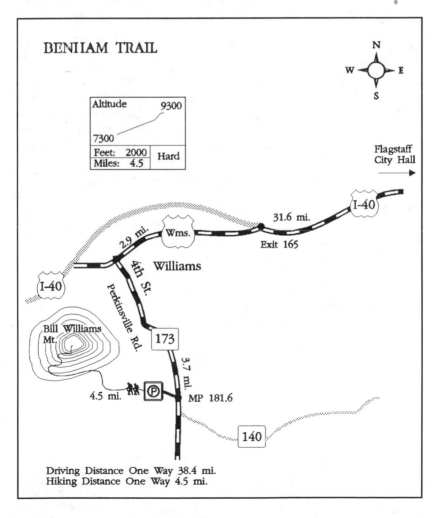

BENHAM TRAIL

Altitude 9300
7300
Feet: 2000 Hard
Miles: 4.5

Flagstaff
City Hall →

I-40

31.6 mi.
Exit 165

Wms.

2.9 mi.

Williams

I-40

4th St.

Perkinsville Rd.

Bill Williams Mt.

173

3.7 mi.

4.5 mi. Ⓟ

MP 181.6

140

Driving Distance One Way 38.4 mi.
Hiking Distance One Way 4.5 mi.

BILL WILLIAMS MOUNTAIN TRAIL

General Information
Location Map F1
Bill Williams Mountain USGS Map
Kaibab (Williams District) Forest Service Map

Driving Distance One Way: 36.5 miles (Time 50 minutes)
Access Road: All cars, All paved except last 0.20 miles
Hiking Distance One Way: 4.4 miles (Time 3 hours)
How Strenuous: Hard
Features: Beautiful forest, High mountain, Views

NUTSHELL: This hike takes you to the top of Bill Williams Mountain outside the Town of Williams, about 30 miles west of Flagstaff.

DIRECTIONS:
From Flagstaff City Hall Go:
　　　　West on Route 66 (Santa Fe) a block, then follow the curve left on Sitgreaves Street under the railroad overpass. The street name will change to Milton Road at the first stoplight. Keep going south on Milton until you are out of town, headed toward Phoenix on I-17. At 2.0 miles you will reach Exit 340B, which is an access ramp onto I-40 West. The sign will say, "Williams and Los Angeles." Get onto I-40 West and stay on it for 31.6 miles, where you will see the Williams Exit, #165. Get off on that and at the stop sign, go left to Williams. Go into downtown Williams. The main street through town is divided. You will be on Railroad Avenue headed west. Stay on this through town. At the 35.7 miles point you will be on a frontage road. There you will see a paved road turning left and going uphill toward Days Inn motel. Take this lefthand road. At 36.3 miles you will reach the turn for the Forest Service's Williams District Ranger Office (also called Camp Clover). Go left at this turn and head toward the camp. At 36.5 miles, just before the fence going into the compound, you will see a road going left. It is signed. Turn left on this road and follow it a short distance until you see a trailhead sign to your right. Pull in there and park.

TRAILHEAD: You will see a sign marking the trailhead at the parking area.

DESCRIPTION: The sign advises the hiker that this trail was built in 1902 as a toll trail and is 3.8 miles long. We presume that this was a toll trail for horses, as there were no automobiles in Williams then and hikers would have been unwilling to pay a toll. It makes a fine modern hiking trail.

　　　　Dick hikes with a pedometer to measure distance, and found a serious discrepancy in the "official" mileage for this hike. The 3.8 miles indicated by the sign takes you to the point where the trail intersects FR 111, the road to the lookout tower, yet the mileposts along the trail treat this segment as being 3.0 miles long. From FR 111 it is another 0.6 miles to the tower.

Whatever the mileage, this is a steep and strenuous trail. The first mile is fairly gradual, going through a nice pine forest, where we were lucky enough to see a bobcat strolling along in front of us. From that point, the trail climbs sharply and the forest changes character, becoming almost a rainforest, with lots of fir and spruce and incredible stands of tall aspen.

Because of this heavy forest you won't get any views until you reach FR 111, but from that point upward, the views are marvellous. Try to make it to the tower, for the views from there are as good as any in the region, since the mountain is situated so that you see interesting country all around.

Using two cars, you can park one at the top for an easy one-way hike or park one at the Bill Williams Trailhead and the other at the **Benham Trailhead**, doing both trails in one day.

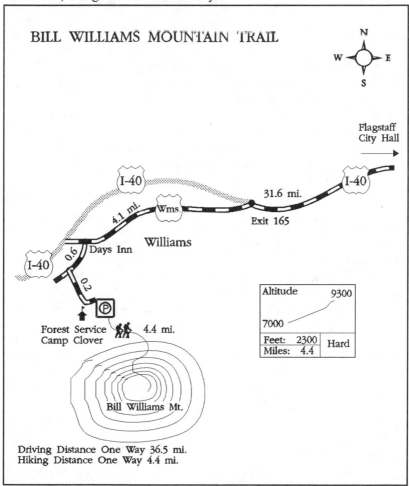

BILL WILLIAMS MOUNTAIN TRAIL

Driving Distance One Way 36.5 mi.
Hiking Distance One Way 4.4 mi.

BISMARCK LAKE ELK PRESERVE

General Information
Location Map E3
Humphreys Peak and Wing Mountain USGS Maps
Coconino Forest Service Map

Driving Distance One Way: 17.2 miles (Time 35 minutes)
Access Road: All cars, Last 7 miles gravel, in good condition
Hiking Distance One Way: 1 mile (Time 30 minutes)
How Strenuous: Easy
Features: Aspen groves, Meadow views

NUTSHELL: Located on the San Francisco Peaks, about 15 miles north of Flagstaff, this short, easy walk displays the alpine beauty of the area.

DIRECTIONS:
From Flagstaff City Hall Go:
 North on Humphreys Street for 0.60 miles, to the stoplight. Then take a left onto a street marked Columbus Avenue, which changes to Ft. Valley Road as it makes a curve to the north. Outside the city limits, the road becomes Highway 180, a major route to the Grand Canyon. At 10.2 miles (MP 225.1), turn right onto FR 151, the Hart Prairie Road, and follow it to the 16.6 point, where it intersects FR 627. Take FR 627 to the right and drive to the 17.2 mile point, where you will find a fenced parking place. Park there.

TRAILHEAD: You will see a sign at a gate in the parking area fence.

DESCRIPTION: The Hart Prairie Road is a loop road that intersects Highway 180 at two points. One point is 10.2 miles north of Flagstaff and the other is 19.6 miles north. If you hear someone talking about getting to a road that is off the Hart Prairie Road, be sure to find out whether they are talking about the upper or lower end of the loop.
 To make this hike, you walk through the fence and follow a road which has been closed, as no vehicle traffic is allowed inside the Bismarck Lake Elk Preserve. At 0.3 miles you will come to Ki Tank. Don't take the fork to the right that appears there. At 0.7 miles, the trail forks again. Take the left fork, which goes uphill to a grassy ledge.
 When you top out on the ledge you find yourself on a sizable meadow ringed with aspen, pine and fir. The lake is hardly deserving of the name most of the time, usually appearing as a cattle tank about 20 feet in diameter except during the spring thaw, when it is at its fullest. In dry Arizona any body of water more than ten feet across is likely to be called a lake.
 The forest is beautiful here. The area gets a lot of moisture, so in

addition to the trees, there are many ferns, mosses, mushrooms and flowers.

The hike is an easy one for the Peaks area, as the climb is gentle, the trail is short, and the altitude is not terribly high.

This is a perfect place for elk, as they have everything they need here: grass, water and shelter. Best time to see them is just at dusk. We have been here three times and have heard but not seen elk each time. If you are in elk country in the autumn, you may hear the bull elks bugling. We have heard this twice at Bismarck Lake Elk Preserve, both times in mid-October. Once it erupted from a thick grove of trees nearby and we just about jumped out of our skins. The elk bugle is a weird sound and if you are unprepared for it, you would have no idea what you are hearing. To us it sounds rather like the hokey trumpeting of elephants that you would hear in a Tarzan movie. The bulls, normally passive, are quite aggressive when they are bugling, so don't bugle back.

The Preserve was created in 1987.

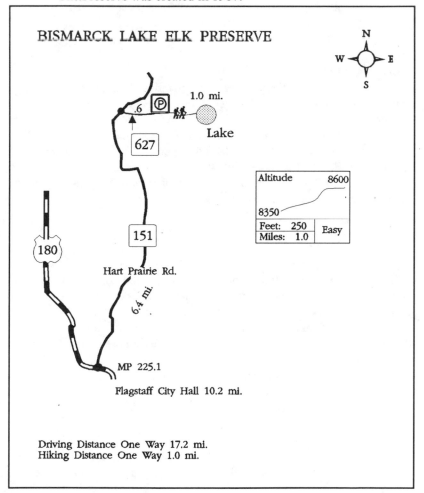

BISMARCK LAKE ELK PRESERVE

1.0 mi.

Lake

627

151

180

Hart Prairie Rd.

6.4 mi.

MP 225.1

Flagstaff City Hall 10.2 mi.

Altitude 8600

8350

| Feet: | 250 | Easy |
| Miles: | 1.0 | |

Driving Distance One Way 17.2 mi.
Hiking Distance One Way 1.0 mi.

BROOKBANK TRAIL

General Information
Location Map E3
Humphreys Pk. & Sunset Crater W. USGS Maps
Coconino Forest Service Map

Driving Distance One Way: 6.5 miles (Time 30 minutes)
Access Road: All cars, Last 2.9 miles medium gravel mountain road
Hiking Distance One Way: 5.0 miles (Time 3 hours)
How Strenuous: Hard
Features: Views, Forests

NUTSHELL: This is a marked and maintained trail that starts at a point on the Elden Lookout Road and climbs to Sunset Park near the top of Mt. Elden north of Flagstaff.

DIRECTIONS:
From Flagstaff City Hall Go:
North on Humphreys Street for 0.60 miles. Turn left at the stoplight onto Columbus Avenue and follow it around a big curve to the north. You will see the street signs call this road Columbus Avenue at first, then Ft. Valley Road and then Highway 180. Stay on Highway 180 to the 3.1 miles point (MP 218.6), where the Schultz Pass Road, FR 420, goes to the right. Follow FR 420. At the 3.6 mile point it curves left where you will see the unpaved Elden Lookout Road (FR 557) going straight. Take the right fork and follow FR 557 to the 6.5 mile point, where you will park.

TRAILHEAD: There is a closed road to your left. The sign is located about twenty yards up this road.

DESCRIPTION: This trail is part of the Dry Lake Hills\Mt. Elden trail system, so it is marked and maintained. The trail goes up a closed ranch road for about a mile, beyond which it turns into a footpath. At the 1.1 mile point you will reach a trail junction. The unmarked trail to your left goes uphill to the **Dry Lake Hills** trail, which is not part of the trail system, but is written up in this book.

Take the right fork here. It will take you around a long loop that hugs the shoulder of one of the hills. At the toe of the loop you will have some good views of the San Francisco Peaks. Then you will curve south and head toward Mt. Elden. You are walking through high north-facing forests of spruce and fir.

At the 3.4 mile point you will reach a trail junction. Here you want to turn right onto the Sunset Trail. The signs here are confusing, so please follow our directions. Our description differs from the Forest Service one.

The trail will take you down a fold between the Dry Lake Hills and Mt. Elden and will then climb up a slope of Mt. Elden through a very nice alpine forest. You will reach a ridge crest on Elden in about a mile. From here the trail goes over the crest a short distance and then follows along on the shoulder of the crest to Sunset Park.

This last half mile was part of a huge man-made forest fire in 1978. Take a good look and contemplate. Only now is the forest starting to heal. One good thing came of the fire, which is that the mountain here is bare so you can get clear views to the east. They are spectacular.

We end the trail at Sunset Park, where you will find another trail junction just above the Elden Lookout Road. You can continue for a mile to the lookout tower, but that makes a long hike. We prefer this hike as a two-car shuttle, parking one at the 6.5 mile point and the other at the 9.4 mile point on the Elden Lookout Road and then hiking down.

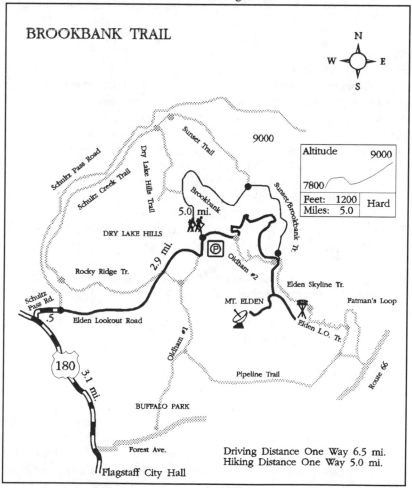

BROOKBANK TRAIL

Driving Distance One Way 6.5 mi.
Hiking Distance One Way 5.0 mi.

BULL BASIN TRAIL

General Information
Location Map E2
Kendrick Peak, Moritz Ridge and Wing Mt. USGS Maps
Coconino Forest Service Map

Driving Distance One Way: 34.55 miles (Time 1.25 hours)
Access Road: All cars, Last 20 miles good gravel road
Hiking Distance One Way: 4.5 miles (Time 3.0 hours)
How Strenuous: Hard
Features: Fine forests, Ten thousand foot peak, Views

NUTSHELL: This trail, located 34.5 miles north of Flagstaff, takes you up the north side of Kendrick Peak, the second highest mountain in the region.

DIRECTIONS:
From Flagstaff City Hall Go:
      North on Humphreys Street for 0.60 miles. Turn left at the stoplight onto Columbus Avenue and follow it around a big curve to the north. You will see the street signs call this road Columbus at first, then Ft. Valley Road and then Highway 180. Stay on Highway 180 to the 14.5 miles point (MP 230), where an unpaved road takes off to the left. Turn left onto this road, FR 245, and follow it to the 17.6 mile point where it intersects FR 171. Turn right on FR 171 and follow it to the 24.8 mile point, where you will see a sign for the Pumpkin Trail. Go just beyond this, to the 24.9 mile point and turn left on FR 171. Follow it to the 27.7 mile point, where it meets FR 144 and turn right on FR 144, taking it to the 29.2 miles point, where it intersects FR 90. Turn right on FR 90 and drive it to the 33.9 mile point, where you will see FR 90A to the right. Take FR 90A to the 34.45 mile point, where you will see a sign marking a road to the right to the Bull Basin trailhead. You can see the parking lot from this point. Turn right, downhill, and you will reach the parking area at 34.55 miles.

TRAILHEAD: Well marked with a sign at the parking area.

DESCRIPTION: There are three trails that take you to the top of Kendrick Peak: The Bull Basin Trail, The **Kendrick Mt. Trail** and The **Pumpkin Trail**. We think Bull Basin is the best, with Pumpkin running a poor third.
      From the parking area you will walk a closed road along the west side of Bull Basin, a large grassy meadow. At 0.9 miles you will come to a trail junction where you will see a trail to the right. The Bull Basin Trail is marked here but the other trail is not. The unmarked trail is The **Connector Trail**.

Up to this point the land has been flat. Beyond it you begin to climb the mountain, with the trail following some old logging roads up to the 1.5 mile point. The forest on this north side of the mountain has as many spruces and firs as pines and seems to have recovered from logging better than pure pine forests do.

Beyond the 1.5 mile point the trail becomes a footpath and begins to climb steeply. The trail is well designed, however, so that the grades are not too steep and the footing is good. The pines begin to thin out and soon you are in a forest of spruce, fir and aspen. We were here in October when the aspen leaves had yellowed and many had fallen, carpeting the forest floor with gold.

At 3.0 miles you will emerge onto a small saddle and follow a ridgeline to the top. From here the forest is all spruce and there are many huge boulders. You will emerge from this dark forest at 4.00 miles at the Old Ranger Cabin, built in 1911-1912 and in remarkably good shape. A trail log is kept inside. From the cabin it is another half mile to the lookout tower.

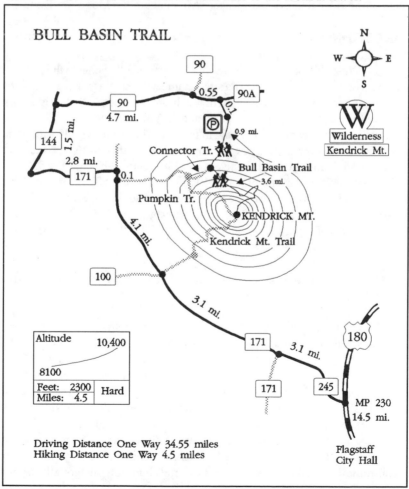

CASNER MOUNTAIN TRAIL NORTH

General Information
Location Map F2
Loy Butte, Sycamore Point USGS Maps
Coconino Forest Service Map

Driving Distance One Way: 28.75 miles (Time 60 minutes)
Access Road: High clearance only, Last 25.0 miles unpaved, rough spots
Hiking Distance One Way: 4.0 miles (Time 2.5 hours)
How Strenuous: Moderate
Features: Views

NUTSHELL: Located 28.75 miles southwest of Flagstaff, this hike follows the top of a ridge that connects Casner Mountain to the Mogollon Rim.

DIRECTIONS:
From Flagstaff City Hall Go:
    West a block on Route 66 (Santa Fe), then south, beneath the railroad overpass on Sitgreaves Street. The street name will change to Milton Road as you go farther. At 0.50 miles you will reach a Y intersection. The right fork is named West Old US Highway 66. Take it. You will soon leave town. At 2.6 miles you will reach a road going to the left. This is the Woody Mountain Road, FR 231. Take it. It is paved about a mile and then turns into a cinder road. At 16.6 miles you will intersect FR 538. Turn right onto FR 538 and follow it to the 25.85 mile point, where FR 538B branches off to the right. Take FR 538B. It follows the path of the huge powerline you can see overhead. The road is pretty good down to the 28.25 mile point but from there it becomes very rough with lots of exposed tire-eating rock. It ends at 28.75 miles at a bare spot on the ridge, where you park.

TRAILHEAD: You walk the power line service road, which is suitable for foot traffic only.

DESCRIPTION: This trail began its life as a sheep driveway. Years later engineers followed this same route to bring a major power line down to the Verde Valley and the sheep trail was converted into a service road for the line.
    A major attraction of this trail is that the ridge you walk is so narrow that you can see off into the Sycamore side or the Sedona side in many places. Both are spectacular. There are very few trees growing along the side of this trail, so it is mostly unshaded and can be hot. Take lots of water.
    At the 0.25 mile point on the hike you will come to a three-point wilderness trail intersection where the Casner Mountain, Mooney and Taylor Cabin trails meet. You can see the Mooney Trail going down diagonally to your

left into the Sedona back country. The Taylor Cabin Trail drops down steeply into Sycamore Canyon on your right.

The Casner Mountain Trail is not level. As it follows the contours of the ridge it dips and rises. At 2.0 miles it makes a major dip into a saddle where you reach bottom at 2.5 miles. From there you begin the mile-long ascent that will take you onto Casner Mountain.

You reach a false top on Casner at 3.5 miles and then make the final push to hike's end, the real top, at 4.0 miles.

The trail continues, going down the mountain on its south face. It is about 3.0 miles to the bottom on the south. Instead of trying to make this a killer day hike, we think it is better described as two hikes. The **Casner Mountain Trail South** is described in our other book, *Sedona Hikes*.

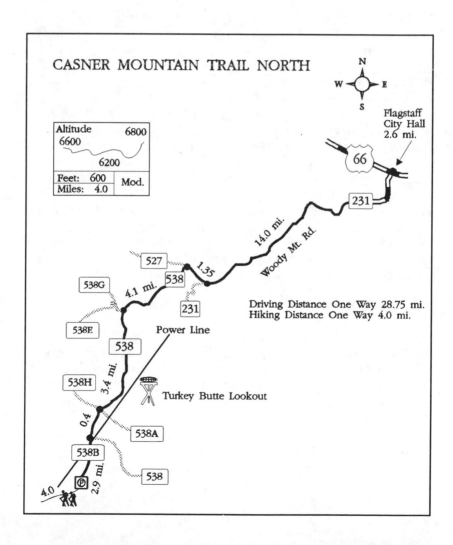

CASNER MOUNTAIN TRAIL NORTH

Altitude 6800
6600
6200
Feet: 600 Mod.
Miles: 4.0

Flagstaff
City Hall
2.6 mi.

66

231

14.0 mi.

Woody Mt. Rd.

527

1.35

538

538G

4.1 mi.

231

538E

Power Line

538

538H

3.4 mi.

Turkey Butte Lookout

0.4

538A

538B

2.9 mi.

538

4.0

Driving Distance One Way 28.75 mi.
Hiking Distance One Way 4.0 mi.

CHAVEZ PASS RUINS

General Information
Location Map G4
Chavez Pass West USGS Map
Coconino Forest Service Map

Driving Distance One Way: 72.4 miles (Time 1.75 hours)
Access Road: All cars, Last 23.2 miles good gravel road
Hiking Distance One Way: 0.75 miles (Time 45 minutes)
How Strenuous: Easy
Features: Extensive Indian ruins at historic site

NUTSHELL: It takes a bit of travelling to reach this ruin located 72.4 miles southeast of Flagstaff, but you will pass through beautiful country and find an impressive ruin.

DIRECTIONS:
From Flagstaff City Hall Go:
          West on Route 66 (Santa Fe) Avenue one block then left (south) on Sitgreaves Street under the railroad overpass. The street name will change to Milton Road as you go south. At 1.7 miles you will reach a stoplight at Forest Meadows Street. Turn right here onto Forest Meadows and go one block to Beulah. Turn left on Beulah and follow it south. Beulah merges onto Highway 89A. At 2.4 miles (MP 401.6), turn left onto the Lake Mary Road. Follow the Lake Mary Road (FH 3) to the 49.4 mile point (MP 297.4), where you turn left on a cindered road, FR 211. Follow this to the 57.6 mile point, where you will meet FR 82. Turn left on FR 82 and follow it to the 68.6 mile point, where the road intersects FR 69B. Turn right on FR 69B and follow it to the 72.4 mile point, just beyond a cattle guard. Park off the road to your right there.

TRAILHEAD: There is no sign or trail. Your objective is the low round hill to your left.

DESCRIPTION: You will travel through heavily timbered country on your approach to this hike until the last six miles, where you break out on top of Anderson Mesa into prairie and juniper land. When you turn east on FR 69B you will enter a region of hills and buttes. This is the historic Chavez Pass area. You will leave ranch land at the cattle guard, where there is a fence, and enter public land. The hill that is your target is easy to find. Look at the map. The arms of the triangle formed by the splitting of FR 69 aim right at the hill.
          The hill is only about 100 feet high and you can climb it just about anywhere. As you near the top you will begin to see profuse potsherds. Then on a bench below the top you will hit the first set of ruins. These are just low

lines of stone outlining the rooms. From the bench you climb to the absolute top, where you will find a large multi-room pueblo ruin. Enjoy looking at the artifacts but leave them there. It is illegal to collect them. Stand here and look east and you can see all the way to the Hopi mesas, getting a sense of the strategic location of this place. It is officially called Nuvakwewtaqa Ruin.

Spanish explorers working their way across northern Arizona in 1583 came this way, following an ancient Indian trail. From Chavez Pass the trail goes west to Stoneman Lake, then into the Verde Valley by way of Beaverhead. This route is one of the few feasible ways that allowed travel, for it provided water, grass and relatively level ground, avoiding major chasms. The Chavez for whom the pass is named was a US Army scout sent into the region in 1863. Ironically, he never came through the pass.

An interesting way to end this trip is to take FR 69 east, going by **Meteor Crater** and coming out on I-40, in 25 miles, from where it's 37.9 miles to Flagstaff.

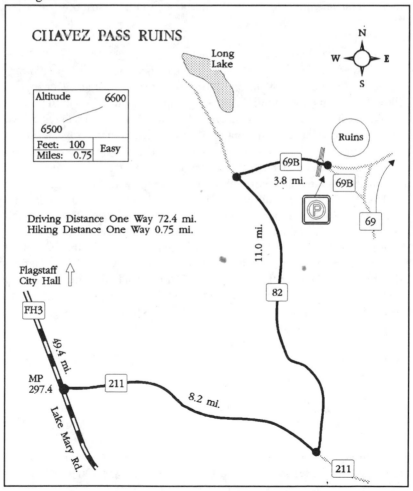

CHAVEZ PASS RUINS

Long Lake

N
W — E
S

Altitude   6600

6500

Feet: 100   Easy
Miles: 0.75

Ruins

69B
3.8 mi.   69B

69

Driving Distance One Way 72.4 mi.
Hiking Distance One Way 0.75 mi.

11.0 mi.

Flagstaff
City Hall

FH3

82

49.4 mi.

MP
297.4   211

8.2 mi.

Lake Mary Rd.

211

CLOVER SPRING

General Information
Location Map F1
Bill Williams Mountain USGS Map
Kaibab (Williams District) Forest Service Map

Driving Distance One Way: 36.5 miles (Time 50 minutes)
Access Road: All cars, All paved except last 0.20 miles
Hiking Distance One Way: 1.25 miles (Time 40 minutes)
How Strenuous: Moderate
Features: Beautiful forest, Views, Spring

NUTSHELL: This hike takes you to a spring on the flank of Bill Williams Mountain outside the Town of Williams, about 30 miles west of Flagstaff.

DIRECTIONS:
From Flagstaff City Hall Go:
       West on Route 66 (Santa Fe) a block, then follow the curve left on Sitgreaves Street under the railroad overpass. The street name will change to Milton Road at the first stoplight. Keep going south on Milton until you are out of town, headed toward Phoenix on I-17. At 2.0 miles you will reach Exit 340B, which is an access ramp onto I-40 West. The sign will say "Williams and Los Angeles." Get onto I-40 West and stay on it for 31.6 miles, where you will see the Williams Exit, #165. Get off on that and at the stop sign, go left to Williams. Go into downtown Williams. The main street through town is divided. You will be on Railroad Avenue headed west. Stay on this through town. At the 35.7 miles point you will be on a frontage road. There you will see a paved road turning left and going uphill toward Days Inn motel. Take this lefthand road. At 36.3 you will reach the turn for the Williams District Ranger Office for the Forest Service (also called Camp Clover). Turn left on this turn and head toward the camp. At 36.5 miles, just before the fence going into the compound, you will see a road going left. It is signed. Turn left on this road and follow it a short distance until you see a trailhead sign to your right. Pull in there and park.

TRAILHEAD: You will see a sign marking the Bill Williams Mountain trailhead at the parking area.

DESCRIPTION: You will hike along the **Bill Williams Mountain Trail** for a distance of 0.67 miles, then the Clover Spring Trail branches off to the left. It is marked by a sign. This first segment of the trail is moderately steep and passes through a typical ponderosa pine forest with lots of oak mixed in. There are a couple of places around the half mile spot where you can look out over the Williams area.

Once you leave the Bill Williams Trail, the Clover Springs trail goes downhill a bit and around the side of the mountain. You will come upon a sign reading, "Clover Spring 1/2 Mile" that is inaccurate, as the spring is only 0.2 miles from that point.

The spring appears on the hillside with no change in the appearance of the terrain, except for a row of green grass to mark where it flows. You are suddenly there, with a small sign to tell you that the place is Clover Spring.

There is a square concrete box at the head of the spring. When full it overflows and runs downhill, cutting a channel. A piece of metal has been placed over the channel. About twenty feet down from the box, a small pool is formed and from there a trickle runs free down the mountainside, tracing a thin green line. The Forest Service tapped Clover Spring in the past and used the water at Camp Clover, but you won't see any pipelines or other evidence of this use.

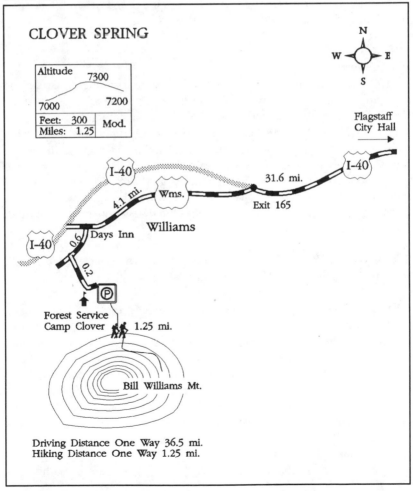

CLOVER SPRING

Driving Distance One Way 36.5 mi.
Hiking Distance One Way 1.25 mi.

COCONINO RIM TRAIL

General Information
Location Map C2
Grandview Point USGS Map
Kaibab (Tusayan) Forest Service Map

Driving Distance One Way: 87.6 miles (Time 2 hours)
Access Road: All cars, Last 15.3 miles good dirt road
Hiking Distance One Way: 3.0 miles (Time 1.5 hours)
How Strenuous: Easy
Features: Grand Canyon views, Arizona Trail link

NUTSHELL: This trail goes along the crest of the Coconino Rim, a long ridge running southeasterly from Grandview Point at the Grand Canyon, 87.6 miles from Flagstaff.

DIRECTIONS:
From Flagstaff City Hall, Go:
          North on Humphreys Street 0.60 miles to a stoplight. Go left on Columbus Avenue and follow the curve north. Street signs will show the street first as Ft. Valley Road, then Highway 180. This is a major road to the Grand Canyon. At 50.4 miles (MP 265.8), you will intersect Highway 64, coming out of Williams, at a place called Valle. Go right at this junction and follow the highway to the 72.3 mile point (MP 235.5), which you will find just as you come into Tusayan. Go right on FR 302 and follow it to the 87.5 mile point, where there is a junction. Take a left on FR 310 there, where the sign says, "G.C.N.P. 1" and in 0.1 mile you will see a sign for the Grandview Lookout to your right. Pull in and park at the base of the fire tower.

TRAILHEAD: You will see a sign at the parking area saying, "Arizona Trail Coconino Rim Section." The trail is marked by posts placed every half mile.

DESCRIPTION: The Arizona Trail is an ambitious project to create a linked series of trails that would allow hikers to walk from Utah to Mexico. A few segments of the trail have already been completed and tied together, starting in the north. This trail is part of the system and for that reason it is difficult to give true mileage for this hike as theoretically it will go to Mexico.
          The Coconino Rim is the uplifted portion of a large fault that created a crescent shaped ridge about 500 feet high running southeasterly from the Grand Canyon, which goes east to west in the area. The hiking trail takes advantage of the rim to bring the hiker into the Grand Canyon off of the main roads and above the desert.
          We recommend that you climb the fire tower before you hike. It

provides great views, whereas the trail has few. Then, you get underway. For the first mile of the trail the Forest Service has provided a series of signs telling about the Dwarf Mistletoe, with examples pointed out in the forest. This is interesting. We were especially taken with the information that the mistletoe propagates by explosively shooting its sticky seeds as far as sixty feet.

You will pass through areas where the mistletoe was not attacked and another where infected trees were removed. In the thinned area you are able to see into the Grand Canyon but it is only a glimpse.

The trail runs through an attractive pine forest, typical of the area, with nothing special to recommend it. The forest is so heavy that you cannot see into the distance. This is the irony of this trail: although it passes through one of the great scenic areas of the world, you can't see more than a few feet through the trees. There are no bare vista points. We turned back at the 3.0 mile post, which made a nice hike. No telling how far the trail actually goes now. We saw a trail marker at the Moqui Stage Station, many miles away.

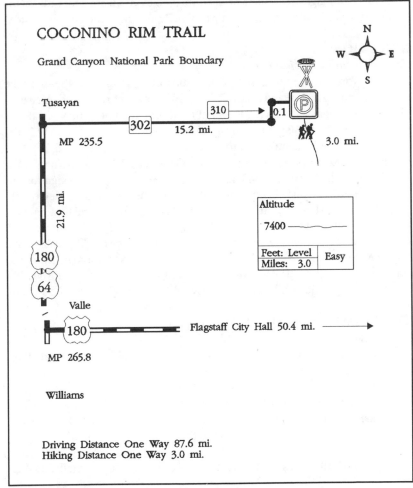

CONNECTOR TRAIL

General Information
Location Map E2
Kendrick Peak, Moritz Ridge and Wing Mt. USGS Maps
Coconino Forest Service Map

Driving Distance One Way: 34.55 miles (Time 1.25 hours)
Access Road: All cars, Last 20 miles good gravel road
Hiking Distance One Way: 2.0 miles (Time 1.0 hour)
How Strenuous: Easy
Features: Nice forest, Views

NUTSHELL: This sidehill trail is located on Kendrick Mountain, 34.55 miles north of Flagstaff. After a brief climb it takes you from **The Bull Basin Trail** on the north side of the mountain to **The Pumpkin Trail** on the west side.

DIRECTIONS:
From Flagstaff City Hall Go:
 North on Humphreys Street for 0.60 miles. Turn left at the stoplight onto Columbus Avenue and follow it around a big curve to the north. You will see the street signs call this road Columbus at first, then Ft. Valley Road and then Highway 180. Stay on Highway 180 to the 14.5 miles point (MP 230), where an unpaved road takes off to the left. Turn left onto this road, FR 245, and follow it to the 17.6 mile point where it intersects FR 171. Turn right on FR 171 and follow it to the 24.8 mile point, where you will see a sign for the Pumpkin Trail. Go just beyond this, to the 24.9 mile point and turn left on FR 171. Follow it to the 27.7 mile point, where it meets FR 144 and turn right on FR 144, taking it to the 29.2 point, where it intersects FR 90. Turn right on FR 90 and drive it to the 33.9 mile point, where you will see FR 90A to the right. Take FR 90A to the 34.45 mile point, where you will see a sign marking the access road to the Bull Basin trailhead. You can see the parking lot from this point. Turn right, downhill, and you will reach the parking area at 34.55 miles.

TRAILHEAD: Use the Bull Basin Trailhead.

DESCRIPTION: From the parking area you will walk a closed road along the west side of Bull Basin, a large grassy meadow. At 0.9 miles you will come to a trail junction where you will see a trail to the right. A line of stones and poles indicating that this is a trail junction is on the ground at this point. **The Bull Basin Trail** is marked with a sign here but the right hand trail is not marked. It is The Connector Trail. Take the right fork and you will be on the Connector.
 The trail moves west along the base of Kendrick Mountain and then

makes a gentle climb. After the climb, you will stay pretty much on the same level for the rest of the hike.

Because the trail is located on the north and west side of the mountain, the forest is more of a spruce and fir forest than a pine forest. It is quite attractive and is a pleasant walk. There are some aspens mixed in.

Along the trail there are some places where there are openings in the trees through which you can get views to the north. The landscape is one of wooded ridges below which a pastel desert begins abruptly and stretches to the Grand Canyon. Depending on how clear the air is, this can be quite a view. About one-tenth of a mile before the trail ends, you will enter a zone where the spruces stop and the pines begin.

The trail terminates where it meets the Pumpkin Trail at a point that is 1.4 miles from the Pumpkin Trailhead. There are signs at this junction. You could hike to the top of Kendrick on the Pumpkin Trail from here.

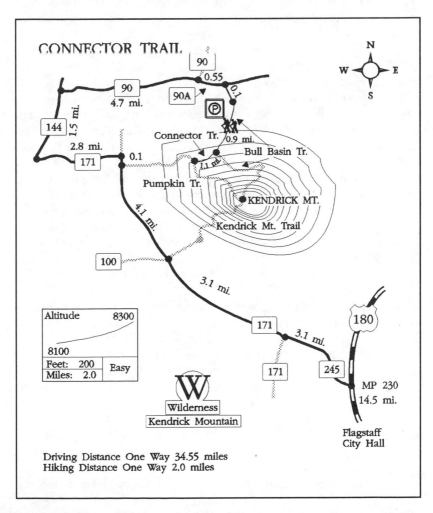

COOKSTOVE TRAIL

General Information
Location Map F3
Mountainaire USGS Map
Coconino Forest Service Map

Drive Distance One Way: 17.1 miles (Time 20 minutes)
Access Road: All cars, All paved
Hiking Distance One Way: 0.75 miles (Time 45 minutes)
How Strenuous: Hard
Features: Views

NUTSHELL: Marked and posted trail located just across Highway 89A from the Pine Flat Campground 17.1 miles south of Flagstaff. It climbs the east wall of Oak Creek Canyon.

DIRECTIONS:
From Flagstaff City Hall Go:
West one block on Route 66 (Santa Fe) then left (south) on Sitgreaves Street under the railroad overpass. As you continue south you will see the street signs calling the street Milton Road, as Sitgreaves Street blends into Milton. At 1.7 miles you reach the intersection of Forest Meadows, where there is a traffic light. Here you turn right. You will see a sign for Highway 89A, which is the road you want. At the next corner turn left on Beulah and follow it out of town. Beulah will connect onto Highway 89A which is the road to Oak Creek Canyon and Sedona. At 13.8 miles (MP 390) you will reach the canyon rim and begin the winding descent. After you have completed the switchbacks and are on the canyon floor, drive to the 17.1 mile point (MP 386.9), the Pine Flat Campground. On your right you will see a structure about five feet high and four feet square made of round stones that houses a spring. Park near it.

TRAILHEAD: On the east side of the road just across Highway 89A from the spring. It is marked by a rusty sign, "Cookstove Trail #143."

DESCRIPTION: The water in the spring at the Pine Flat campground is potable. In fact, it is delicious pure water. You will see many people stop off here and fill bottles and jugs for drinking water. We do this ourselves every time we go into Oak Creek Canyon. It is better than any water you can buy.
This trail is typical of all trails in upper Oak Creek Canyon that climb the east wall of the canyon: namely, it goes virtually straight up with little finesse. Similar trails are **Harding Spring, Purtymun** and **Thomas Point.** They are all strenuous hikes.
The trail starts right by the highway and immediately begins to climb.

At first the trail parallels Cookstove Draw. At 0.1 miles you get a great view down into the draw, where there is a small waterfall during snowmelt and after hard rains. Then the trail veers away from Cookstove Draw as it rises.

The forest through which this trail passes is typical for upper Oak Creek Canyon, with pine at the beginning, changing into mixed pines and firs as you climb and the altitude increases.

The trail does a little zigging and zagging. When you top out, you are in a spot where you get good views of the west wall of Oak Creek Canyon, but the views are not as good as the views you get at the top of the Harding Spring trail.

Hikes in the upper canyon are usually cool, often being 10 to 15 degrees cooler than hikes in Sedona. The altitude at the rim is about 6600 feet, almost as high as Flagstaff, and the climate is similar. These hikes can often be pleasant in summer when hiking in Sedona would be too hot.

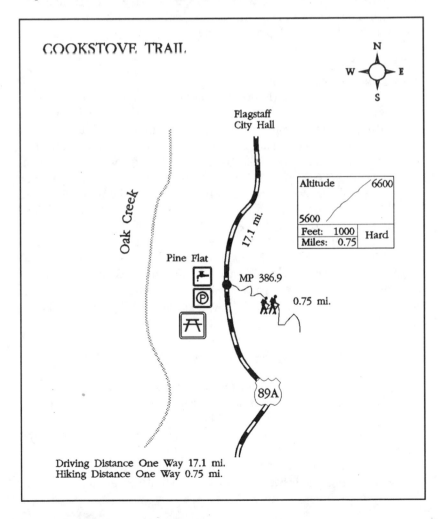

DAVENPORT HILL TRAIL

General Information
Location Map F1
Bill Williams Mountain USGS Map
Kaibab (Williams District) Forest Service Map

Driving Distance One Way: 42.3 miles (Time 60 minutes)
Access Road: All cars, Last 4.0 miles good gravel road
Hiking Distance One Way: 2.5 miles (Time 1.25 hours)
How Strenuous: Moderate
Features: Beautiful forest, Lake

NUTSHELL: This hike starts at the Dogtown Lake Campground near Williams. You follow the Dogtown Nature Trail for a quarter of a mile, then branch off to climb to the top of Davenport Hill.

DIRECTIONS:
From Flagstaff City Hall Go:
 West on Santa Fe (Route 66) a block, then follow the curve left on Sitgreaves Street under the railroad overpass. The street name will change to Milton Road at the first stoplight. Keep going south on Milton until you are out of town, headed toward Phoenix on I-17. At 2.0 miles you will reach Exit 340B, which is an access ramp onto I-40 West. The sign will say "Williams and Los Angeles." Get onto I-40 West and stay on it for 31.6 miles, where you will see the Williams Exit, #165. Get off on that and at the stop sign, go left to Williams. Go into downtown Williams and turn left at Fourth Street, where you will see a sign reading, "Ski Area, White Horse Lake." Follow Fourth Street, which will take you out of town into a valley. Here the road is still paved and is designated FR 173. At 38.5 miles turn left onto FR 140. You will see a sign for "Dogtown Lake" here. Take FR 140 to the 41.3 mile point, where you turn left on FR 132. You will reach the campground at 42.3 miles. At the office turn left and then left again. You park at the parking area on the shore of the lake.

TRAILHEAD: As you get out of your car you will see the trail sign.

DESCRIPTION: Dogtown Lake (named after a Prairie Dog colony) is a pretty lake in a scenic basin. You start on the nature trail, which takes you along the valley where a stream would flow if it hadn't been dammed to form the lake. The valley is marshy and lush. Descriptive signs along the trail tell about things of interest.
 At about a quarter of a mile, just after you have passed over a bridge and the trail begins to loop back to camp, you will find the Davenport Hill Trail

branching to the left. There is a sign reading "Davenport Hill Trail No. 63, Top of Davenport Hill 2.5."

You will walk along a level bench to the one mile point, where you cross a road. You are now at the foot of the hill and begin to climb. The trail follows the contours of the hill intelligently so as to moderate the grade. This involves winding around the hill, which also gives you different viewpoints, though the forest is so thick that you only get glimpses toward Bill Williams Mountain and toward Davenport Lake. You reach an intermediate top at 1.5 miles, a good resting point, then begin the final ascent. Toward the top you hike through a dense forest of oak, pine, fir and spruce. It is really lovely.

At the top the forest returns to the prevailing Ponderosa pine belt. The trail takes you north to the farthest point on the hill where it stops at a large cairn. There is a sign here reading, "Davenport Hill, Elevation 7805." The views are disappointing because the forest is so thick, but it's a great place for a picnic.

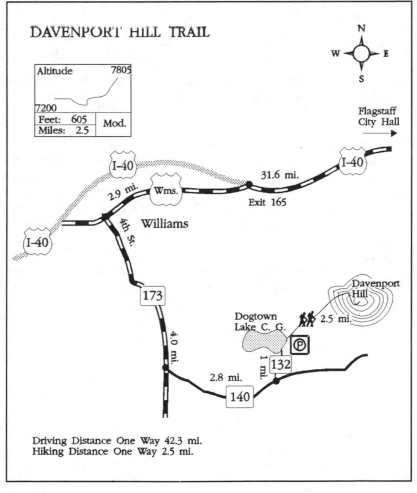

DOGTOWN NATURE TRAIL

General Information
Location Map F1
Bill Williams Mountain USGS Map
Kaibab (Williams District) Forest Service Map

Driving Distance One Way: 42.3 miles (Time 60 minutes)
Access Road: All cars, Last 4.0 miles good gravel road
Hiking Distance, Complete Loop: 0.40 miles (Time 30 minutes)
How Strenuous: Easy
Features: Self-guided nature trail, Lake

NUTSHELL: This hike starts at the Dogtown Lake Campground near Williams. You make a loop from the lake, enjoying the scenery and explanatory signs along the way.

DIRECTIONS:
From Flagstaff City Hall Go:
> West on Santa Fe (Route 66) a block, then follow the curve left on Sitgreaves Street under the railroad overpass. The street name will change to Milton Road at the first stoplight. Keep going south on Milton until you are out of town, headed toward Phoenix on I-17. At 2.0 miles you will reach Exit 340B, which is an access ramp onto I-40 West. The sign will say "Williams and Los Angeles." Get onto I-40 West and stay on it for 31.6 miles, where you will see the Williams Exit, #165. Get off on that and at the stop sign, go left to Williams. Go into downtown Williams and turn left at Fourth Street, where you will see a sign reading, "Ski Area, White Horse Lake." Follow Fourth Street, which will take you out of town into a valley. Here the road is still paved and is designated FR 173. At 38.5 miles turn left onto FR 140. You will see a sign for "Dogtown Lake" there. Take FR 140 to the 41.3 mile point, where you turn left on FR 132. You will reach the campground at 42.3 miles. At the office turn left and then left again. You park at the parking area on the shore of the lake.

TRAILHEAD: As you get out of your car you will see a sign reading, "Nature Trail," to your right.

DESCRIPTION: Dogtown Lake (named after a Prairie Dog colony) is a pretty lake in a scenic basin. The nature trail takes you along the valley where a stream would flow if it hadn't been dammed to form the lake. The little valley is marshy and lush. Descriptive signs along the trail tell about things of interest, covering everything from telling the age of trees from their rings, to local flora, to why the old logging stumps are so high (because the lumberjacks used hand saws and could not work while stooped way over).

The trail is quite easy. It dips into the valley, which it crosses on a charming wooden bridge. After you climb out of the valley on the other side, you are on flat land again. At about the 0.20 miles point you will find the **Davenport Hill Trail** branching to the left. There is a sign there reading, "Davenport Hill Trail No. 63, Top of Davenport Hill 2.5."

At this point, the Dogtown Trail curves to the right and heads back toward the campground, passing through an attractive pine forest.

This is such a short trail that it would not be worth a drive from Flagstaff. However, it is easy to do it while you are hiking the more ambitious Davenport Hill Trail. On the longer trail you start out on the Dogtown Nature Trail until you come to the junction mentioned above. On the way back from the top of Davenport Hill, just take the remainder of the loop to go back to your parking place and you will do both trails in one outing.

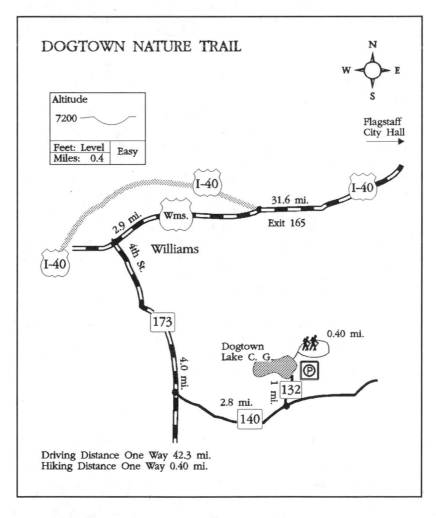

DOGTOWN NATURE TRAIL

Altitude
7200
Feet: Level — Easy
Miles: 0.4

Flagstaff
City Hall

Williams

Driving Distance One Way 42.3 mi.
Hiking Distance One Way 0.40 mi.

DONEY TRAIL

General Information
Location Map E3
Wupatki SW USGS Map
Coconino Forest Service Map

Driving Distance One Way: 42 miles (Time 60 minutes)
Access Road: All cars, All paved
Hiking Distance One Way: 0.50 miles (Time 30 minutes)
How Strenuous: Easy
Features: Views, Indian ruins

NUTSHELL: This is a short easy trail located near the Wupatki National Monument northeast of Flagstaff. It takes you to the top of two cinder cones that give great unobstructed views of a fascinating volcanic field. You will also see some vestigial Indian ruins on this hike.

DIRECTIONS:
From Flagstaff City Hall Go:

East, curving to north on Santa Fe (Route 66). As you leave the city limits you will see that Santa Fe (Route 66) is also Highway 89. Follow Highway 89 north out into the country. At 16.4 miles (MP 430.3) you will reach the entrance to Sunset Crater National Monument. Turn right on the road into Sunset Crater. This road is also known as FR 545. At 18.4 miles you will reach a ticket booth where you will have to pay admission. Just beyond that is the Visitor Center, which is worth a look.

At 26.0 miles you reach the Painted Desert Vista. This is a lookout point where we recommend stopping to enjoy the view. Under the right lighting conditions it is superb. At 37.8 miles you enter the Wupatki National Monument, which adjoins Sunset Crater, and you will see the road to the Wupatki Visitor Center to your left. This center is also worth a look.

Keep following FR 545 to the 41.9 mile point, where you will see a road to your left going to the Doney Picnic Ground. Take it. At 42.0 miles you will reach the parking area, where you should park.

TRAILHEAD: You will see a sign at the parking area.

DESCRIPTION: The trail is obvious when you start the hike. It climbs twin cinder cones, one higher than the other. The trail leads to a saddle between the two cones at 0.13 miles. Here you can decide whether to go left to the lower cone or right to the higher one. We recommend that you go left first. It's less than 0.10 miles to the left top and is a climb of only 100 feet. You will see some informative signs along the path. Just below the top you will see the smallest, crudest Indian ruin imaginable. There are good views from the top and a bench to sit on.

Then it's on to the higher cone. It is 200 feet higher than the parking lot, so you get better views than you can from the lower cone. However, each summit offers a different angle so both are worthwhile. On the trail you will see a small partially excavated pit house. At the top you will find a bench where you can sit and enjoy the views. There is a nice sign there with a sketch identifying the mountains you see to the west.

Because these tops are bare cinder cones your view is unobstructed. To the north you can see the Vermilion Cliffs and when the light is right you get a sense of the great cleft that is the Grand Canyon. To the east, you look at the Painted Desert. To the west you see the San Francisco Peaks and a long line of volcanic mountains, hills and cones. To the south you look at the Sunset Crater area.

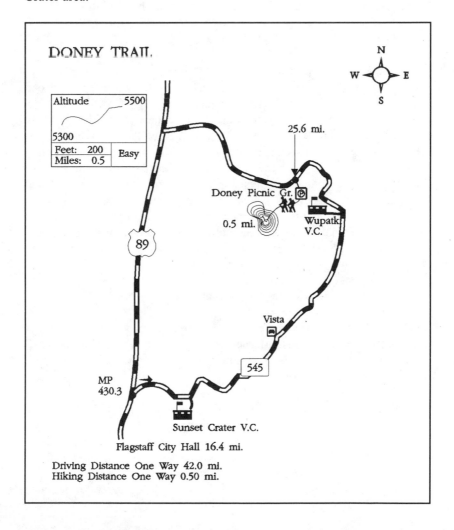

DONEY TRAIL.

Altitude 5500
5300
Feet: 200
Miles: 0.5
Easy

25.6 mi.

Doney Picnic Gr.
0.5 mi.
Wupatki V.C.

89

Vista

545

MP 430.3

Sunset Crater V.C.

Flagstaff City Hall 16.4 mi.

Driving Distance One Way 42.0 mi.
Hiking Distance One Way 0.50 mi.

DORSEY SPRING TRAIL

General Information
Location Map F2
Sycamore Point USGS Map
Coconino Forest Service Map

Driving Distance One Way: 22.95 miles (Time 60 minutes)
Access Road: High clearance for last 0.65 miles
Hiking Distance One Way: 2.3 miles (Time 1.50 hours)
How Strenuous: Moderate
Features: Hidden spring, Virgin forests

NUTSHELL: Located about 25 miles southwest of Flagstaff, this trail takes you part of the way into Sycamore Canyon to a beautiful spring.

DIRECTIONS:
From Flagstaff City Hall Go:
　　　　West a block on Santa Fe (Route 66), then south, beneath the railroad overpass on Sitgreaves Street. The street name will change to Milton Road as you go farther. At 0.50 miles you will reach a Y intersection. The right fork is named West Old US Highway 66. Take it. You will soon leave town. At 2.6 miles you will reach a road going to the left. This is the Woody Mountain Road, FR 231. Take it. It is paved about a mile and then turns into a cinder road. At 16.6 miles you will intersect FR 538. Turn right onto FR 538 and follow it to the 22.3 mile point, where it intersects the Kelsey Spring Road, FR 538G. Take 538G. The roads to this point are good, but beyond it they are rough. At 22.7 miles you hit another intersection where FR 538E forks to the left. This is the Dorsey Spring Road. Turn left onto it and follow it to its end at 22.95 miles, where you will find a parking lot.

TRAILHEAD: You will see a big sign at the parking area.

DESCRIPTION: The Dorsey Spring Trail does not take you into the inner gorge of Sycamore Canyon like its nearby neighbors the **Kelsey Spring Trail** and the **Winter Cabin Trail** do. It stops at Dorsey Spring. Also unlike those trails, the parking lot is not located at the canyon's rim.
　　　　From the parking area you will walk a closed jeep road. At 0.25 miles you will see a closed road to the **Hog Hill** trailhead forking to the left. At 1.8 miles you will reach the rim. From the rim area you will get a few views into the depths of the canyon, the only place on this trail where that is possible.
　　　　You will hike down into Sycamore along a side canyon. It is fairly steep but the footing is decent and you only have to go half a mile, to the 2.3 mile point. The spring is on a small shelf to your left. The water has been

channeled so it flows from a black plastic pipe. The spring is usually dependable but the Forest Service recommends purifying its water. From the place where the water comes out of the pipe you will see a thin river of green grass running down a long way, ultimately into Sycamore.

A few yards below the spring there is a large shelf of land, a beautiful idyllic spot.

You will also find markers for the **Kelsey-Winter Trail** coming through this large shelf of land. Dorsey Spring is located about midway between Kelsey Spring and Winter Cabin Spring on the Kelsey-Winter Trail. You can go north along Kelsey-Winter about 2.0 miles to **Babe's Hole** and into the gorge of Sycamore Canyon via Geronimo Spring or you can go south about 2.0 miles to **Winter Cabin** and into the Sycamore Canyon gorge via Ott Lake, so it is an ideal resting place in between.

Treat springs with special care. They are immensely important to wildlife. Though water looks pure, the giardia risk is ever present.

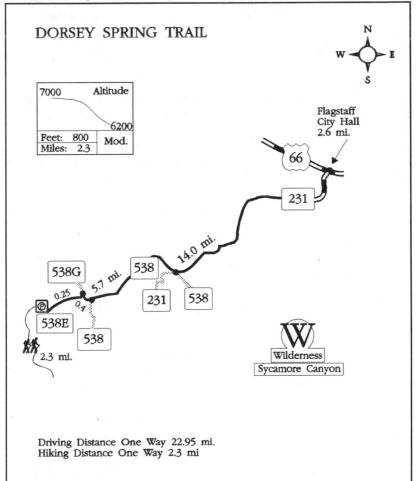

DORSEY SPRING TRAIL

Driving Distance One Way 22.95 mi.
Hiking Distance One Way 2.3 mi

DOW SPRING TO POMEROY TANKS

General Information
Location Map F2
Bill Williams Mountain and Garland Prairie USGS Maps
Kaibab (Williams District) Forest Service Map

Driving Distance One Way: 28.2 miles (Time 45 minutes)
Access Road: All cars, Last 12.4 miles good gravel road
Hiking Distance, Complete Loop: 10.15 miles (Time 5.5 hours)
How Strenuous: Moderate
Features: Cabin ruins, Canyon springs, Views, Waterfall, Historic road

NUTSHELL: This hike is located in the area west of Flagstaff. It takes you along the rim of Sycamore Canyon from its source to the gigantic chasm that it becomes, explores fascinating rock pools and follows a bit of the historic Overland Road.

DIRECTIONS:
From Flagstaff City Hall Go:
 West a block on Santa Fe (Route 66), then south, beneath the railroad overpass on Sitgreaves Street. The street name will change to Milton Road. At 0.50 miles you will reach a Y intersection. The right fork is named West Old US Highway 66. Take it. You will soon leave town, driving on a stretch of fabled Highway 66. At the 4.8 mile point you will merge onto Interstate-40 West. Look for Exit 178, "Parks Road" and take it. It is at the 18.0 mile point. From the exit turn left and go toward Garland Prairie. When you cross the railroad tracks you will be on FR 141, the main road through Garland Prairie. Stay on it to the 27.6 miles point, where it meets FR 131. Turn left on FR 131 and take it to the 28.0 mile point, where you will see an unmarked jeep trail to the right. Take this and follow it to the 28.2 mile point where you will find a parking area. Park.

TRAILHEAD: There is a large sign with a map at the parking area.

DESCRIPTION: From the parking place at Dow Spring walk toward the canyon, where you will find the **Sycamore Rim Trail** at the rim. This hike is essentially the south half of the Sycamore Rim Trail plus the Overland Road. It is a much better dayhike than the official Sycamore Rim Trail, which has you climb KA Hill.
 Note the little canyon in which Dow Spring is located. It seems insignificant but it is the source of mighty Sycamore Canyon and one of the joys of this trail is seeing how the canyon develops from a baby into a giant.
 In 1.0 miles be sure to look into the canyon. There you will see a series

of beautiful pools fed by LO Spring. Unusual lily pads grow in these pools. Beyond, the canyon starts to deepen, coming to its fullest depth at the 3.65 mile point. There you will find yourself at Sycamore Vista, also referred to as Double Spring (Tank). You have to detour south for 0.25 miles to go to the actual vista point from the main trail.

From here you will climb a rocky hillside and go down into another canyon. At 5.65 miles you will reach Sycamore Falls, where you will see a trail coming in from the Sycamore Falls parking area. These falls run only in the spring. From here walk north along the canyon until you come to Pomeroy Tanks at 6.9 miles. These are like the rock pools of LO Spring. As you continue you will cross the canyon and go toward its head. At 7.35 miles you will reach the Overland Road. Here you leave the Sycamore Rim Trail and follow the Overland Road to the right (east) to the 9.35 miles point, where it once more meets the Sycamore Rim Trail. Here you turn right (south) and take the Sycamore Rim Trail back to Dow Spring, which you will reach at 10.15 miles.

DOW SPRING TO POMEROY TANKS

N
W ← → E
S

Altitude	
	6700
6600	
Feet: 100	Mod.
Miles: 10.15	

Flagstaff City Hall via I-40 to Exit 178 is 18.0 mi. ▶

9.6 mi. on FR 141
from Parks Road
Exit on I-40

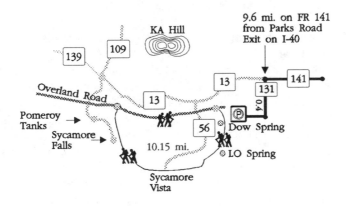

KA Hill

139   109

Overland Road

13   13   141   131

0.4

Pomeroy Tanks →

Sycamore Falls →

56   ℗   Dow Spring

10.15 mi.   ⊚ LO Spring

Sycamore Vista

Driving Distance One Way 28.2 mi.
Hiking Distance, Complete Loop 10.15 mi.

DRY LAKE HILLS

General Information
Location Map E3
Humphreys Peak and Flagstaff West USGS Maps
Coconino Forest Service Map

Driving Distance One Way: 8.0 miles (Time 30 minutes)
Access Road: All cars, Last 4 miles good dirt road
Hiking Distance One Way: 1.75 miles (Time 60 minutes)
How Strenuous: Moderate
Features: Views

NUTSHELL: Located about 10 miles north of Flagstaff, this moderate hike takes you through beautiful forests and meadows to a superb lookout point.

DIRECTIONS:
From Flagstaff City Hall Go:
 North on Humphreys Street a distance of 0.60 miles to the stoplight at Columbus Ave. Turn left here. The street you will be on bears three names: Columbus, Ft. Valley Road and Highway 180. It goes around a big curve and heads north, taking you out of town. At 3.1 miles (MP 218.6) the Schultz Pass Road (FR 420) branches off to the right. Take it. At 3.6 miles it curves to the left. The paving ends soon after the curve. At 8.0 miles you will be well up in the mountains. A sideroad drops off sharply to your right into a gully here. Take this road, which is marked FR 789, down to a gate. You will want to park by the gate. Don't try to drive FR 789 even if the gate should be unlocked.

TRAILHEAD: No trail signs. You walk the road, FR 789.

DESCRIPTION: The old road (FR 789) passes through a lovely mixed forest of aspen, spruce, fir and pine. It is moist in this forest, so there are many flowers, ferns and other botanicals. At 0.90 miles you will come out into a clearing where there is a broad meadow. This is the first of the Dry Lakes. In the spring it will hold water from snow melt but during the rest of the year it will live up to its name and be dry. At the entrance to this first meadow are a couple of fenced ponds that hold water year around.
 The first meadow was the site of the Brookbank Ranch, built in the late 1800s. Into the 1960s the old abandoned ranch house and some other structures were still there. In the late 60s and early 70s, however, many old cabins in the Peaks area were torn down and these days few remain. Treat the remaining cabins with respect when you find them. They are very fragile.
 At 1.0 miles you will see a trail going off to your left. This connects with the **Brookbank Trail**. We have seen mountain bikers take this. At 1.5

miles you have reached the end of the first Dry Lake. Here the road branches left and right and the trail ahead seems blocked by a hump. If you walk over this hump and go straight ahead you will come to the second Dry Lake. It is a bit smaller than the first, but is worth a look.

A more interesting experience is to take the road to the left. It goes to a rocky outcrop that is a fine viewpoint from which to get views of Mt. Elden and East Flagstaff. This is the end of the line. Coming back you'll have prime views of the Peaks.

The best way to show someone where the Dry Lake Hills are is to take them to Macy's for a cup of coffee. A good idea anyway. When you're finished, go outside and have them look up Beaver Street. It forms a frame aiming right at the Dry Lake Hills. We have tried this several times and it always works. "Oh, so that's what those are."

This is not an officially named trail, but we have given it our name, as it seems to fit. Brookbank Meadow is privately owned.

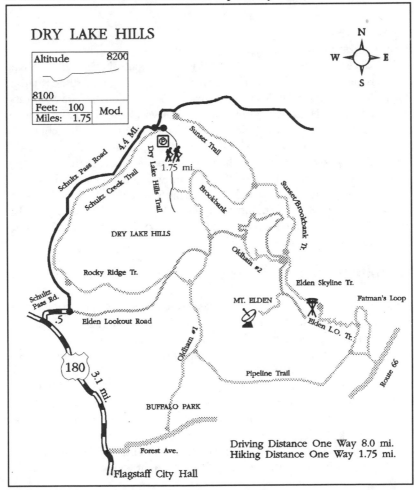

EAGLE ROCK

General Information
Location Map E2
Parks USGS Map
Kaibab (Williams) Forest Service Map

Driving Distance One Way: 24.5 miles (Time 40 minutes)
Access Road: All cars, Last 1.2 miles good gravel road
Hiking Distance, Complete Loop: 6.5 miles (Time 3.5 hours)
How Strenuous: Moderate
Features: Beautiful forests

NUTSHELL: This hike is located in Spring Valley, west of Flagstaff. It takes you through an interesting forest.

DIRECTIONS:
From Flagstaff City Hall Go:
 West a block on Route 66 (Santa Fe), then south, beneath the railroad overpass on Sitgreaves Street. The street name will change to Milton Road as you go farther. At 0.50 miles you will reach a Y intersection. The right fork is named West Old US Highway 66. Take it. You will soon leave town, driving on a stretch of fabled Highway 66. At the 4.8 mile point you will merge onto Interstate-40 West. Look for Exit 178 at the 18.0 mile point, and take it. Turn right at the stop sign and travel to the 18.1 mile point, where there is a second stop sign. Turn left here and go to the 18.8 mile point, where you will see the Parks Store to your right. Turn right here, on the Spring Valley Road (FR 141). It is paved to the 23.2 mile point, and is a good gravel road beyond. At 24.5 miles you will see a sign for the Cross Country Ski Trail. Turn left here into the parking lot and park.

TRAILHEAD: You will see a large wooden signboard with a trail map.

DESCRIPTION: The Forest Service has created three cross-country ski trails in this area. The trails are marked in the trees. You begin this hike by following RS Hill Trail for about a mile. It is marked by blue triangles.
 You will start on a road after going through a gate. Be sure to watch for the place at about 0.40 miles where the trail veers off to the left, away from the road. You will at times be on roads and at other times will be offroad all through this hike. Be sure to follow the triangles. It becomes almost like a game locating and following them especially in those areas where the timber tress are marked with blue paint, making it hard to see the triangles.
 At 0.75 miles you will reach a beautiful meadow. In the middle of the meadow is Shoot-Em-Up-Dick Tank. To your right you will look down the

valley at a big mountain, Kendrick Peak. At the other side of the meadow you will come onto FR 76 and walk it for a short distance until you reach the sign where the **Eagle Rock Trail** forks to the left.

You will now be following red triangles. The next part of the hike takes you cross country about a quarter of a mile, to a road, FR 104. You turn left and follow FR 104 into some beautiful backcountry.

Beyond the 1.5 mile point it will be clear to you that you are headed for a pass between hills. This is Eagle Rock Pass. Before the pass you will see an unmarked sideroad to your left. Look left and you will see Eagle Rock. The sideroad doesn't go to Eagle Rock as it would seem, however. It peters out in about 0.25 miles.

From the pass you make a fairly steep descent on a foot trail, joining a road at the bottom, which you follow through a pine forest to a point where the **RS Hill Trail** joins. Turn right here and follow its blue triangles home.

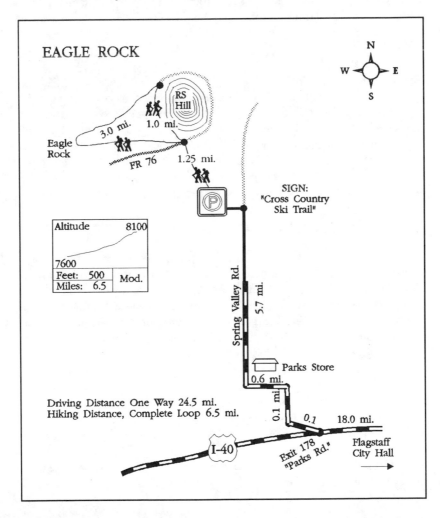

ELDEN LOOKOUT TRAIL

General Information
Location Map E3
Flagstaff East USGS Map
Coconino Forest Service Map

Driving Distance One Way: 5.2 miles (Time 10 minutes)
Access Road: All cars, All paved
Hiking Distance One Way: 3.0 miles (Time 2 hours)
How Strenuous: Hard
Features: Views

NUTSHELL: This marked and maintained trail runs from the base of Mt. Elden in East Flagstaff to the top of the mountain where a fire lookout tower is located.

DIRECTIONS:
From Flagstaff City Hall Go:
East on Route 66 (Santa Fe). Highway 89 runs concurrently with Route 66 (Santa Fe) as the highway goes through Flagstaff, so you will see road signs with both designations. At 5.2 miles (MP 419.5) just beyond the Flagstaff Mall, you will see a sign for the "Mt. Elden Trailhead" and a paved driveway to your left into a parking lot bounded by a pole fence. Pull in there and park.

TRAILHEAD: There is a sign with map at the gate in the parking lot.

DESCRIPTION: This trail is part of the Dry Lake Hills\Mt. Elden trail system.
You will meet the **Fat Man's Loop Trail** branching to the right shortly after you begin. After that you will come to two fences that have pass-through gates. Go through them. You will see clearly by now that you are walking directly toward Mt. Elden. In about a quarter mile you will reach the junction with the **Pipeline Trail**, which goes left. For about the first mile you will pass through a pine forest. The trail rises as it approaches the mountain. At the top of this approach, which is the apex of the Fat Man's Loop, you will see a sign showing the Elden Lookout Trail going uphill.
From this point to the top, about two miles, the trail is very steep. There is hardly a level stretch anywhere. You will note that a lot of work has been done on this trail. In some places "stairs" have been built and in others cribbing has been used to hang the trail out over space. Mt. Elden is so steep and so rocky that constant maintenance is needed to keep this trail open. Every year it must be cleared of fallen trees, rockslides, etc. We appreciate the work the Forest Service does on this trail.

The forest through which you pass on your way to the top is not heavy. This is due to the terrain and a 1978 forest fire. Consequently there are many open spaces for great views. You look out north and east into East Flagstaff, Doney Park, the Sunset Crater area, and far in the distance, the Painted Desert.

The three mile point at the top where the sign indicating the end of the trail is located is not the absolute top of Mt. Elden. You will find a sign there indicating that the lookout tower is 0.25 miles away. If you have enough energy left for it, by all means, make this final ascent, because the views at the top are as good as any in the Flagstaff area. If a ranger is in the tower you may be invited up. Go. You won't regret it.

We like this hike much better going down, not only because it's easier on the heart, but because the views are before you, unfolding. You don't have to look over your shoulder as you do going up. Using two cars, you can park one at the tower and one at the trailhead and hike downhill.

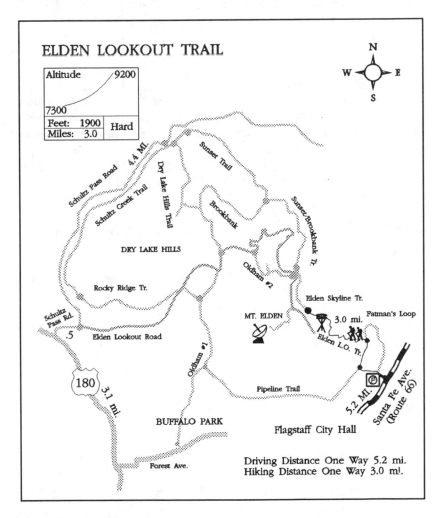

ELDEN PUEBLO

General Information
Location Map E3
Flagstaff East USGS Map
Coconino Forest Map

Driving Distance One Way: 6.4 miles (Time 10 minutes)
Access Road: All cars, All paved
Hiking Distance One Way: 0.10 miles (Time 30 minutes)
How Strenuous: Easy
Features: Indian ruins

NUTSHELL: Interesting Indian ruins, presently being excavated. Located just north of Flagstaff, this is more of a sightseeing excursion than a hike, as you do very little walking.

DIRECTIONS:
From Flagstaff City Hall Go:
East on Route 66 (Santa Fe). Highway 89 runs concurrently with Route 66 (Santa Fe) as the highway goes through Flagstaff, so you will see road signs with both designations. At 6.4 miles (MP 420.7), as you are leaving town and starting to get out into the country, you will see a sign, "Elden Pueblo Ruins" and a gravel drive going into the trees to your left just before the stoplight at the junction of Highway 89 and the Townsend-Winona Road. This is the entrance to the parking area for Elden Pueblo. Pull in there and park.

TRAILHEAD: There are no trail signs. A path starts at the south end of the parking lot. It is easy to find.

DESCRIPTION: The parking lot is bounded by crisscrossed logs, so you will know you have the right place if you see them. There is a road going through a gate to your right (north) from the parking lot. It does go to the ruin, but it is the long way around, intended for vehicles only, so that they can loop around and avoid driving right on the site of the ruins. You will find signs directing you to the pueblo site.

The ruins are very near the highway and you will soon see them when you begin to walk the footpath. They are undergoing restoration but this is sporadic and there is no way of knowing on any particular day whether anyone will be there. If no one is present you are welcome to help yourself and wander around. Unfortunately there are no self-guiding signs.

At times the Forest Service sponsors amateur digs at Elden Pueblo, when the public is invited to come out and work for a day under the guidance of professional archaeologists. Look for announcements in the Flagstaff newspaper or call the Elden Pueblo Project Manager, Northern Arizona Natural History Association, (602) 523-9642 for recorded information on these digs. It's your chance to find out what archaeology is really like.

A look at this site shows you how much work goes into excavation. You can appreciate better what has happened at some fully restored places such as Wupatki or Tuzigoot when you look at the work here. Elden Pueblo was discovered years ago and the prominent federal archaeologist Jesse Fewkes considered it a major site worthy of maximum attention in the 1920s but for some reason it has languished for many years with almost no heed paid to it. It is a sizable site. The more they dig here, the bigger the ruin seems and the present thought is that there may be an older ruin under the surface ruin.

In addition to the highly publicized Indian ruins such as Wupatki there are many smaller ruins like Elden Pueblo located northeast of Flagstaff.

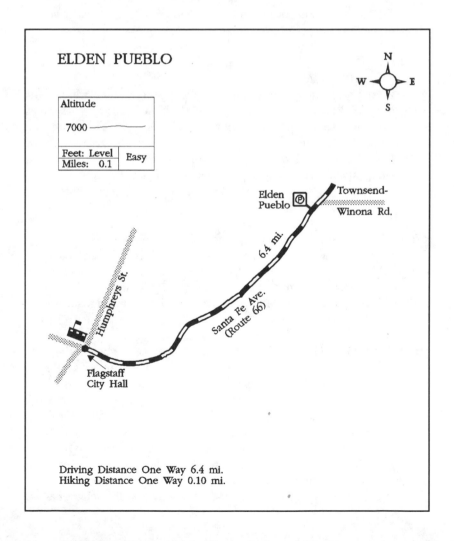

ELDEN PUEBLO

Altitude

7000

Feet: Level
Miles: 0.1   Easy

N
W — E
S

Elden
Pueblo   Townsend-
Winona Rd.

6.4 mi.

Humphreys St.

Santa Fe Ave.
(Route 66)

Flagstaff
City Hall

Driving Distance One Way 6.4 mi.
Hiking Distance One Way 0.10 mi.

ELDEN RED HILLS (HEART) TRAIL

General Information
Location Map E3
Flagstaff East & Sunset Crater West USGS Maps
Coconino Forest Service Map

Driving Distance One Way: 7.0 miles (Time 15 minutes)
Access Road: All cars, Last 0.1 mile good dirt road
Hiking Distance One Way: 3.85 miles (Time 2.5 hours)
How Strenuous: Moderate to Hard
Features: Unusual red and white hills, Rock formations, Views

NUTSHELL: This trail, located just 7.0 miles from City Hall, takes you up a red hill on the east face of Mt. Elden.

DIRECTIONS:
From Flagstaff City Hall Go:
East on Route 66 (Santa Fe). Highway 89 runs concurrently with Route 66 (Santa Fe) as the highway goes through Flagstaff, so you will see road signs with both designations. At 6.4 miles (MP 420.7), as you are leaving town and starting to get out into the country, you will see the stoplight at the junction of Highway 89 and the Townsend-Winona Road. Look for a dirt road (FR 9129) going into the trees to your left one half mile beyond the stoplight, at 6.9 miles (MP 421.1). Take this dirt road to the parking area at the fence, at 7.0 miles.

TRAILHEAD: There are lath-type trail signs. You will also see a sign through the fence saying , "Sandy Seep Vehicle Closure. This area closed to motor vehicles to protect the critical Sandy Seep deer winter range and to offer non-motorized recreation opportunities." Go through the opening in the fence and walk a few yards to your left, where you will pick up an old road. Follow the road.

DESCRIPTION: The road is easy to walk and makes a good hiking path because it has been closed to motor vehicles. At about one third of a mile you will come to the back fence. The road turns right here. Keep following it. The road will wind through the forest and at about one mile you will come to a hill. The road curves around it. At 1.5 miles you will see a trail sign leave the road to the left. Get off the road and follow the footpath. **Sandy Seep** is to your right.

You will walk into a ravine and then up to another closed road that leads to Mt. Elden. Note that the soil here is red. There are two redrock hills looking like importations from Sedona to your right and a red foothill projecting from the face of Mt. Elden. At 2.1 miles you will reach the base of the red foothill, where there is a water tank. You will also see a plastic pipe going up a canyon to tap a spring.

From this point the trail switchbacks up the red hill to the top of Mt. Elden. The trail is nicely laid out, with the switchbacks making the grade moderate. Kudos to Flagstaff's Frank Davies, who promoted this trail.

Sherry, with her photographer's eye, says this part of the trail is *visually exciting*. There are many bold and unusual lava dike formations, burnt trees like totems, vast views to the east, finger ridges running parallel to the hill you are climbing and other delights.

You will come to the top of Mt. Elden at a point on the **Sunset Trail** that is 0.56 miles from its end, just above the Elden Lookout Road. If you are hardy, you could do the **Elden Skyline Trail** over to the lookout tower and then take the **Elden Lookout Trail** to the bottom.

This is a dandy two-car hike, parking one at the bottom and one at the top, then hiking down. Now unnamed, this will likely be the Heart Trail.

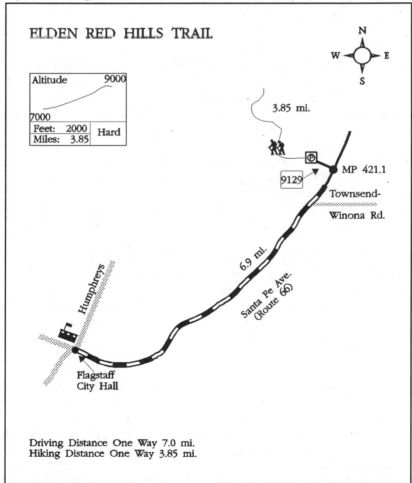

ELDEN RED HILLS TRAIL

Altitude 9000
7000
Feet: 2000
Miles: 3.85 Hard

3.85 mi.

9129

MP 421.1

Townsend-
Winona Rd.

6.9 mi.

Santa Fe Ave.
(Route 66)

Humphreys

Flagstaff
City Hall

Driving Distance One Way 7.0 mi.
Hiking Distance One Way 3.85 mi.

ELDEN SKYLINE TRAIL

General Information
Location Map E3
Humphreys Pk. & Sunset Crater W. USGS Maps
Coconino Forest Service Map

Driving Distance One Way: 9.4 miles (Time 40 minutes)
Access Road: All cars, Last 5.8 miles medium gravel mountain road
Hiking Distance One Way: 1.00 miles (Time 35 minutes)
How Strenuous: Moderate
Features: Unsurpassed views of Flagstaff

NUTSHELL: This trail starts at Sunset Park near the top of Mt. Elden and goes to a point just below the lookout tower.

DIRECTIONS:
From Flagstaff City Hall Go:
North on Humphreys Street for 0.60 miles. Turn left at the stoplight onto Columbus Avenue and follow it around a big curve to the north. You will see the street signs call this road Columbus Avenue at first, then Ft. Valley Road and then Highway 180. Stay on Highway 180 to the 3.1 miles point (MP 218.6), where the Schultz Pass Road, FR 420, goes to the right. Follow this road. At the 3.6 miles point it curves left where you will see the unpaved Elden Lookout Road (FR 557) going straight. Take the right fork and follow FR 557 to the 9.4 mile point, where you will park in an area off the right shoulder.

TRAILHEAD: Across the road you will see a footpath going uphill to the skyline. At the crest you will find signs.

DESCRIPTION: This trail is considered officially to be the last leg of the Sunset Trail. We feel that it is a much better experience to treat it as a separate trail. Elden Skyline Trail is our name, not the Forest Service name.
The place where the trail starts is a junction of the **Sunset Trail** and the **Oldham Trail No. 2** and you will find signs for each of them here. Go to the right, on the Sunset Trail.
This whole area on top of Mt. Elden shows the results of what a forest fire can do. Hundreds of acres of prime forest were burned away in 1978 in the catastrophic Radio Fire. The area is just now beginning to heal.
Your trail will take you along the crest of Mt. Elden, climbing uphill a bit a first and then dipping. Almost all the way you will have tremendous views. You look down on East Flagstaff, the Doney Park area and off toward the Sunset Crater area. On a clear day you can see the Painted Desert off in the distance.

One of the first trees to come back after a forest fire is the aspen and you will find groves of young aspens along this trail. They have replaced the spruce that predominated here before the fire.

At about the three-quarter mile point, the trail comes very close to the road going to the fire lookout, but then it veers away from it. At the 1.00 mile point you will reach the place where this trail meets the **Elden Lookout Trail** coming up from East Flagstaff.

This is the end of the trail, but at this point you have two options. The first is to take the Elden Lookout Trail up to the fire tower, which is a quarter mile hike. The views from the tower are superb. If a ranger is in the tower you may be invited up. Go up if you get the chance. You won't soon forget what you see from there.

The other option is to bushwhack your way out to the end of a rocky knob that is to your left at the junction. This is only about one-tenth of a mile and it takes you to another excellent viewpoint.

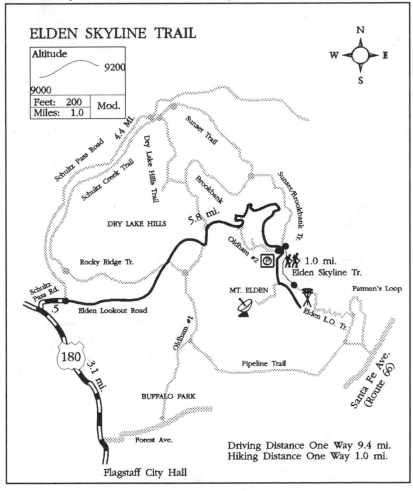

ELDEN SKYLINE TRAIL

Driving Distance One Way 9.4 mi.
Hiking Distance One Way 1.0 mi.

FAT MAN'S LOOP

General Information
Location Map E3
Flagstaff East USGS Map
Coconino Forest Service Map

Driving Distance One Way: 5.2 miles (Time 10 minutes)
Access Road: All cars, All paved
Hiking Distance, Complete Loop: 2.4 miles (Time 1.5 hours)
How Strenuous: Moderate
Features: Views

NUTSHELL: This maintained trail located in East Flagstaff at the base of Mt. Elden is designed to provide moderate exercise for a "fat man." It provides good scenery and views.

DIRECTIONS:
From Flagstaff City Hall Go:
    East on Route 66 (Santa Fe). Highway 89 runs concurrently with Route 66 (Santa Fe) as the highway goes through Flagstaff, so you will see road signs with both designations. At 5.2 miles (MP 419.5) just past the Flagstaff Mall, you will see a sign for the "Mt. Elden Trailhead" and a paved driveway to your left into a parking lot bounded by a pole fence. Pull in there and park.

TRAILHEAD: There are trail signs at the gate in the parking lot fence.

DESCRIPTION: The Forest Service has developed a trail system around the Mt. Elden\Dry Lake Hills areas in Flagstaff and this trail connects with others in that system. You will find trail information at the trailhead. Fat Man's Loop is a nice trail, well marked, The footing is good. As the name suggests, the trail makes a loop. It is not flat, as it climbs to a high point beyond midway and then descends.
    Start out on the main trail and watch for a fork at 0.15 miles. There Fat Man's branches to the right. At 0.30 miles you will come to a pole fence with a squeeze through opening designed to pass humans but not horses. At this point the trail, which up to now has been heading toward Mt. Elden, turns to the right and moves parallel to the base of the mountain. Just beyond this gate, a secondary trail intersects at right angles. Don't turn left or right here. Go straight. At 0.40 miles you hit another trail junction. This is posted with a sign saying, "Fatman's Loop, Elden Lookout." You want to go left here, toward Mt. Elden. Soon after this, the trail winds around and under a giant old alligator-bark juniper tree, which is quite a sight. Since these trees live to be very old, this one must be ancient to have grown so large.

At 0.90 miles you have climbed high enough so that you begin to get some views. To your right the open plain is Doney Park. To your left you see immense cliffs on Mt. Elden. These are made of basaltic columns of lava caused by huge volcanic outbursts two million years ago. All through this area you will see basalt boulders, some of them big as a house and your trail will wind through a nifty crevice between boulders. As you climb even higher, you can see Sunset Crater to the north.

You reach the high point of the trail at 1.5 miles, where there is another trail junction. The path to the right is the **Elden Lookout Trail**, which is not for fat men as it is a very steep climb. You take the trail to the left, from where it is all downhill back to the starting point.

At 2.0 miles you will reach another junction where there is a sign reading, "**Pipeline Trail No. 42, Oldham Trail No. 1**, Buffalo Park 4." Just beyond this point is another pole fence with a squeeze through. From there you saunter back to your car.

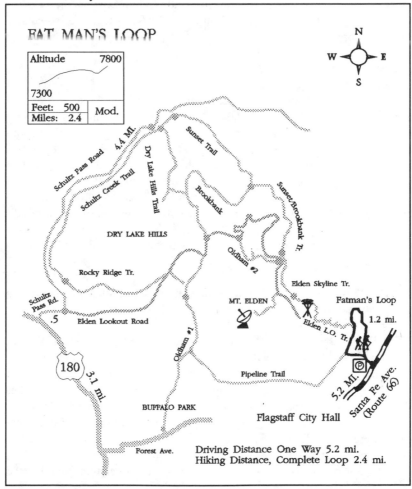

FAT MAN'S LOOP

Altitude 7800
7300
Feet: 500 | Mod.
Miles: 2.4

Driving Distance One Way 5.2 mi.
Hiking Distance, Complete Loop 2.4 mi.

FISHER POINT

General Information
Location Map F3
Flagstaff East USGS Map
Coconino Forest Service Map

Driving Distance One Way: 7.2 miles (Time 15 minutes)
Access Road: All cars, Last 0.10 miles good gravel road
Hiking Distance One Way: 3.0 miles (Time 90 minutes)
How Strenuous: Moderate
Features: Caves, Beautiful canyon

NUTSHELL: Located south of Flagstaff, only a few miles out on the Lake Mary Road, this hike requires a brief climb into Walnut Canyon, then an easy walk along the canyon bottom. It features impressive cliffs and a cave that is fun to explore.

DIRECTIONS:
From Flagstaff City Hall Go:

West on Route 66 (Santa Fe) one block and then south (left) on Sitgreaves Street under the railroad overpass. As you continue south you will see the street signs calling the street Milton Road, as Sitgreaves blends into Milton. At 1.7 miles you reach the stoplight at Forest Meadows, where you turn right. At the next corner turn left on Beulah and follow it out of town. Beulah will connect onto Highway 89A. At the 2.4 miles point (MP 401.6) you will see the turnoff to the Lake Mary Road to your left. Take it and follow the Lake Mary Road to the 7.1 mile point where you will see a gravel road to your left. Turn left onto the gravel road and take it about 300 feet, where you will see another gravel road to your right. Turn right and take the road to the 7.2 miles point. Park there.

TRAILHEAD: There are no trail signs. You will see a path marked by cairns going down into a canyon. This is the trail you want.

DESCRIPTION: The trail descends a side canyon to the floor of Walnut Canyon. Walnut Canyon National Monument is several miles downstream. There is a fairly steep drop into the canyon bottom. You reach the streambed at 0.40 miles. Cross the streambed and you will find an old road on the other side. Go left on the road. It is your hiking path. The canyon is wide as you begin, but the farther you go, the deeper and narrower it gets. There are some truly impressive cliffs and if you have an eye for line, you will love the crazy cracks, streaks and angles caused by erosion of the cliff faces.

The trail goes fairly straight for about 2 miles and then curves to the right. Just beyond the curve, to your left, is Fisher Point, where there is a half cave under an enormous boulder. Walk on past the boulder to a place where the trail seems to end at a screen of willows.

This screen is at a bend in Walnut Canyon. The trail continues but completely changes character. It goes from a jeep road to a foot trail. The canyon becomes very narrow and you wind your way back and forth across the streambed. At 2.5 miles the trail goes past a large cave to your right. This is fun to explore, and even has an "escape hatch" out the back. At 2.7 miles there is a smaller cave that is partly hidden. It is uphill to your right. Look for a short trail to it taking off from the streambed where the bed is wide and full of coarse sand.

We recommend stopping at the 3.0 miles point, where you will find a large Ponderosa with a silver stripe painted around it. From that point the trail disappears and you have to bushwhack. The channel is choked and becomes impassable beyond the 3.0 mile point.

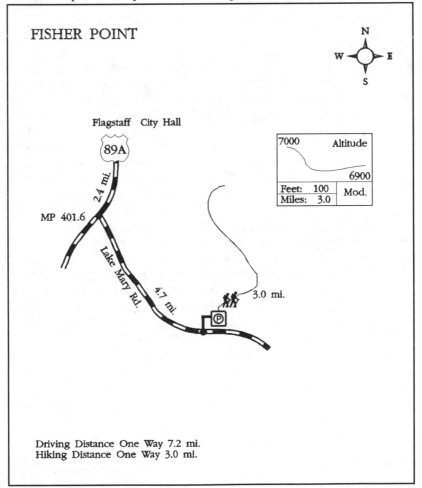

FISHER POINT

N
W — E
S

Flagstaff City Hall

89A

7000   Altitude

6900

| Feet: | 100 | Mod. |
| Miles: | 3.0 | |

2.4 mi.

MP 401.6

Lake Mary Rd.

4.7 mi.

3.0 mi.

P

Driving Distance One Way 7.2 mi.
Hiking Distance One Way 3.0 mi.

GOVERNMENT KNOLL

Driving Distance One Way: 25.9 miles (Time 45 minutes)
Access Road: All cars, Last 11 miles medium gravel road
Hiking Distance One Way: 0.5 miles (Time 30 minutes)
How Strenuous: Moderate
Features: Views

NUTSHELL: This cinder cone located at the north end of Government Prairie 25.9 miles west of Flagstaff provides beautiful views of Kendrick Mountain and the San Francisco Peaks. It is easy to reach and to climb.

DIRECTIONS:
From Flagstaff City Hall Go:
West a block on Route 66 (Santa Fe), then south, beneath the railroad overpass on Sitgreaves Street. The street name will change to Milton Road as you go farther. At 0.50 miles you will reach a Y intersection. The right fork is named West Old US Highway 66. Take it. You will soon leave town, driving on a stretch of fabled Highway 66. At the 4.8 mile point you will merge onto Interstate-40 West. Look for Exit 185, "Transwestern Rd., Bellemont" and take it. It is at the 10.8 mile point. From the exit turn right and go to the frontage road, where you turn left onto FR 146. You are now following another stretch of U.S. 66. Stay on this to the 18 mile point, where you will see FR 107 fork right. Take FR 107 and follow it to the 23.2 mile point, just beyond a bare hill we call **Rain Tank Hill** (unnamed on government maps). Here you will find FR 793 to the right. It has no sign at the entrance and looks primitive but it is a decent road when it is dry. Turn right and follow FR 793. It will take you north across the prairie. At 23.9 miles you will see a sign marked 793 and 81. Take the left fork here. There is a gate at 24.1 miles. Go through it. At 24.3 miles you will pass the **Beale Road on Government Prairie**. Look for markers showing the right of way of this historic road as you pass. You can also see the old wagon tracks. At 25.4 miles you will come to Horseshoe Tank at the base of Government Knoll. The road splits here. Take the left fork and drive along the north side of the hill. When you come to the 25.9 mile point you will see a V-shaped notch in the hill with boulders at the bottom of the V. Park there.

TRAILHEAD: There is no trail. You walk up the hill through the notch.

DESCRIPTION: These cinder hills are all extinct volcanoes. From a distance they look symmetrical like a perfect cone or anthill. As you explore them you will find that most of them have a low side with a V-shaped opening gouged out by lava flow. Such is the case with Government Knoll.

Once you climb past the notch you are on the inside of the crater. Walk uphill to your left (north) on a gentle slope that is a natural ramp to the top. The highest point of the hill is the north side.

The hike is not long or overly hard. All you can see until you crest out are the sides of the crater. Then you break over the top and are presented with a genuine "*Aha!*" panorama.

This hill is located at the north end of Government Prairie so you are close to Kendrick Mountain and the San Francisco Peaks and have superlative views of them. We were here on a late September afternoon. It was perfectly silent and calm. The golden fields of the prairie stretched away smooth as velvet. It was gorgeous and very refreshing, deeply peaceful.

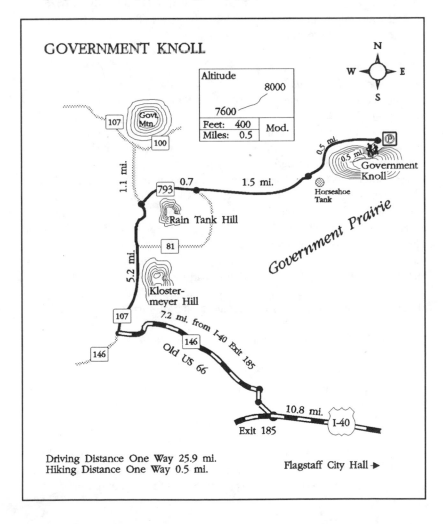

GOVERNMENT KNOLL

Driving Distance One Way 25.9 mi.
Hiking Distance One Way 0.5 mi.

Flagstaff City Hall →

GRAND FALLS

General Information
Location Map E4
Grand Falls USGS Map
Coconino Forest Service Map

Driving Distance One Way: 38.6 miles (Time 1 hour)
Access Road: All cars, Last 9.3 miles medium dirt road
Hiking Distance One Way: 0.75 miles (Time 45 minutes)
How Strenuous: Moderate
Features: Waterfall

NUTSHELL: Located 38.6 miles east of Flagstaff, Grand Falls is Arizona's biggest waterfall, with a drop higher than Niagara's. Admire it from the top and then hike down to the water.

DIRECTIONS:
From Flagstaff City Hall Go:
        East, curving to north on Route 66 (Santa Fe). As you leave the city limits you will see that Route 66 (Santa Fe) is also Highway 89. Follow Highway 89 north. At 6.5 miles (MP 420.5) you will reach the last stoplight in town at the junction of the Townsend-Winona Road. Turn right here onto the Townsend-Winona Road and follow it to the 14.7 miles point (MP 428.6) where it intersects Leupp Road. Turn left on the Leupp Road and take it to the 29.3 miles point (MP 443.5), where Navajo Route 70 joins it to the left. You will see a sign for the Grand Falls church and there is a mangled cattle guard at the highway. From here you follow Navajo Route 70 to the 38.3 miles point. The road surface is black cinders. These sometimes cause loose pockets where traction is not good. The road is very dusty. At 38.3 miles there is an unmarked turn uphill to the left. Take it (it's rough) and you will top out at 38.6 miles where you will see some picnic shelters. Park here near the rim. If you drive all the way to the river, you have missed the uphill turn.

TRAILHEAD: 375 feet from the last picnic shelter.

DESCRIPTION: Take this trip only when the river, the Little Colorado, is carrying lots of water, which means during spring snowmelt in March and April. When you reach the parking area, park at the first cluster of shelters. Some shelters are picnic tables and others are viewpoints. From this place you will see other shelters downstream. You can drive to the last one, but the road to that point is really rough. We prefer to keep the car at the top and walk the rest of the way. When you reach the last shelter, you will see a jeep road that appears to go right to the rim. This is the trailhead. It is unmarked.

The trail is crude and goes abruptly to the river bottom. Once there you can walk along the shore toward the falls and, depending on how muddy it is, you can get quite close to the falls. If you get close enough to be hit by spray you will find that the water is almost as much soil as liquid and when it dries on you it leaves a film of dirt. The high dirt content of the water accounts for the color and thickness of the falls, which look exactly like cocoa. The falls spill over two major levels.

We have seen daredevils work their way around so that they can stand under the falls at their extreme end but this can be very dangerous and you should not try it unless you have a strong death wish.

The canyon walls at the bottom are interesting. The wall the falls spill over is sandstone, whereas the wall on your side of the river is lava. Roden Crater erupted and poured this lava into the riverbed, damming the river and changing it to its present course.

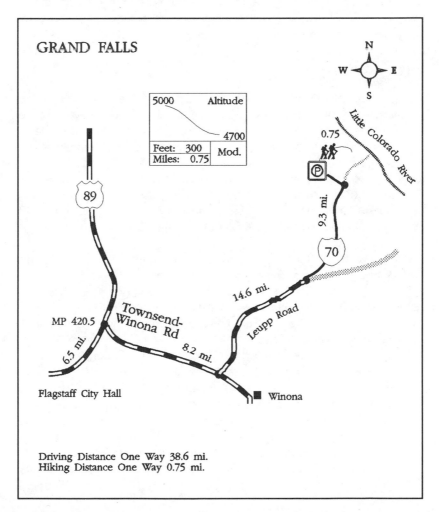

GRAND FALLS

Driving Distance One Way 38.6 mi.
Hiking Distance One Way 0.75 mi.

GRIFFITHS SPRING CANYON

General Information
Location Map F3
Mountainaire USGS Map
Coconino Forest Service Map

Driving Distance One Way: 7.5 miles (Time 20 minutes)
Access Road: All cars, Last 0.25 miles good dirt road
Hiking Distance One Way: 0.80 miles (Time 30 minutes)
How Strenuous: Easy
Features: Beautiful canyon

NUTSHELL: This small canyon is located just south of Flagstaff. Because water usually runs through the canyon all year, a rarity in Arizona, the streambed is a haven for wildlife and supports diverse plantlife.

DIRECTIONS:
From Flagstaff City Hall Go:
West on Route 66 (Santa Fe) one block then left (south) on Sitgreaves Street under the railroad overpass. As you continue south you will see the street signs calling the street Milton Road, as Sitgreaves blends into Milton. At 1.7 miles you reach the stoplight at Forest Meadows, where you turn right. At the next corner turn left on Beulah and follow it out of town. Beulah will connect onto Highway 89A which is the road to Oak Creek Canyon and Sedona. At 7.2 miles (MP 396.8) on Highway 89A you will see an unmarked access road to your left. Take it. Just off the highway there is an unlocked gate. Go through it and stay on the dirt road to the 7.5 miles point. Park.

TRAILHEAD: No trail signs. You will see the canyon floor down to your left. Walk into it and go downstream (to the right).

DESCRIPTION: From the gate, you want to drive about 0.25 miles, to a point where the road forks. The road is a bit rough but a passenger car can handle the road when it is dry. Park at the fork. The right fork just peters out in about 0.10 miles. Walk the left fork, which goes down into the canyon.
The canyon is narrow and there is usually a little stream running through it. There is no developed hiking trail but you can follow the bed of an old logging railroad in most places and game trails in others. You will cross the stream several times, which could be troublesome if it is carrying much water. In some areas the canyon walls are high Malpais (basaltic lava) cliffs cut and cracked into very attractive lines and angles. In other places the walls are low and open. The forest is mostly pine but there are copses of oak and others of aspen.

On a hike in August we saw lots of flowers, among them potentillas, wild roses, asters, penstemons, Indian paintbrushes, lupines, evening prim- roses, linarias, cranesbills and many others. There was also an abundance of elk sign.

The hike ends on a jarring note at 0.80 miles where the canyon is blocked by an earthfill which supports a road into the south end of Forest Highlands subdivision. There is a huge culvert you could walk through but we suggest that you do not, as you emerge into the disheartening sight of Lindbergh Springs, which used to be a lovely place but now is disfigured by the road building. This is a pretty hike until you round the final bend.

This canyon became the center of a controversy in 1991 due to the desire of the developers of Forest Highlands to acquire the canyon area to add to their subdivision. Nature lovers are trying to block this move so that it can be preserved as a pristine habitat. After seeing what happened to Lindbergh Springs, we have to side with the conservationists.

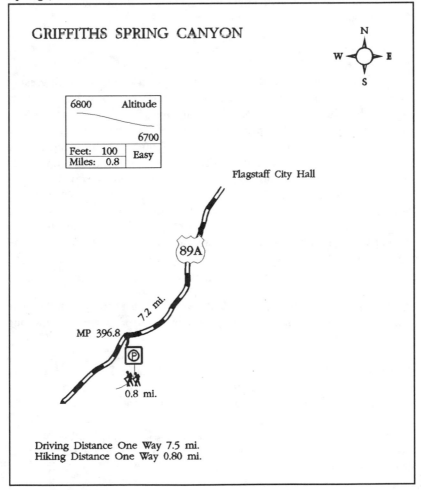

GRIFFITHS SPRING CANYON

6800	Altitude
	6700

Feet:	100	Easy
Miles:	0.8	

Flagstaff City Hall

89A

7.2 mi.

MP 396.8

0.8 mi.

Driving Distance One Way 7.5 mi.
Hiking Distance One Way 0.80 mi.

HARDING SPRING TRAIL

General Information
Location Map F3
Mountainaire and Munds Park USGS Maps
Coconino Forest Service Map

Drive Distance One Way: 18.4 miles (Time 35 minutes)
Access Road: All cars, All paved
Hiking Distance One Way: 0.80 miles (Time 45 minutes)
How Strenuous: Hard
Features: Views

NUTSHELL: This is a marked and posted trail located just across Highway 89A from the Cave Spring Campground 18.4 miles south of Flagstaff. It climbs the east wall of Oak Creek Canyon.

DIRECTIONS:
From Flagstaff City Hall Go:
          West one block on Route 66 (Santa Fe) then left (south) on Sitgreaves Street under the railroad overpass. As you continue south you will see the street signs calling the street Milton Road, as Sitgreaves Street blends into Milton. At 1.7 miles you reach the intersection of Forest Meadows, where there is a traffic light. Here you turn right. You will see a sign for Highway 89A, which is the road you want. At the next corner turn left on Beulah and follow it out of town. Beulah will connect onto Highway 89A which is the road to Oak Creek Canyon and Sedona. At 13.8 miles (MP 390) you will reach the canyon rim and begin the winding descent. After you have completed the switchbacks and are on the canyon floor, drive to the 18.4 mile point (MP 385.6), the Cave Spring Campground. Parking is scarce in the campground and you will probably have to park on the shoulder of the highway.

TRAILHEAD: On the east side of Highway 89A just across from the Cave Spring Campground entrance. It is marked by a rusty sign reading, "Harding Spring Trail #51."

DESCRIPTION: There is no official parking area for this hike. Cars park all along the shoulders of the road wherever there is a wide spot. If you are lucky you might find a parking spot in the Cave Spring Campground but don't count on it. Camping in the campground requires the payment of a fee.

          Since you will be so near the Cave Spring Campground after you park, you might as well walk into the campground and take a look at Cave Spring. It is an interesting place.

Like the other trails going up the east wall of upper Oak Creek Canyon the Harding Spring trail goes virtually straight up with little finesse. You start in a pine and spruce forest and then get into a more open area as you climb above tree line. Then you get into a region of pine forest again at the top.

The trail zigzags in such a way that it isn't a killer, like the **Purtymun Trail.** It is more like the **Cookstove Trail** or the **Thomas Point Trail.**

The trail was built in the late 1800s to provide access to the canyon rim so that families living down in the canyon could get to the top and go to Flagstaff. They could lead a horse on such a trail or hike it but it was not a wagon road, as you will see when you take it. They would leave a wagon chained to a tree at the top and hitch the horse to it for the trip to town and return. When they brought their goods back, they would park the wagon and pack the goods down by horseback. Such a trip often took several days and was considered to be a major undertaking. Most of the east rim hikes are like that.

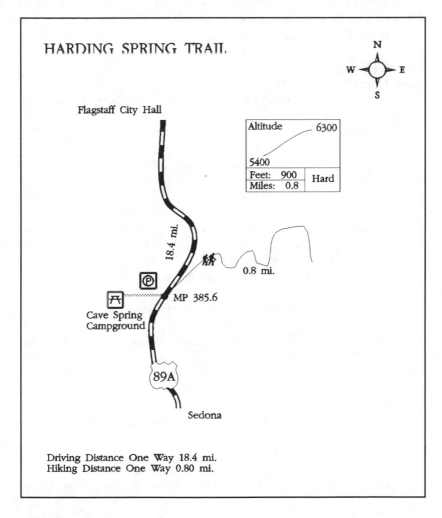

HOG HILL TRAIL

General Information
Location Map F2
Sycamore Point USGS Map
Coconino Forest Service Map

Driving Distance One Way: 22.95 miles (Time 60 minutes)
Access Road: High clearance for last 0.65 miles
Hiking Distance One Way: 2.15 miles (Time 1.50 hours)
How Strenuous: Moderate
Features: Easy access to Winter Cabin via old road

NUTSHELL: This trail into Sycamore Canyon 23.0 miles southwest of Flagstaff is unique among the upper canyon trails because it follows an old road rather than a footpath into the canyon.

DIRECTIONS:
From Flagstaff City Hall Go:
　　　West a block on Route 66 (Santa Fe), then south, beneath the railroad overpass on Sitgreaves Street. The street name will change to Milton Road as you go farther. At 0.50 miles you will reach a Y intersection. The right fork is named West Old US Highway 66. Take it. You will soon leave town. At 2.6 miles you will reach a road going to the left. This is the Woody Mountain Road, FR 231. Take it. It is paved about a mile and then turns into a cinder road. At 16.6 miles you will intersect FR 538. Turn right onto FR 538 and follow it to the 22.3 mile point, where it intersects the Kelsey Spring Road, FR 538G. Take 538G. The roads to here are good, but beyond this point they are rough. At 22.7 miles you hit another intersection where FR 538E forks to the left. This is the Dorsey Spring Road. Turn left onto it and follow it to its end at 22.95 miles, where you will find a parking lot.

TRAILHEAD: You will see a big sign at the parking area.

DESCRIPTION: You begin this hike by walking along the **Dorsey Spring Trail**. The beginning part of this trail is an old road that has been closed to vehicles. At 0.25 miles you will see a sign saying, "Hog Hill Trailhead 1/2" and a road forking to the left. Take this road to the left and follow it to the 0.75 mile point where you will reach a fence. The fence is officially the trailhead, although there is no marker or sign of any kind there except for Wilderness Area boundary signs.

　　　Go through the gate at the fence and continue to walk along the old road. The road becomes worse and worse as you go. There are no signs, markers or blazes along the way. We did find a few cairns. Pay attention and you should have no trouble following the road.

At 0.85 miles you will see the canyon rim nearby to your right. From here the road begins to descend steeply. It makes a decent hiking trail but you don't see how anyone could ever have driven it. The grade is very sharp and the surface consists of exposed rock all the way. You will never leave the road and go off onto a footpath.

The trail is not scenic. It passes through a typical pine forest and goes down the canyon businesslike. At 2.0 miles you will come to a sidecanyon.

We were here in October and saw many red leaves on the trees in the canyon. It turns out that they are maples. Originally the road crossed the canyon but washouts have erased it. The trail splits here. Take the right fork along the streambed. You will emerge in just a few yards onto a bare spot less than 0.1 mile above Winter Cabin. You can see the cabin roof. The trail ends at 2.15 miles at the cabin.

Of all the trails in upper Sycamore Canyon, we like this the least.

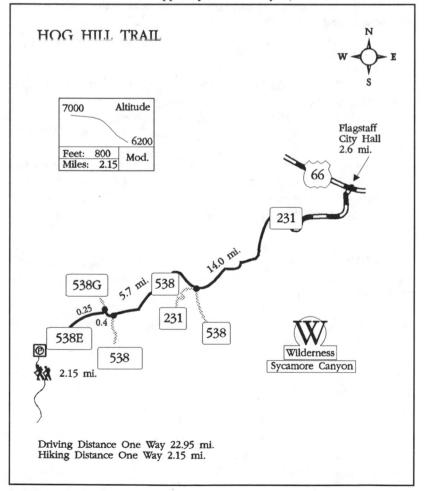

HUMPHREYS TRAIL

General Information
Location Map E3
Humphreys Peak USGS Map
Coconino Forest Service Map

Driving Distance One Way: 14.8 miles (Time 30 minutes)
Access Road: All cars, All paved
Hiking Distance One Way: 4.5 miles (Time 3 hours)
How Strenuous: Hard, Steep climb, High altitudes
Features: Highest point in Arizona, Alpine forests, Unsurpassed views

NUTSHELL: Starting from the Snow Bowl located about 15 miles north of Flagstaff, this strenuous climb takes you to the top of the San Francisco Peaks, the highest point in Arizona.

DIRECTIONS:
From Flagstaff City Hall Go:
   North on Humphreys Street for 0.60 miles. Turn left at the stoplight onto Columbus Avenue and follow it around a big curve to the north. You will see the street signs call this road Columbus at first, then Ft. Valley Road and then Highway 180. Stay on Highway 180 to the 7.3 miles point (MP 223), where the road to the Snow Bowl branches off to the right. It is well posted. Follow the Snow Bowl road to the top at 13.8 miles. You will encounter a first parking area there. Disregard the trail sign you will see at the first parking area. Drive beyond the first parking place to the highest parking area at the 14.8 miles point and park there by the big chairlift, which looks like a giant black spider.

TRAILHEAD: You will find the trailhead at the end of the deck at the chairlift (Skyride) office. It is posted. This is the older trailhead. The one you saw posted below was added only recently and is not as good.

DESCRIPTION: At 0.66 miles the old trail and the new trail meet in the forest and thereafter are the same.
   The forest in the first couple of miles of this trail is a heavy one of fir, spruce and aspen. There are many fallen timbers, making a tangle on the forest floor. The trees are tall, shutting out most of the sun and allowing no views.
   As you go higher, the forest opens and you will encounter small meadows which permit views to the west. At about the 10,500 foot point the aspens begin to disappear. You can see from here into the Snow Bowl area. What appear to be roads there are actually the ski runs cut through the trees. The major peak that you will see is Mt. Agassiz.

At 3.75 miles the only trees are twisted and stunted bristlecone pines. There is no cover and the footing is not very good. You must stay on the trail here. At 4.0 miles you reach the rim where the Humphreys Trail joins the **Weatherford Trail** coming in from your right. You can look into the Inner Basin of the Peaks here and enjoy a splendid view. You can also see to the east for the first time on the hike for views of Sunset Crater and the Painted Desert.

The mountain top will be different from what you imagined. You are above timberline. It is bare and almost always windy and cold. The footing is terrible, being a mixture of loose gravel and rough jagged lava. You can't really walk along the crest.

To get to the top of Mt. Humphreys you take the path to the left. The top is 0.50 miles away. The altitude is over 12,000 feet. This and the roughness of the trail make the crest hike hard. Allow a half hour for it. Take good boots, warm clothing and plenty of water. Allow lots of time. If you are properly prepared this is one of Arizona's best hikes.

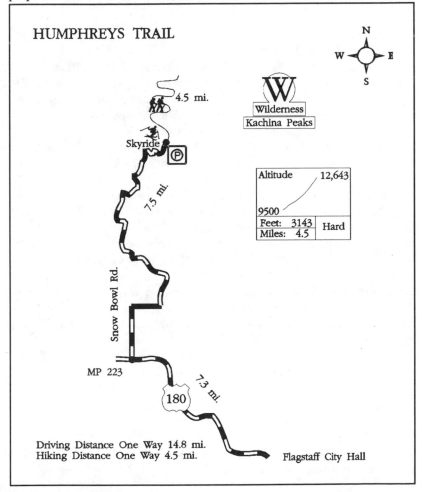

HUMPHREYS TRAIL

N
W E
S

4.5 mi.

Wilderness
Kachina Peaks

Skyride

Altitude   12,643
9500
Feet: 3143   Hard
Miles: 4.5

7.5 mi.

Snow Bowl Rd.

MP 223

180

7.3 mi.

Driving Distance One Way 14.8 mi.
Hiking Distance One Way 4.5 mi.

Flagstaff City Hall

I-40 PARKS NATURE TRAIL

General Information
Location Map E2
Parks USGS Map
Coconino Forest Service Map

Driving Distance One Way: 13.8 miles (Time 20 minutes)
Access Road: All cars, All paved
Hiking Distance, Complete Loop: 0.25 miles (Time 30 minutes)
How Strenuous: Easy
Features: Easy nature trail located at a highway rest stop

NUTSHELL: This hike is the easiest (and least interesting) in the book, a flat ramble on a paved trail adjacent to an interstate highway rest stop.

DIRECTIONS:
From Flagstaff City Hall Go:
    West a block on Route 66 (Santa Fe), then south, beneath the railroad overpass on Sitgreaves Street. The street name will change to Milton Road as you go farther. At 0.50 miles you will reach a Y intersection. The right fork is named West Old US Highway 66. Take it. You will soon leave town, driving on a stretch of fabled Highway 66. At the 4.8 mile point you will merge onto Interstate-40 West. Follow I-40 to the 13.8 mile point (MP 182.7) where you will see signs marking a rest stop. Pull in here and park.

TRAILHEAD: As you drive into the rest stop you will see one sign marking the parking area for buses and trucks and another one for cars. Take the road for cars. It makes a loop and comes back onto the interstate highway. About midway through the loop you will see the large wooden sign marking the trailhead to your right. There are several parking spaces nearby.

DESCRIPTION: At the entrance to the hiking trail there is a signboard with a map of the trail. There is also a box that is supposed to contain brochures describing the identified points of interest along the trail. These points are marked by a couple of dozen numbered posts.
    When we visited the place in September, 1991, there were no pamphlets in the box. The trail takes off into the woods and is paved all the way. You never get very far from the highway and you will hear highway noises the whole time. At least the woods muffle the noises.
    The area through which the trail passes is not particularly interesting. It is a typical pine forest with a flat floor. Without the brochure, it is very hard to imagine finding two dozen points of interest in such an uninteresting piece of ground. We were hard pressed to find things worthy of discussion.

The trail was installed by the Kaibab District of the Forest Service and is a great idea. We need hiking trails of all kinds, from the long and strenuous to the short and easy. You could even roll a wheelchair around this trail with little trouble. The problem is that the people who would most profit from using this trail won't know about it: the travellers on I-40, many of whom would love the chance to get out, stretch their legs and breathe some fresh air. There are no signs along the highway announcing the presence of the trail. People who read this book will know about the trail but are quite unlikely to try it because there are so many superior trails. We have to give the Forest Service an E for Effort on this trail but can't really recommend it. We have seen it written up in two other hike books, so we include it.

Even though this trail is called the I-40 Parks Nature Trail, it is not located at the Parks exit, which is Exit 178, located 4.2 miles west of this rest stop.

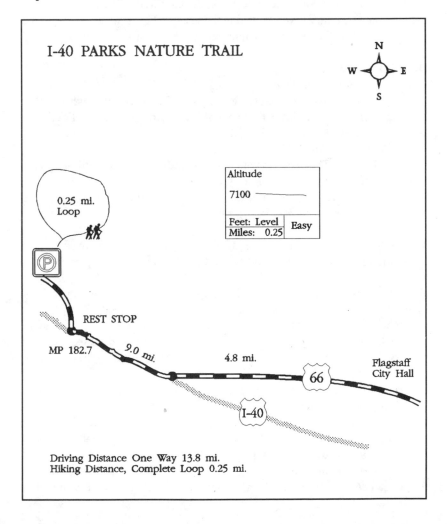

I-40 PARKS NATURE TRAIL

N
W — E
S

0.25 mi.
Loop

Altitude

7100 ————

Feet: Level
Miles: 0.25   Easy

REST STOP

MP 182.7   9.0 mi.   4.8 mi.   66   Flagstaff City Hall

I-40

Driving Distance One Way 13.8 mi.
Hiking Distance, Complete Loop 0.25 mi.

INNER BASIN TRAIL

General Information
Location Map E3
Humphreys Peak and Sunset Crater West USGS Maps
Coconino Forest Service Map

Driving Distance One Way: 21.6 miles (Time 45 minutes)
Access Road: All cars, Last 4.5 miles medium dirt road
Hiking Distance One Way: 2.0 miles (Time 1 hour)
How Strenuous: Hard, Steep Climb, High altitudes
Features: High mountain, Alpine forests, Great views

NUTSHELL: The San Francisco Peaks located north of Flagstaff are an extinct volcanic crater with an opening to the east. This trail takes you up the valley formed by that eastern opening into the heart of the crater.

DIRECTIONS:
From Flagstaff City Hall Go:
East on Route 66 (Santa Fe). This will take you through the city, heading first easterly and then north out of town. Route 66 (Santa Fe) is also Highway 89. At 17.1 miles (MP 431.2) turn left onto FR 552 and take it to the 18.3 mile point. Turn to the right there, also FR 552. You will see a sign for Lockett Meadow. This road is a winding narrow dirt road which climbs up the face of the mountain. At 21.3 miles you reach Lockett Meadow. There you will see a road to your right into a camping area. Take this and park anywhere around the 21.6 mile point.

TRAILHEAD: To find the trailhead you must drive all the way back into the trees among the campsites. The trailhead is posted with a big sign.

DESCRIPTION: The trail is a road that was used by the City of Flagstaff for maintenance vehicles, because the Inner Basin of the Peaks is the city's watershed. This makes the trail wide and easy to walk. Even so, at these altitudes, the hike will be more strenuous than you would think, given its relatively short distance. You will be climbing constantly.

The Inner Basin of the Peaks has a tremendous amount of water because all the water from snow melting inside the crater gathers in the bowl. There are several springs in the basin. The early settlers of Flagstaff realized the importance of the basin as a water supply for the town and sewed up all the water rights. As a result most of the water is captured and channelled and you will see very little of it on the surface.

The vegetation here is very lush, as the basin is moist. You will pass through a beautiful forest of aspen, spruce and fir, with many ferns and other low growing plants.

At the 1.5 mile point you will come to Jack Smith Spring where there are two green cabins. There is a faucet outside the larger cabin from which you can drink delicious cold spring water. The altitude at Jack Smith is 9400 feet.

You will find a hiker's log in an ammo can here and you are requested to enter your name and other information. The spring is a crossroads and you will see a sign showing FR 146 going to the left to what we call the **Tunnel Trail** and ending at the Schultz Pass Road 8.5 miles away. To the right FR 146 (also known as the Abineau Pipeline Trail) goes about 5.25 miles to a point on the north face of Mt. Humphreys. Along the way it intersects the **Bear Jaw Trail** at 3.0 miles and the **Abineau Trail** at 5.0 miles.

Instead of taking a fork, go straight ahead. At 2.0 miles you will break out of the timber into a bare area. This is the Inner Basin. You will have awesome views of the inside of the crater and distant views to the east and some great exploring.

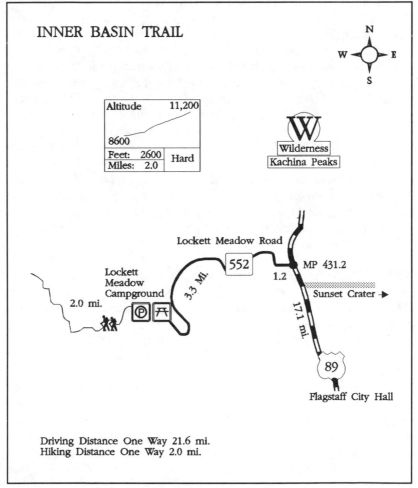

INNER BASIN TRAIL

Driving Distance One Way 21.6 mi.
Hiking Distance One Way 2.0 mi.

KA HILL

General Information
Location Map E2
Bill Wms Mt. & Garland Prairie USGS Maps
Kaibab (Williams District) Forest Service Map

Driving Distance One Way: 30.9 miles (Time 45 minutes)
Access Road: All cars, Last 12.4 miles good gravel road
Hiking Distance, Complete Loop: 5.70 miles (Time 3.0 hours)
How Strenuous: Moderate
Features: Views, Historic road

NUTSHELL: This hike is located in an area west of Flagstaff bordering Garland Prairie, just north of Sycamore Canyon.

DIRECTIONS:
From Flagstaff City Hall Go:
    West a block on Route 66 (Santa Fe), then south, beneath the railroad overpass on Sitgreaves Street. The street name will change to Milton Road as you go farther. At 0.50 miles you will reach a Y intersection. The right fork is named West Old US Highway 66. Take it. You will soon leave town, driving on a stretch of fabled Highway 66. At the 4.8 mile point you will merge onto Interstate-40 West. Look for Exit 178, "Parks" and take it. It is at the 18.0 mile point. From the exit turn left and go toward Garland Prairie. When you cross the railroad tracks you will be on FR 141, the main road through Garland Prairie. Stay on it to the 27.6 miles point, where it meets FR 131. At this point the road going straight ahead will be FR 13. Take FR 13 to the 30.9 point, where you will see a small wooden sign marking the Sycamore Rim Trail to your right. Park there.

TRAILHEAD: The trail is marked with the sign where you park.

DESCRIPTION: This hike could loosely be described as the north half of the **Sycamore Rim Trail.**
    As you begin the hike you will notice that you are climbing, but the trail has been located and engineered well to take advantage of the terrain. You will be fairly high up the hill before you note that you have done a considerable climb. From the 1.5 mile point the trail steepens and gets a bit more difficult but it is still a fine trail. You will come out on the top at a point slightly below the true summit and walk along the crest. The top is wooded but there are a few thin spots where you can see out. The views to the north and east are good, out over Garland Prairie. You will reach the absolute top at 1.92 miles and find a trail marker with altitude there. From this point you descend the east face

of the hill. The trail is steeper here.

You will reach FR 13 at 3.05 miles. Go south of it on the trail to the 3.42 mile point, to intersect the **Overland Road,** an historical road built in 1863 so that followers of a Prescott gold rush could reach Prescott from the Beale Road. The Overland started about where Flagstaff now is and ran for 85 miles. It was difficult and disliked. After the railroad came through northern Arizona in 1882 the road was abandoned. Historians have done a good job recently locating the right of way and marking it with cairns, brass caps and posts bearing a burro symbol.

Turn right (west) on the Overland Road and follow it to the 5.42 mile point where it intersects the Sycamore Rim Trail again. Here you will turn right (north) and return to your parking place at 5.70 miles.

The Sycamore Rim Trail has you hike a twelve mile circuit omitting the Overland Road. We found this twelve miler to be very demanding, so have broken it into two sections, KA Hill and **Dow Spring to Pomeroy Tank.**

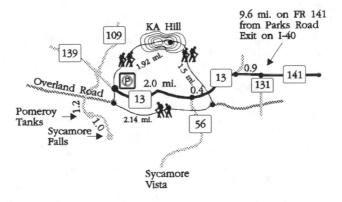

KA HILL

Altitude 7287 | 6600 | Feet: 687 Miles: 5.70 | Mod.

Flagstaff City Hall via I-40 to Exit 178 is 18.0 mi. ▶

9.6 mi. on FR 141 from Parks Road Exit on I-40

KA Hill

109

139

1.92 mi.

1.5 mi.

13   0.9   141

131

Overland Road

2.0 mi.   0.4

13

Pomeroy Tanks

1.2

2.14 mi.

56

1.0

Sycamore Falls

Sycamore Vista

Driving Distance One Way 30.9 mi.
Hiking Distance, Complete Loop 5.70 mi.

KACHINA TRAIL

General Information
Location Map E3
Humphreys Peak USGS Map
Coconino Forest Service Map

Driving Distance One Way: 14.0 miles (Time 40 minutes)
Access Road: All cars, All paved
Hiking Distance One Way: 6.0 miles (Time 3 hours)
How Strenuous: Moderate if done as recommended
Features: High mountains, Alpine forests, Excellent views

NUTSHELL: This mildly strenuous hike across the south face of the San Francisco Peaks a dozen miles north of Flagstaff displays the best the Peaks have to offer. **A personal favorite.**

DIRECTIONS:
From Flagstaff City Hall Go:
          North on Humphreys Street for 0.60 miles. Turn left at the stoplight onto Columbus Avenue and follow it around a big curve to the north. You will see the street signs call this road Columbus at first, then Ft. Valley Road and then Highway 180. Stay on Highway 180 to the 7.3 miles point (MP 223), where the road to the Snow Bowl branches off to the right. It is well posted. Follow the Snow Bowl road to the top at 13.8 miles where you will see a trail sign and encounter a parking area. Turn right and drive to the end of this large graveled parking area and park.

TRAILHEAD: You will see a large sign announcing the trail at the end of the parking lot.

DESCRIPTION: This trail starts at the 9300 foot level and winds its way across the south face (Flagstaff side) of the Peaks, dropping to 8800 feet at trail's end. This is a very gradual hike for the Peaks where every trail tends to be very steep. Nevertheless, the high elevation may make this a tougher hike than the mileage would indicate for those unaccustomed to high altitudes.
          The trail starts in a lovely forest of fir, spruce and aspen. This is a good trail to take in the fall to see the changing aspen leaves.
          You will see some interesting basalt cliffs at 1.5 miles. In places you will find clearings that give you views out over the countryside.
          Just beyond the 4.0 mile point you will enter Friedlein Prairie which is a beautiful meadow area, visible from Flagstaff, from where it looks like a triangle with the point at the top. You will walk along the foot of the triangle. From the bottom of the prairie you get some breathtaking views up the

mountain, which seems huge from this vantage point.

The trail ends at a road that extends from the end of the Friedlein Prairie Road to the **Weatherford Trail** trailhead. This road was blocked in October 1990 so that vehicles cannot drive it anymore. This is an unfortunate decision for the Forest Service to make, because the road was the best access to the Weatherford Trail. It is easy to hike, however.

The Kachina Trail is a major hike if you must turn around at the end and go back 6.0 miles uphill to your starting point. The best way to do this hike is to use a two-car shuttle. Park one car at the end of the Friedlein Prairie Road where the roadblock is. There is a parking area there that will hold several cars. For directions showing how to get to the end of the Friedlein Prairie Road see the entry for the **Weatherford Trail**. Park the other car at the Kachina Trail trailhead as mentioned at the beginning of this hike description.

This has become a very popular trail. Please keep dogs on a leash if you bring them along, and don't carve on the aspens, it opens them to infection.

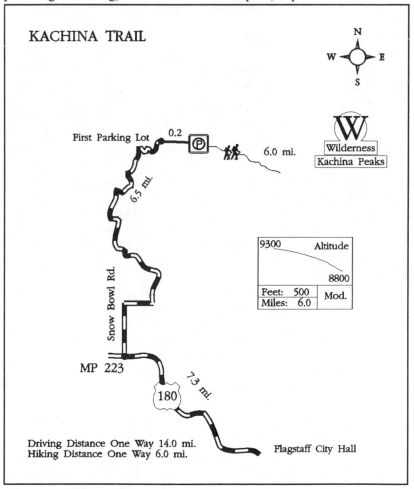

KELSEY SPRING TRAIL

General Information
Location Map F2
Sycamore Point USGS Map
Coconino Forest Service Map

Driving Distance One Way: 24.1 miles (Time 1 hour)
Access Road: High clearance needed for last 1.8 miles
Hiking Distance One Way: 0.50 miles (Time 30 minutes)
How Strenuous: Moderate
Features: Views, Sycamore Canyon access

NUTSHELL: Located about 25 miles southwest of Flagstaff, this is a scenic trail in its own right as well as being an access trail into Sycamore Canyon.

DIRECTIONS:
From Flagstaff City Hall Go:
West one block on Route 66 (Santa Fe), then left (south) beneath the railroad overpass on Sitgreaves Street. The street name will change to Milton Road as you go farther. At 0.50 miles you will reach a Y intersection. The right fork is named West Old US Highway 66. Take it. You will soon leave town. At 2.6 miles you will reach a road going to the left. This is the Woody Mountain Road, FR 231. Take it. It is paved about a mile and then turns into a cinder road. At 16.6 miles you will intersect FR 538. Turn right onto FR 538 and follow it to the 22.3 mile point, where it intersects the Kelsey Spring Road, FR 538G. Take 538G. This road is very rough. At 22.7 miles you hit another intersection where a road forks to the left. This is FR 538E, the Dorsey Spring Road. Stay on FR 538G and follow it to its end at 23.7 miles, where it meets FR 527A. Turn left onto the Kelsey Trail road to the 24.1 mile point, the parking area. This last 0.4 mile stretch is terrible, a tire-eating hell of exposed rock.·

TRAILHEAD: You will see a big sign at the parking area.

DESCRIPTION: The Kelsey Spring Trail is marked and maintained by the Forest Service and is in good condition. Start this hike by going to the rim of Sycamore Canyon rather than taking the main trail down into the canyon. You will see an unmarked but distinct footpath going to the rim to the left of the main trail. The main trail goes down into the canyon, whereas the rim trail stays on top. Sycamore Canyon deserves the overworked adjective "awesome" and the rim here is a great vantage point from which to see it. After you fill your eyes then go back to the main trail and make your descent.
The trail down is fairly steep but the footing is good and it passes

through a beautiful forest. At 0.50 miles you will reach a meadow onto which Kelsey Spring flows after running out of a concrete box. Take a look around and you will find the remains of an old cabin. There isn't much left, no standing walls, just some lumber and rubble. If you want to see an interesting cabin, try the nearby **Winter Cabin Trail.**

The shelf of land on which the spring is located is a veritable Shangri-La, a tranquil remote haven away from the cares of the world. Visit this place on a fine summer day when the spring is flowing, flowers are blooming and birds are singing and you won't want to come back out. It is idyllic.

From the site of the spring the trail goes on down another 0.7 miles to **Babe's Hole**, (highly recommended, **A personal favorite**) then down another 1.5 miles to Geronimo Spring, where you are at the inner gorge of Sycamore Canyon.

Springs and cabins are both fragile. Treat them with respect. Camp no closer than 200 feet to a spring. Drinking the water is risky: giardia.

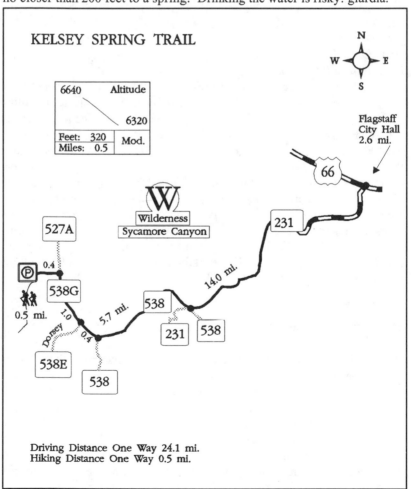

KELSEY-WINTER CABIN TRAIL

General Information
Location Map F2
Sycamore Point USGS Map
Coconino Forest Service Map

Driving Distance One Way: 24.1 miles (Time 1 hour)
Access Road: High clearance needed for last 1.8 miles
Hiking Distance One Way: 5.45 miles (Time 3 hours)
How Strenuous: Moderate
Features: Springs, Pristine forests, Views

NUTSHELL: This trail is located in Sycamore Canyon, 24.1 miles southwest of Flagstaff. It takes you along the side of the canyon between Kelsey Spring and Winter Cabin.

DIRECTIONS:
From Flagstaff City Hall Go:
West one block on Route 66 (Santa Fe), then left (south) beneath the railroad overpass on Sitgreaves Street. The street name will change to Milton Road as you go farther. At 0.50 miles you will reach a Y intersection. The right fork is named West Old US Highway 66. Take it. You will soon leave town. At 2.6 miles you will reach a road going to the left. This is the Woody Mountain Road, FR 231. Take it. It is paved about a mile and then turns into a cinder road. At 16.6 miles you will intersect FR 538. Turn right onto FR 538 and follow it to the 22.3 mile point, where it intersects the Kelsey Spring Road, FR 538G. Take 538G. This road is very rough. At 22.7 miles you hit another intersection where a road forks to the left. This is FR 538E, the Dorsey Spring Road. Stay on FR 538G and follow it to its end at 23.7 miles, where it meets FR 527A. Turn left onto the Kelsey Trail road to the 24.1 mile point, the parking area. This last 0.4 mile stretch is terrible, a tire eating hell of exposed rock.

TRAILHEAD: You will see a big sign at the parking area.

DESCRIPTION: From the parking area you hike down the **Kelsey Spring Trail**. You will reach Kelsey Spring at 0.5 miles. Then go down the trail to **Babe's Hole**, a personal favorite, at 1.2 miles. Go on down the trail to 1.3 miles, where you reach a trail junction. The Kelsey-Winter Trail goes left, while the trail to Geronimo Spring goes right.

From this point, the trail moves along the side of the canyon within a one hundred foot band, with minor ups and downs. The first portion of the trail is in a forest, but at about the 1.7 mile point you will reach a clear area.

This is nice for variety and gives good views of Sycamore Canyon. Then you enter into a wooded area again.

You will reach Dorsey Spring at 2.9 miles. The trail turns left and goes uphill to the actual spring, getting there at 3.10 miles. Before the spring, in a flat area, there is a sign showing the way to Winter Cabin.

The second leg of the trail from **Dorsey Spring** to **Winter Cabin** follows the same lateral course but is more interesting. There are more open spots, high cliffs on your left, a Thumb Butte on your right. There is about a half mile where you pass narrowly through scrub oak and locust, meaning thorns and sharp edged leaves. Bare arms and legs will be scratched here. You will reach Winter Cabin at 5.45 miles.

You can reverse your course when you reach Winter Cabin and go back to the Kelsey Spring trailhead or you can hike 1.5 miles up to the Winter Cabin trailhead (where you have thoughtfully parked a second car).

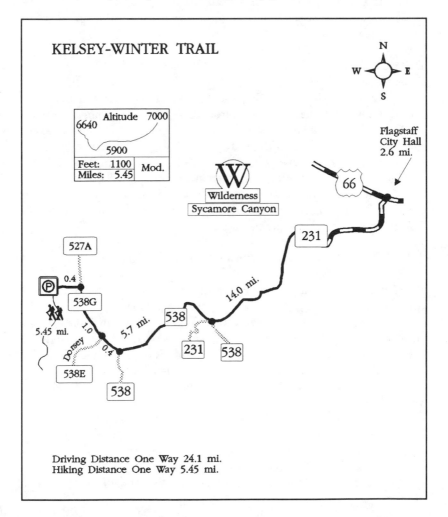

KELSEY-WINTER TRAIL

Altitude 7000
6640
5900
Feet: 1100   Mod.
Miles: 5.45

Wilderness
Sycamore Canyon

Flagstaff
City Hall
2.6 mi.

66

231

527A

14.0 mi.

0.4

538G

5.7 mi.

538

1.0

Dorsey

0.4

231   538

5.45 mi.

538E

538

Driving Distance One Way 24.1 mi.
Hiking Distance One Way 5.45 mi.

KENDRICK MT. TRAIL

General Information
Location Map E2
Kendrick Peak and Wing Mt. USGS Maps
Coconino Forest Service Map

Driving Distance One Way: 21.1 miles (Time 45 minutes)
Access Road: All cars, Last 6.6 miles good gravel road
Hiking Distance One Way: 4.6 miles (Time 3.0 hours)
How Strenuous: Hard
Features: Ten thousand foot peak, Views

NUTSHELL: Located 21.1 miles north of Flagstaff, Kendrick Peak is next tallest to the San Francisco Peaks. This trail switchbacks to the summit where you get great views.

DIRECTIONS:
From Flagstaff City Hall Go:
North on Humphreys Street for 0.60 miles. Turn left at the stoplight onto Columbus Avenue and follow it around a big curve to the north. You will see the street signs call this road Columbus at first, then Ft. Valley Road and then Highway 180. Stay on Highway 180 to the 14.5 miles point (MP 230), where an unpaved road takes off to the left. Turn left onto this road, FR 245, and follow it to the 17.6 mile point where it intersects FR 171. Turn right on FR 171 and follow it to the 20.7 mile point, where you will see a sign for the Kendrick Trail. Turn right on the drive to the trailhead, which you will reach at 21.1 miles. Park in the parking area.

TRAILHEAD: Well marked with a sign at the parking area.

DESCRIPTION: The Forest Service has developed nice facilities at the trailhead, with a good parking lot, trash dump and toilet.
As you start this trail you will walk along a footpath to the 0.7 mile point, where you join an old road, now closed. As is usual, hiking an old road is good news, for roadbuilders of years ago had to hold a gentle grade so that the engines of the old cars could make it. This road is no exception.
The forest for the first mile or so has been heavily logged and is not very attractive. As you go higher, you rise above the logging zone and get into very attractive woods of mixed conifers and large aspen groves.
The trail follows an unending series of switchbacks and climbs, climbs, climbs. There are several open spaces from which to enjoy views southward across Government Prairie.
At 2.00 miles the road ends and you follow a footpath. This is a good

path, following the contours of the mountain intelligently and providing good footing. It was built as a working trail so that rangers could reach the fire lookout tower by horseback.

From a distance you will notice that Kendrick Peak has one definite sharp point, not a series of peaks like its neighbor, the San Francisco Peaks. You will reach a flat area just below the absolute peak at about 4.1 miles. Here you will find the Old Lookout Cabin, with an explanatory sign. It was built in the years 1911-1912 and is remarkably preserved considering the harsh winters it endures. You can go inside and sign your name in a log book. The **Bull Basin Trail** terminates just behind the cabin.

From this flat there is one last climb to the tower, reached at 4.6 miles. One nice thing about the Kendrick hike is that you never rise above timber line. At the base of the tower you can see over the trees, but when you climb it, you get tremendous views, some of the best in the region.

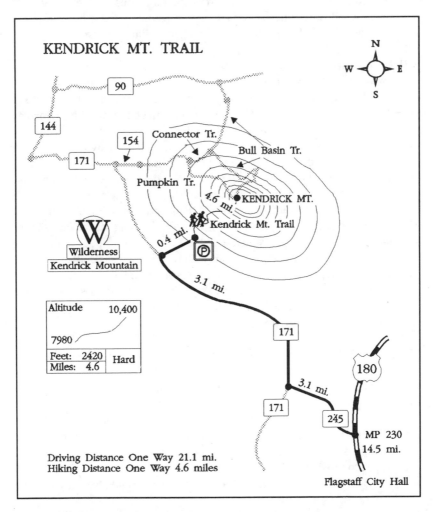

KEYHOLE SINK

General Information
Location Map E2
Williams USGS Map
Coconino Forest Service Map

Driving Distance One Way: 22.8 miles (Time 40 minutes)
Access Road: All cars, All paved
Hiking Distance One Way: 0.55 miles (Time 20 minutes)
How Strenuous: Easy
Features: Hidden pond, Cliffs with rock art

NUTSHELL: This easy hike is located in the Parks area, 22.8 miles west of Flagstaff. It follows a little canyon into a picturesque rounded box. Water is dammed there by cliffs on which are scratched Indian rock art.

DIRECTIONS:
From Flagstaff City Hall Go:
        West a block on Route 66 (Santa Fe), then south, beneath the railroad overpass on Sitgreaves Street. The street name will change to Milton Road as you go farther. At 0.50 miles you will reach a Y intersection. The right fork is named West Old US Highway 66. Take it. You will soon leave town, driving on a stretch of fabled Highway 66. At the 4.8 mile point you will merge onto Interstate-40 West. Look for Exit 178, Parks Road, at the 18.0 mile point, and take it. Turn right at the stop sign and travel to the 18.1 mile point, where there is a second stop sign. Turn left here. You are now on the fabled old U.S. Highway 66 heading west. At the 18.8 mile point you will see the Parks Store to your right. Keep going west to the 22.8 mile point. At the 22.4 mile point you will see the road to the Oak Hill Snow Play Area. This is 0.40 miles from your target. When you reach the 22.8 mile point, you will see a cinder road going down off the right side at an acute angle. Pull off onto this road and park. High clearance vehicles can drive about 0.40 miles on this road, but protruding sharp rocks are rough on tires.

TRAILHEAD: There are no signs, but the way is easy. Just follow the road.

DESCRIPTION: In about 0.10 miles from the highway you will see a road branching off to the right. Do not take this. Follow the left fork. The road will follow a small canyon that winds around into a bottom, where you will see a stand of young aspen trees lining the floor of the canyon. Keep following the road as it goes into the canyon. The road will become very rough. You will see a place to your right where a forest fire burned a few trees in 1991.
        Beyond this point you will follow a game trail into the canyon. The

way is obvious. You will come to a fence made of aspen logs. Here the aspens stop and you will be looking into a charming little bowl where the canyon ends against basalt cliffs some thirty to forty feet high. The floor of the bowl is covered with grass.

Walk toward the farthest, blackest cliff. In wet years there will be a pond of water at its base, because the cliff acts as a natural dam for all the water flowing into the canyon. We saw this place in September, 1990, when there had been a lot of rain and there was a good sized pond there. In September, 1991, it was dry.

As you face the cliff, look for rock art on the cliff faces to the left of the blackest face. There are two major panels. If you look carefully, you will see a few more figures scattered here and there.

This is a natural waterhole for game and you will see elk and deer sign around it. It would also be a trap for game that were cornered in the box.

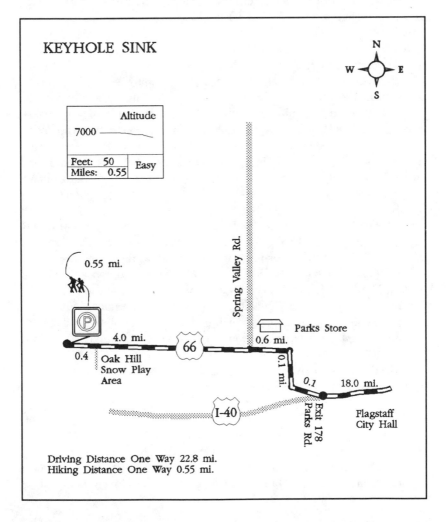

KLOSTERMEYER HILL

General Information
Location Map E2
Parks USGS Map
Kaibab (Williams) Forest Service Map

Driving Distance One Way: 22.7 miles (Time 45 minutes)
Access Road: All cars, Last 11 miles medium gravel road
Hiking Distance One Way: 0.5 miles (Time 30 minutes)
How Strenuous: Moderate
Features: Views

NUTSHELL: You make a brief climb to the top of a bare hill on the west side of Government Prairie 22.7 miles west of Flagstaff for gorgeous views.

DIRECTIONS:
From Flagstaff City Hall Go:
West a block on Route 66 (Santa Fe), then south, beneath the railroad overpass on Sitgreaves Street. The street name will change to Milton Road as you go farther. At 0.50 miles you will reach a Y intersection. The right fork is named West Old US Highway 66. Take it. You will soon leave town, driving on a stretch of fabled Highway 66. At the 4.8 mile point you will merge onto Interstate-40 West. Look for Exit 185, "Transwestern Rd., Bellemont" and take it. It is at the 10.8 mile point. From the exit turn right and go to the frontage road, where you turn left onto FR 146. You are now following another stretch of U.S. 66. Stay on this to the 18 mile point, where you will see FR 107 fork right. Take FR 107 and follow it to the 21.7 mile point. Here you will see FR 81 going to the right. Take FR 81. The USGS map shows the old alignment of this road. Presently it goes just north of the hill heading due east. At the 22.45 mile point you will see FR 81 fork. Take the right fork, headed toward the hill. You will soon come to two water tanks. If you are in a low clearance vehicle, park there, at 22.7 miles. If you have high clearance, follow the primitive road you see turning right before the fence and following the fence line uphill. You can drive uphill almost to the aspen grove, another 0.2 miles.

TRAILHEAD: There is no trail. Because of the terrain, it is easy to find your way. Just head uphill.

DESCRIPTION: The hill is steep but you don't have to hike far. Soon you will be in an aspen grove and will see that there is a saddle above it. When you emerge onto the saddle, turn to the right and hike up to the top of the knob.

Once you are at the top of the hill, you will be treated to one of the finest panoramas imaginable. Before you lies the open plain of Government Prairie, bounded on all sides by deep pine woods and ringed with mountains and hills. Why are there such open areas when so much of the country is covered with pines?

This whole scene is something special, a real treat to the eye accustomed to uniform pine forests. In the fall the grass is high and has turned tawny. Everything seems smooth, golden and sinuous, punctuated here and there with bright shows of turning aspen leaves. The golden carpet flows right over these bald hills as if they were deliberately placed interest mounds intended to provide visual delight.

The views to the north are best because you see little sign of human habitation though you can't see far because of Kendrick Peak and the San Francisco Peaks. To the south the country is equally fine but there are many homes and the effect is diminished by them. As if in compensation, however, you can see a long way.

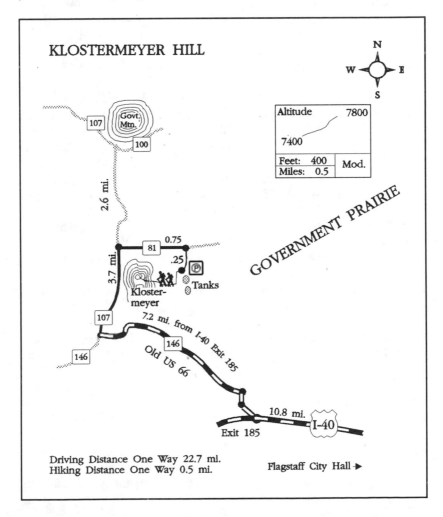

LAKEVIEW TRAIL

General Information
Location Map G3
Mormon Lake USGS Map
Coconino Forest Service Map

Driving Distance One Way: 24.5 miles (Time 35 minutes)
Access Road: All cars, All paved
Hiking Distance One Way: 1.25 miles (Time 40 minutes)
How Strenuous: Moderate
Features: Beautiful forest, Excellent views

NUTSHELL: This hike gently climbs a ridge radiating south from Mormon Mountain. At the ridge top you are treated to sweeping views of Mormon Lake and the surrounding countryside.

DIRECTIONS:
From Flagstaff City Hall Go:
West one block on Route 66 (Santa Fe), then left (south) on Sitgreaves Street under the railroad overpass. The street name will change to Milton Road as you go south. At 1.7 miles you will reach a stoplight at Forest Meadows Street. Turn right here onto Forest Meadows and go a block to Beulah. Turn left on Beulah and follow it south. Beulah merges onto Highway 89A. At 2.4 miles (MP 401.6), turn left onto the Lake Mary Road. Follow the Lake Mary Road to the 19.3 mile point (MP 323.6), where you turn right onto the Mormon Lake Road. At 24.3 miles, on the Mormon Lake Road, you will see a sign marked "Double Springs Campground, Lakeview Trail." Turn right here and follow the gravel road that goes into the campground to the 24.5 miles point where there is a parking area around the public restroom. Pull in and park.

TRAILHEAD: You will see a sign marking the trail to your left just before you reach the parking area.

DESCRIPTION: This area is used for cross-country skiing in the winter and you will see metal squares nailed to trees along the way marking the various ski trails.

At the beginning of the trail you will encounter a little stream, a rarity in northern Arizona. There is a line of stepping stones across the stream, making it easy to cross. Once across, you will see the trail heading uphill to your right. In about one tenth of a mile you will see the official trailhead sign for the Lakeview Trail. The trail is narrow but in good condition. It is well maintained. This is rocky soil, but the footing is pretty comfortable.

The forest around Mormon Mountain is particularly beautiful. In addition to the ubiquitous Ponderosa pine, there is much oak and you will also see some aspen. Flowers and shrubs grow in profusion. Benches have been thoughtfully placed at the beginning, halfway and top of the trail. Since this is a moderately easy hike, you can take your time. No need to hustle. Stop at the benches to catch your breath and enjoy the experience.

For nine-tenths of the hike, you cannot understand why the trail has been given the name Lakeview. Then, as you near the top, you can see why. The trail has been climbing gradually up a ridge. As you come to the top of the ridge, you find that its top is a lava cliff. Around the perimeter no pine trees grow, so you have unobstructed views.

You can walk around the ridgetop and enjoy great views. As the name suggests, Mormon Lake is fully in view. Depending upon the wetness of the preceding winter, you will either see a lot of water or a great big pasture with a small pond in the center. Wooded hills and ridges surround the lake and provide a pretty sight.

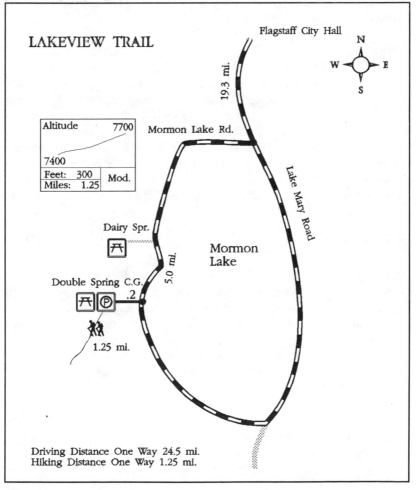

LAKEVIEW TRAIL

Flagstaff City Hall

19.3 mi.

Altitude 7700

7400
Feet: 300   Mod.
Miles: 1.25

Mormon Lake Rd.

Lake Mary Road

Dairy Spr.

Mormon
Lake

Double Spring C.G. .2

5.0 mi.

1.25 mi.

Driving Distance One Way 24.5 mi.
Hiking Distance One Way 1.25 mi.

LAVA FLOW TRAIL

General Information
Location Map E3
Wupatki SW USGS Map
Coconino Forest Service Map

Driving Distance One Way: 22.1 miles (Time 30 minutes)
Access Road: All cars, All paved
Hiking Distance, Complete Loop: 1.0 mile (Time 45 minutes)
How Strenuous: Easy
Features: Views, Extinct volcanos, Self-guided nature trail

NUTSHELL: This is an easy trail located in the Sunset Crater National Monument 20 miles northeast of Flagstaff. It takes you on a fascinating self-guided nature walk through a volcanic field.

DIRECTIONS:
From Flagstaff City Hall Go:
East, curving to north on Route 66 (Santa Fe). As you leave the city limits you will see that Route 66 (Santa Fe) is also Highway 89. Follow Highway 89 north out into the country. At 16.4 miles (MP 430.3) you will reach the entrance to Sunset Crater National Monument. Turn right on the road into Sunset Crater. This road is also known as FR 545. At 18.4 miles you will reach a ticket booth where you will have to pay admission. Just beyond that is the Visitor Center, which is worth a look. At 21.9 miles you will see a road branching off to your right marked Lava Flow Trail Drive. Take it. It leads to a parking area at 22.1 miles.

TRAILHEAD: You will see a sign at the parking area.

DESCRIPTION: This trail is designed as a self-guided walk with points of interest keyed to a guide booklet that is available from the dispenser located at the beginning of the trail. You can take a booklet free. If you decide to keep it, then you put fifty cents into the dispenser at the end of the trail. If you don't want to keep the booklet then you return it to the dispenser.

The trail is paved for a short distance. In fact the Park Service has created a paved stub of a trail for wheelchair bound visitors. A nice gesture. On the main trail, once the paving ends, the trail surface is composed of black cinders. You would have no trouble walking the trail in street shoes but you would scuff them up plenty if you did. Jogging shoes or light trail shoes are excellent footgear for this hike.

A hiker could hurry around the trail in thirty minutes but we recommend that you take your time. Use the booklet and read it at the appropriate stopping points that are described in the booklet. These points really are interesting and even people who don't like museums or educational walks should find something to enjoy. These black cinder locations have a special feeling that some people respond to very positively. In winter you can sometimes see some startlingly special effects when white drifts of snow form stark contrasting patterns against the black cinders.

Until the 1960s visitors could hike to the top of Sunset Crater. Finally climbing on the crater had to be stopped because of the severe erosion that the multitudes of hikers were causing to the face of the crater. The sides of the crater are covered with deep loose black cinders and are therefore unstable. They kept sluffing away from the trails. It is too bad people can't enjoy the experience anymore as we did when we were kids, but it is justifiable under the circumstances.

One of the features of this trail is an ice cave, a lava tube such as you encounter on the **Lava River** and **Slate Lake Lava Cave** hikes.

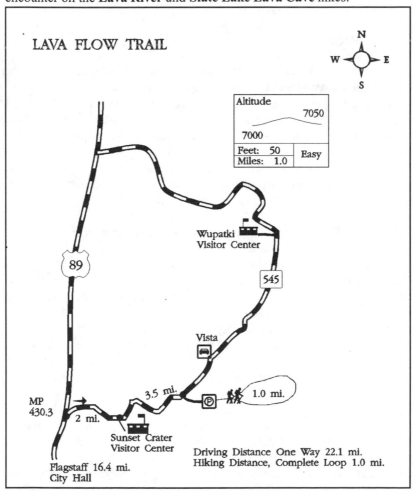

LAVA RIVER CAVE

General Information
Location Map E2
Wing Mountain USGS Map
Coconino Forest Service Map

Driving Distance One Way: 19 miles (Time 40 minutes)
Access Road: All cars, Last 4.5 miles good gravel road
Hiking Distance One Way: 0.70 miles (Time 1 hour)
How Strenuous: Moderate
Features: Unusual underground lava tube

NUTSHELL: This underground lava tube located 19 miles northwest of Flagstaff is a unique experience.

DIRECTIONS:
From Flagstaff City Hall Go:
North on Humphreys Street for 0.60 miles. Turn left at the stoplight onto Columbus Avenue and follow it around a big curve to the north. You will see the street signs call this road Columbus at first, then Ft. Valley Road and then Highway 180. Stay on Highway 180 to the 14.5 miles point (MP 230), where an unpaved road takes off to the left. Turn left onto this road, FR 245, and follow it to the 17.6 mile point where it intersects FR 171. Turn left onto FR 171 and follow it to the 18.6 mile point, where it intersects FR 171A. Turn left on 171A and follow it to the 19.0 mile point where you will find the parking area.

TRAILHEAD: Look for a large ring of stones circling a pit at the parking area. This is the entrance to the cave.

DESCRIPTION: Even if you know nothing about volcanos it is obvious that this part of Northern Arizona is an ancient volcanic field. Craters and cinder cones dot the landscape everywhere. The mighty San Francisco Peaks themselves are a huge volcanic crater.

Lava tubes are formed when the outer portion of a river of lava cools while the interior is still hot and flowing. Under the right conditions the outer skin will form a hard shell and the inner core will flow right on through like water going through a straw, leaving an empty tube.

That's what you will find on this trip. The Forest Service has made an attractive entrance down into the tube using native stone to form a natural stairway. You have to duck to get into the opening but then the tube deepens so that you can stand upright. The height of the tube is not uniform, however, and there are low and high places along the way. The tube goes on for about

0.70 mile, lowering as it goes. The coldest spot is near the entrance and you may find ice there. The cave was discovered in 1915 by lumberjacks who were logging nearby.

You must come properly prepared for this hike. It can be dangerous if you are unprepared. Once you get a short way past the daylight coming in from the entrance you are in absolute darkness. The floor, ceiling and walls are all extremely rough and uneven and you have to watch your step. It is also cold. This means that every member of your party should dress warmly and carry lights. We recommend that each person have two good flashlights equipped with fresh batteries.

We have heard a horror story of a hiker who went into Lava River Cave with one flashlight. He got into the cave about halfway and then dropped and broke his light. When this happened he freaked out, panicked and bashed himself up considerably trying to rush back to the entrance. A word to the wise is sufficient.

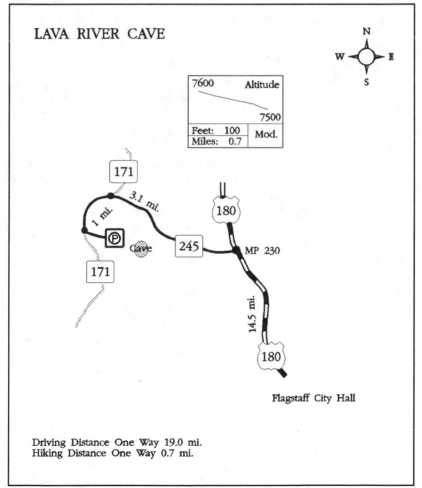

LAVA RIVER CAVE

| 7600 | Altitude |
| | 7500 |

| Feet: 100 | Mod. |
| Miles: 0.7 | |

171

3.1 mi.

1 mi.

180

245 MP 230

171

14.5 mi.

180

Flagstaff City Hall

Driving Distance One Way 19.0 mi.
Hiking Distance One Way 0.7 mi.

LEDGES TRAIL

General Information
Location Map G3
Mormon Lake USGS Map
Coconino Forest Service Map

Driving Distance One Way: 23.3 miles (Time 30 minutes)
Access Road: All cars, All paved except last 0.3 miles
Hiking Distance, Complete Loop: 1.5 miles (Time 45 minutes)
How Strenuous: Moderate
Features: Views

NUTSHELL: This is a nice trail at the base of Mormon Mountain, about 20 miles southeast of Flagstaff. It takes you through a pine forest to The Ledges, a ragged basalt cliff, from where you have fine views of Mormon Lake.

DIRECTIONS:
From Flagstaff City Hall Go:
　　　　West on Route 66 (Santa Fe) one block then left (south) on Sitgreaves Street under the railroad overpass. The street name will change to Milton Road as you go south. At 1.7 miles you will reach a stoplight at Forest Meadows Street. Turn right here onto Forest Meadows and go one block to Beulah. Turn left on Beulah and follow it south. Beulah merges onto Highway 89A. At 2.4 miles (MP 401.6), turn left onto the Lake Mary Road. Follow the Lake Mary Road to the 19.3 mile point (MP 323.6), where you turn right onto the Mormon Lake Road. At 23.0 miles, on the Mormon Lake Road, you will see a sign marked "Dairy Springs Amphitheater." Turn right here and follow the gravel road to the 23.3 miles point where there is a parking area.

TRAILHEAD: There is a large sign at the parking lot marking the trailhead.

DESCRIPTION: This area is used for cross-country skiing in the winter and you will see signs and triangles nailed to trees along the way marking the various ski trails. The triangles for the Ledges Trail are silver.
　　　　From its start the trail gradually ascends a hill. The sides of the trail here are lined with rocks. You will see some houses below you toward Mormon Lake. At about 0.25 miles you begin to see the lake and it will be in sight most of the way from this point.
　　　　In wet years Mormon Lake is a sizable body of water and at such times it supports a lot of boating and fishing. In dry years you can practically walk across it and the boat docks stick up out of the ground a long way from water. Mormon Lake is a natural lake. It was originally called Mormon Dairy Lake because of the Mormon pioneers who ran a dairy here for several years. Over

the years the name of the lake was shortened to Mormon Lake. Dairy Springs is another legacy from that time.

The trail goes through a forest of pine, oak and spruce. It reaches its apex at 0.75 miles and then begins to descend. At 0.90 miles you come onto the ledges for which the trail is named. The name is descriptive of the way this place looks, as the gray basalt stone has layered in such a way as to form ledges. Few things grow in this bare rock, so this is a good viewpoint. After the ledges the trail goes downhill toward the Mormon Lake Road.

At about 1.0 miles you will come to a group of homes. These are summer homes and if you are making the hike in the summer you may be greeted by inquisitive dogs or children. Many paths through this area make following the main trail difficult. No worries. Just keep working your way downhill toward the highway, which you can see plainly. When you reach the highway, go right (west) and you will return to the driveway entrance in about 0.20 miles, from where it is about 0.1 mile back to your car.

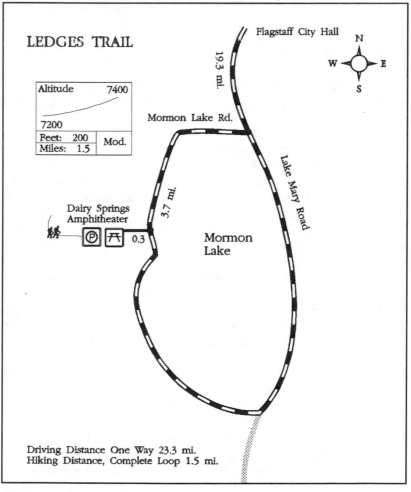

LITTLE ELDEN

General Information
Location Map E3
Sunset Crater West USGS Map
Coconino Forest Service Map

Driving Distance One Way: 11.3 miles (Time 30 minutes)
Access Road: All cars, Last 2.1 miles good gravel road
Hiking Distance One Way: 2.3 miles (Time 1.5 hours)
How Strenuous: Moderate
Features: Beautiful spring, Cliffs, Views

NUTSHELL: Starting at Little Elden Spring about 11 miles north of Flagstaff, this trail takes you south around the base of Little Elden Mt. into a scenic bowl.

DIRECTIONS:
From Flagstaff City Hall Go:
　　　　East on Route 66 (Santa Fe). Highway 89 runs concurrently with Route 66 (Santa Fe) as the highway goes through Flagstaff, so you will see road signs with both designations. At 6.4 miles you will pass the last stoplight in town at the Winona-Townsend Road. Continue on Highway 89 to the 9.2 mile point (MP 423.3) where a gravel road (FR 556) takes off to the left. Pull in on this. You will see a sign identifying it as Elden Springs Road. Drive this to the 11.3 miles point, where you will see the spring to your left. You may have to park on the right side of the road because of the deep ditch on the left side.

TRAILHEAD: There are no trail signs. Go up and visit the spring, it is only a few yards away. When you come back, turn right (east) as you go through the squeeze-through gate and follow the fence about 40 yards to its end. There you will go through a take-down gate. This is where the trail starts.

DESCRIPTION: Little Elden is not a freestanding mountain but is the north wing of Mt. Elden. The fire lookout tower is on the south wing. In between the wings there is an arc which forms a fascinating basin filled with unusual features. This trail takes you to that basin.
　　　　You start the trail at Little Elden Spring, a lush spot, then soon move away from that into a more arid life zone supporting pines, junipers and scrub oak. The area is rather bare because of the terrible Radio Fire that raged through here in 1978. The bareness does give you open views.
　　　　The face of Little Elden looks like a huge rock pile full of eye-catching formations, lines, crevices and mystery. Is that a cave you see or only a seam? The rock is a light rust color. At 0.40 miles you will reach a fork. Go right

Kendrick Peak from Wild Bill Hill

Front Cover: *The San Francisco Peaks from White Horse Hills*

Government Prairie From Wild Bill Hill

Pictograph at Veit Spring

Secret Canyon

Wupatki Ruin

Doney Crater

Grand Falls

Tunnel Road

Lockett Meadow

Dry Lake Hills

South Rim of The Grand Canyon

there, toward the mountain.

At 0.80 miles the trail crosses a road. Stay on the footpath. At 1.00 miles you will come to a second road. Leave the footpath here and go left on the road.

The road serpentines to the base of a hill at 1.5 miles, where you will find the soil is deep white sand. This is the **Sandy Seep** area. At 1.75 miles, between that hill and the next, you will see a faint road to your right go into a ravine and up. Follow that path, which is marked. You will meet another road. Turn right and follow that road, which heads straight for the mountain, passing through an area of red soil and hills that look like a Sedona landscape.

At 2.3 miles you will reach a large green water tank where this hike ends. You will see trail markers for the **Elden Red Hills Trail** here. It is 1.8 miles to the top.

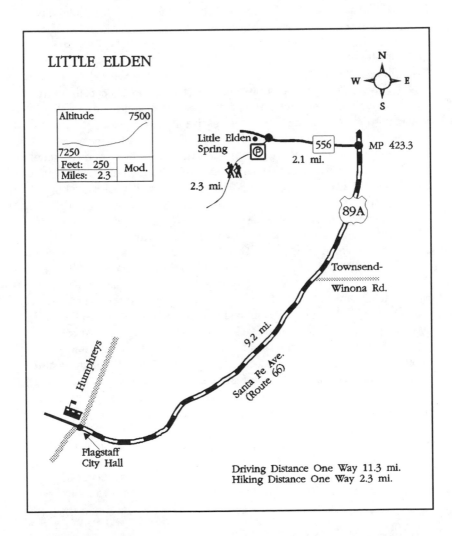

LITTLE ROUND MOUNTAIN

General Information
Location Map F2
Loy Btt., Sycamore Pt., Wilson Mt. USGS Maps
Coconino Forest Service Map

Driving Distance One Way: 30.5 miles (Time 1.5 hours)
Access Road: High clearance, Last 6.7 miles terrible roads
Hiking Distance One Way: 1.5 miles (Time 1 hour)
How Strenuous: Moderate
Features: Glorious views off Mogollon Rim into redrock country

NUTSHELL: Located 30.5 miles southwest of Flagstaff, this little-known destination takes you to one of the best viewpoints on the Mogollon Rim.

DIRECTIONS:
From Flagstaff City Hall Go:
        West a block on Route 66 (Santa Fe), then south, beneath the railroad overpass on Sitgreaves Street. The street name will change to Milton Road as you go farther. At 0.50 miles you will reach a Y intersection. The right fork is named West Old US Highway 66. Take it. You will soon leave town. At 2.6 miles you will reach a road going to the left. This is the Woody Mountain Road, FR 231. Take it. It is paved about a mile and then turns into a cinder road. Take FR 231 to the 23.2 mile point, where you will reach a junction. Go left here, still on FR 231. At the 23.8 miles point you turn right onto FR 539, a dirt road going uphill. You will see a big steel pole gate there. You follow FR 539 to its end, but it is poorly marked, so follow directions carefully. At 25.1 miles you come to a junction. Go left here (you will see a pole gate to your right). At 25.8 you reach another fork where there is a marker for FR 6249 to the right. Go left here. At 26.5 miles you will reach a tank marked Rattle (not Rattle*snake*) Tank; take the left fork here. At 27.1 miles there is another fork, where you go right (don't take the road with the pole gate marked FR 6273). At 27.6 miles you will reach Rattlesnake Tank, where you go left. At 28.3 miles you reach a fork where you go right. At 28.6 miles you will hit another fork, where you go right. At 29.0 miles there is a junction. You will see an unnamed tank and a fence to your right. Turn left here. At 30.3 miles you will see Li'l Round Tank to your left at a fork. Go left here. At 30.5 miles you will reach the Little Round Mountain sign, where you park.

TRAILHEAD: At the Little Round Mountain sign where you park.

DESCRIPTION: Before you take the hike, drive on to the end of the road, through the camping areas on out to the very end, another 0.15 miles. Here you will emerge onto a lookout that is sublime, one of our favorite viewpoints. You are looking from the Mogollon Rim into the Sedona redrock country, which is very beautiful.

From the promontory, drive back to the trailhead and begin the hike. The trail is baffling. It starts out fine, well marked and easy to follow, looking like a major hiking trail. It goes downhill and up through a thick beautiful forest. At about one mile, just as you come to the top of the first upgrade, you will see a trail going to the left. It does not look like the main trail, but it is. Take it. It leads you to the rim and then seems to end indecisively. From there just work your way around the rim enjoying the views to your heart's content and then return the way you came.

The other fork of the trail tops out on a mesa and then mysteriously terminates with no apparent rhyme or reason in a place that isn't even scenic. Don't bother with it.

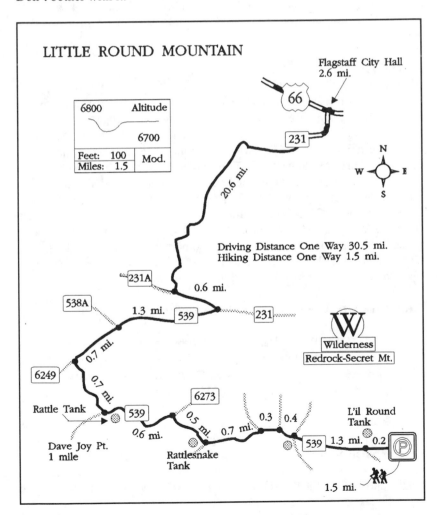

LITTLE ROUND MOUNTAIN

Flagstaff City Hall 2.6 mi.

66

231

6800 Altitude
6700
Feet: 100 Mod.
Miles: 1.5

20.6 mi.

N
W — E
S

Driving Distance One Way 30.5 mi.
Hiking Distance One Way 1.5 mi.

231A 0.6 mi.

538A 1.3 mi. 539 231

W
Wilderness
Redrock-Secret Mt.

6249 0.7 mi.

0.7 mi.

6273

Rattle Tank 539 0.5 mi. 0.7 mi. 0.3 0.4 L'il Round Tank

0.6 mi.

Dave Joy Pt. 1 mile

Rattlesnake Tank

539 1.3 mi. 0.2 P

1.5 mi.

MAXWELL TRAIL

General Information
Location Map G3
Calloway Butte USGS Map
Coconino Forest Service Map

Driving Distance One Way: 58.0 miles (Time 1.5 hours)
Access Road: All cars, Last 8.9 miles good gravel road
Hiking Distance One Way: 0.80 miles (Time 45 minutes)
How Strenuous: Hard
Features: Views, Beautiful pristine stream, Remote canyon

NUTSHELL: This is one of the few trails into West Clear Creek, a remote canyon 58 miles southeast of Flagstaff. The hike is short but steep and very beautiful.

DIRECTIONS:
From Flagstaff City Hall Go:
　　　　West on Route 66 (Santa Fe) one block then left (south) on Sitgreaves Street under the railroad overpass. The street name will change to Milton Road as you go south. At 1.7 miles you will reach a stoplight at Forest Meadows Street. Turn right here onto Forest Meadows and go one block to Beulah. Turn left on Beulah and follow it south. Beulah merges onto Highway 89A. At 2.4 miles (MP 401.6), turn left onto the Lake Mary Road. Follow the Lake Mary Road to the 49.1 mile point (MP 297.8), where you turn right onto a gravel road, FR 81. Follow FR 81 to the 56.0 mile point, where you reach a fork. Take the left fork. You will see a sign for the Maxwell Trail at the fork. Keep driving to the 58.0 mile point. Here you will find some campsites and a parking area. The road goes another 0.25 miles but the last stretch is very rough. You may want to park at 58.0 miles and walk the rest of the road.

TRAILHEAD: There is a sign at the parking area at the end of the road.

DESCRIPTION: West Clear Creek is a tributary of the Verde River. Its headwaters are on the uplands of the Mogollon Rim, where this hike takes place. Located in a remote area, West Clear Creek canyon cuts a course running from east to west. At its low end it joins the Verde River near Camp Verde.

　　　　Getting to the trailhead you will drive through a pine forest that has plenty of open parks. These make good grazing areas for cattle and have been used for ranching ever since settlement of the country began in the late 1800s. The area has been thoroughly logged too, including some of the wild backcountry along FR 81. This logging is unsightly and spoils the remote appearance of the area.

When you get to the trailhead you can get glimpses into the canyon. These tell you that it is very steep. The walls of the canyon are a buff colored sandstone with pink tints. It looks a lot like **Walnut Canyon** near Flagstaff.

The trail takes you by a serpentine route to the canyon bottom where there is an unspoiled stream, living up to its name, Clear Creek. Along the way you walk right in the shadow of enormous cliffs.

The canyon at the bottom is rather narrow and there appear to be no developed trails along the streambed. It is possible to do some hiking at the bottom but this means boulder hopping and wading. Some very hardy, well-prepared types are able to hike the canyon from top to bottom, but this is definitely not for beginners. Don't even think of trying it unless you are thoroughly ready for it. The preferred entry is several miles downstream.

You will be enthralled by the quiet beauty of this canyon, especially at creekside. Look out for poison ivy and keep an eye out for snakes.

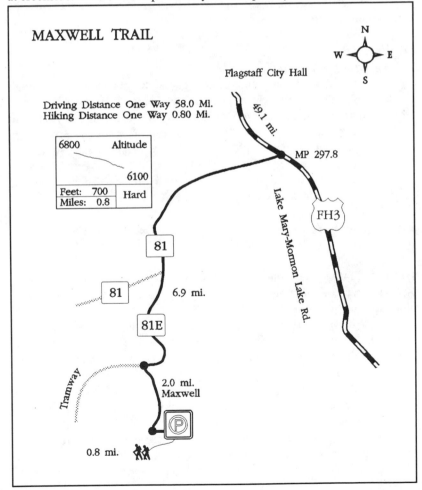

MAXWELL TRAIL

Flagstaff City Hall

Driving Distance One Way 58.0 Mi.
Hiking Distance One Way 0.80 Mi.

6800   Altitude

6100

Feet: 700   Hard
Miles: 0.8

49.1 mi.

MP 297.8

Lake Mary-Mormon Lake Rd.

FH3

81

81

6.9 mi.

81E

Tramway

2.0 mi.
Maxwell

0.8 mi.

METEOR CRATER

Driving Distance One Way: 43.9 miles (Time 1 hour)
Access Road: All cars, All paved
Hiking Distance, Complete Loop: 2.5 miles (Time 1.25 hours)
How Strenuous: Moderate
Features: Trip around rim of world-famed attraction

NUTSHELL: You hike around the rim of Meteor Crater, located 43.9 miles east of Flagstaff, getting a good view of the inside of the crater and the surrounding countryside.

DIRECTIONS:
From Flagstaff City Hall Go:
　　　　East on Route 66 (Santa Fe). Highway 89 runs concurrently with Route 66 (Santa Fe) as the highway goes through Flagstaff, so you will see road signs with both designations. At 4.1 miles you will see a sign to your right marking the entrance to Interstate-40. Take this entrance and at 4.3 miles turn left on the Interstate-40 East Exit. This will place you on I-40 headed east. At 37.9 miles (MP 233.6) you will reach the Meteor Crater turn, Exit 233. Turn right on this and follow the paved road to Meteor Crater. You will reach the parking lot at the Visitor Center at 43.9 miles.

TRAILHEAD: You must go through the Visitor Center to gain access to this trail.

DESCRIPTION: Although Meteor Crater has all the appearance of a National Park or Monument, it is privately owned. You have to pay an admission fee to get in.
　　　　When you arrive at the parking place you will find steps leading you into the ticket office where there is a snack bar and curio store. If you pay the admission fee, you can then go up to the next level where the museum and entrance to the crater is located.
　　　　Take a few minutes and tour the museum. It explains the phenomenon of the crater nicely. Until you see the exhibits, it is easy to underestimate the tremendous force generated by the meteorite hitting the ground. The museum highlights the use of the crater to prepare American astronauts for their landing on the moon in the Apollo flights in the 1960s.
　　　　When you leave the museum and go outside to the crater you will see

three areas to your left. The middle one is a platform cantilevered out over the edge with several lensless "telescopes" aimed at points of interest. Below that there is a covered viewpoint. Above it there is a high platform with a real telescope. The trail starts at the high platform.

From the trailhead you simply walk around the rim of the crater. You can see the trail clearly. Eight markers have been placed along the trail keyed in to points of interest. Due to the roughness of the terrain, the trail does not absolutely stay on top of the rim at all times, but dips around obstacles.

It is interesting to see the crater from different angles as you circumnavigate it, and you will observe signs of old mining and ranching activity as you make the circle. You are totally exposed to the sun on this trail. There is no shade. There is a lot of white rock and soil that reflects sun back at you. The altitude is about 5700 feet, fairly low for northern Arizona. These all add up to one thing: this can be a very hot hike. Formerly hikers could go down to the crater's floor, but this is now forbidden.

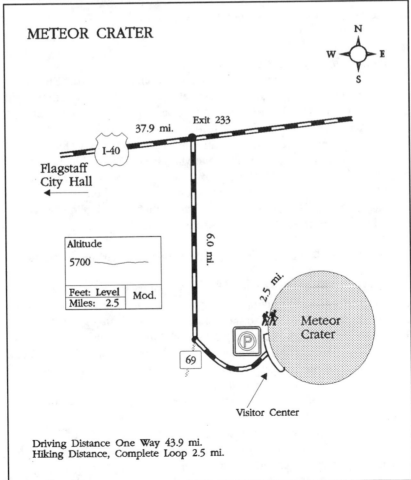

MORMON LAKE NATURE TRAIL

General Information
Location Map G3
Mormon Lake USGS Map
Coconino Forest Service Map

Driving Distance One Way: 23.3 miles (Time 30 minutes)
Access Road: All cars, All paved
Hiking Distance, Complete Loop: 0.50 miles (Time 30 minutes)
How Strenuous: Easy
Features: Relaxing nature trail through attractive forest

NUTSHELL: This is a short undemanding trail at the base of Mormon Mountain about 20 miles southeast of Flagstaff. Numbered posts mark the locations of interesting plants along the path.

DIRECTIONS:
From Flagstaff City Hall Go:
        West one block on Route 66 (Santa Fe) then left (south) on Sitgreaves Street under the railroad overpass. The street name will change to Milton Road as you go south. At 1.7 miles you will reach a stoplight at Forest Meadows Street. Turn right here onto Forest Meadows and go a block to Beulah. Turn left on Beulah and follow it south. Beulah merges onto Highway 89A. At 2.4 miles (MP 401.6), turn left onto the Lake Mary Road. Follow the Lake Mary Road to the 19.3 mile point (MP 323.6), where you turn right onto the Mormon Lake Road. At 23.0 miles, on the Mormon Lake Road, you will see a sign marked "Dairy Springs Amphitheater." Turn right here and follow the gravel road to the 23.3 miles point where there is a parking area.

TRAILHEAD: There is a large sign at the parking lot marking the trailhead.

DESCRIPTION: This area is used for cross-country skiing in the winter and you will see signs and triangles nailed to trees along the way marking the various ski trails. This is also the trailhead for **The Ledges** and **Mormon Mountain** trails, which you will find described in this book.
        This nature trail is very gentle. There are signs to mark the way. Look for 4 x 4 posts painted red which have been inserted along the trail. These are numbered. The numbers refer to trees and plants located along the course of the trail. We did not find any booklets or other materials identifying the plants by number.
        The trail goes through a cool forest composed mostly of Ponderosa pine with some fir and spruce. The forest feels very friendly and pleasant. This is a nice hike if you just want to stretch your legs.

Mormon Lake is a natural lake. In can be quite sizeable after a few wet years. During the 1920s it was a popular fishing resort and boat docks were built. There was also a hunting lodge. In the days before air conditioners, many Phoenix residents came to the north during the summers for relief from the desert heat and built summer cabins. Many of the old cabins you see in the area are relics of those days. The Forest Service at times has had an active summer program for residents and visitors. It built an amphitheater as a stage for lectures. You will see signs for the amphitheater and will drive right by it on the way to the trailhead. You might want to give it a look.

The area got its name from Mormon pioneers who came into northern Arizona from Utah in the 1870s. The area was too cold for reliable farming but they found the lake to be suitable for a dairy and ran one there for years, selling their products in Flagstaff and settlements to the east. For many years Flagstaff residents called the place Mormon Dairy Lake but it was shortened to Mormon Lake over time.

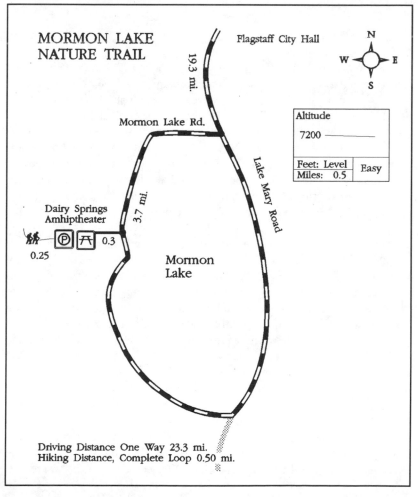

MORMON MOUNTAIN

General Information
Location Map G3
Mormon Lake USGS Map
Coconino Forest Service Map

Driving Distance One Way: 23.3 miles (Time 30 minutes)
Access Road: All cars, All paved
Hiking Distance One Way: 2.25 miles (Time 75 minutes)
How Strenuous: Moderate
Features: Beautiful forest

NUTSHELL: This hike takes you to the top of the dominant mountain on the landscape 20 miles southeast of Flagstaff.

DIRECTIONS:
From Flagstaff City Hall Go:

West one block on Route 66 (Santa Fe), then left (south) on Sitgreaves Street under the railroad overpass. The street name will change to Milton Road as you go south. At 1.7 miles you will reach a stoplight at Forest Meadows Street. Turn right here onto Forest Meadows and go a block to Beulah. Turn left on Beulah and follow it south. Beulah merges onto Highway 89A. At 2.4 miles (MP 401.6), turn left onto the Lake Mary Road. Follow the Lake Mary Road to the 19.3 mile point (MP 323.6), where you turn right onto the Mormon Lake Road. At 23.0 miles, on the Mormon Lake Road, you will see a sign marked "Dairy Springs Amphitheater." Turn right here and follow the gravel road to the 23.3 miles point where there is a parking area.

TRAILHEAD: There is a large sign at the parking lot marking the trailhead.

DESCRIPTION: This area is used for cross-country skiing in the winter and you will see signs and triangles nailed to trees along the way marking the various ski trails. This is also the trailhead for **The Ledges** and **Mormon Lake Nature Trail** hikes, which you will find described in this book.

This trail is gentle and wide at the start. The path of the ski trail is marked by graphics and metal triangles nailed to trees. White triangles mark the path you want to follow on this hike. The trail climbs through a lovely forest of pine, oak and fir, with some aspen located near the top. From the half mile point to the one mile point the grade is very steep but the rest of the trail is not particularly steep for a mountain trail.

Just before you reach the top, you pass through a very attractive old growth forest, but the top is disappointing, as it has been logged. As with many mountains, reaching the top is deceptive. You come to a point where you clearly stop climbing and level out on what appears to be a crest only to find that it is merely a fold or a bench. This happens on this hike. You will not reach a point where you can definitely say to yourself, *"This is the top."*

One of the attractions of a mountain hike is being rewarded with great views at the summit of the mountain. Unfortunately that does not happen here because the trees are so tall and thick that they block your view. We stopped at the 2.25 mile point but the path goes on, probably over to the fire tower and radio-TV transmitters that are located on this mountain. These towers and transmitters are eyesores and are out of sight if you stop at the 2.25 mile point.

You will see a sign at the area where we recommend stopping that is marked *1.5 miles* to the start. The sign is short by 0.75 miles.

We took this hike on a fine October day and were gratified to see many groves of aspen with changing leaves. We also saw several deer.

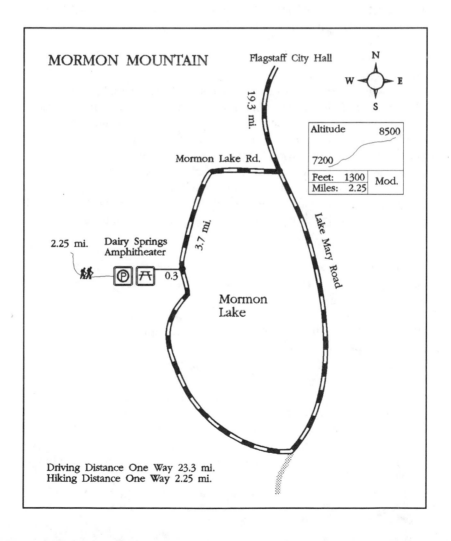

MORMON MOUNTAIN

Flagstaff City Hall

19.3 mi.

Mormon Lake Rd.

Altitude   8500

7200

Feet: 1300 | Mod.
Miles: 2.25

Lake Mary Road

2.25 mi.   Dairy Springs Amphitheater

3.7 mi.

0.3

Mormon Lake

Driving Distance One Way 23.3 mi.
Hiking Distance One Way 2.25 mi.

OAK CREEK VISTA

General Information
Location Map F3
Mountainaire USGS Map
Coconino Forest Service Map

Driving Distance One Way: 14 miles (Time 20 minutes)
Access Road: All cars, All paved
Hiking Distance, Complete Loop: 0.20 miles (Time 30 minutes)
How Strenuous: Easy
Features: Sightseeing spot, Signs explaining flora and fauna

NUTSHELL: More of a stroll than a hike, this easy trail is located 14 miles south of Flagstaff on the rim of Oak Creek Canyon.

DIRECTIONS:
From Flagstaff City Hall Go:
> West one block on Route 66 (Santa Fe) then left (south) on Sitgreaves Street under the railroad overpass. As you continue south you will see the street signs calling the street Milton Road, as Sitgreaves Street blends into Milton. At 1.7 miles you reach the intersection of Forest Meadows, where there is a traffic light. Here you turn right. You will see a sign for Highway 89A, which is the road you want. At the next corner turn left on Beulah and follow it out of town. Beulah will connect onto Highway 89A which is the road to Oak Creek Canyon and Sedona. At 13.7 miles (MP 390) you will see the road to Oak Creek Vista to your left. Pull in on that road and park. It is paved and there are many parking spaces.

TRAILHEAD: The trail is paved, of all things. Pick it up from the parking lot at any point. It makes a loop, so you can join it anywhere you like and come back to where you started.

DESCRIPTION: The Forest Service has made an attractive viewpoint out of the old highway alignment, which used to go through here. On a busy weekend when the weather is good, you will find Indians selling jewelry on blankets they have laid out along the sides of the path.

> The path follows around a bend in the canyon rim. Several standpoints have been established along the rim with signs at each point. The signs explain the history, biology, zoology and geology of the area. You will get some impressive views into the canyon depths from these standpoints.

> The canyon is very deep below this part of the rim, probably one thousand feet or more. The area directly below the viewpoints is actually Pumphouse Wash, a tributary of Oak Creek Canyon, rather than Oak Creek

Canyon itself. You will pass over Pumphouse Wash when you drive down through Oak Creek Canyon. It is spanned by the first big bridge you come to, just below the Sterling Springs Fish Hatchery.

At the canyon rim, the rock you see is a thick cap of grey basalt (lava) at the top with white or buff sandstone cliffs below the grey. The redrock for which Sedona is famous occurs in lower strata. The basalt cliff faces here are favorite spots for rope climbers. Look for them on the cliff faces to the east (on your left) on the same wall of the canyon you are standing on.

An interesting sight is Highway 89A corkscrewing around the toe of a fin as it works its way downhill and comes out onto the floor of Oak Creek Canyon.

This is a very gentle and satisfying walk, an easy stroll for Aunt Maude or other visiting relatives. Kids even seem to like it. It gives an appreciation of the size and depth of Oak Creek Canyon and you just might pick up a jewelry bargain at the same time.

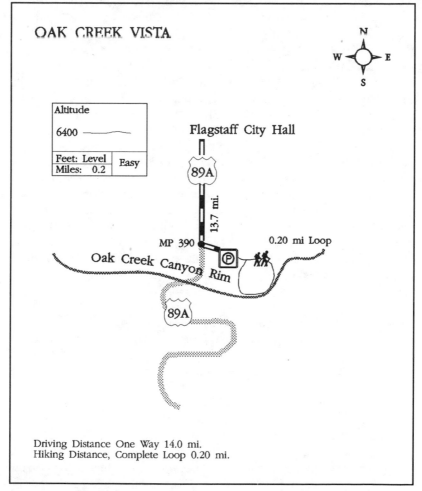

Driving Distance One Way 14.0 mi.
Hiking Distance, Complete Loop 0.20 mi.

OLD CAVES CRATER

General Information
Location Map E3
Sunset Crater West USGS Map
Coconino Forest Map

Driving Distance One Way: 9.5 miles (Time 20 minutes)
Access Road: All cars, Last 0.9 miles medium cinder road
Hiking Distance One Way: 0.75 miles (Time 30 minutes)
How Strenuous: Easy
Features: Indian ruins, Strange volcanic caves

NUTSHELL: Old Caves Crater is a cinder hill located east of Flagstaff. You walk a closed road to the top of the crater to find a fascinating series of natural caves that were used as dwellings by the ancient Indians.

DIRECTIONS:
From Flagstaff City Hall Go:
        East on Route 66 (Santa Fe). Highway 89 runs concurrently with Route 66 (Santa Fe) as the highway goes through Flagstaff, so you will see road signs with both designations. At 8.6 miles (MP 422.9) you will be well out into the country. There you will see the Silver Saddle Road coming in from the right. Take this road (it is paved) to the 9.1 mile point, where you will see unpaved FR 9148R taking off to the left toward a hill. Turn left on FR 9148R and take it to the 9.3 mile point, where you will find a V fork. Take the right fork. At 9.5 miles you will come to a small black cinder pit that has been used as a dump. Go past it uphill, bypassing the road to the left you will see. You will come to a place at about 9.5 miles where the road splits into a V where it meets a cross road. Take the left fork and park just beyond the crossroad, where you will see a road going uphill. Park at the crossroad and do not try to drive farther, as the road is composed of deep loose vehicle-bogging black cinders beyond.

TRAILHEAD: There are no trail signs. The road becomes difficult to drive after the 9.5 mile point, so you park and then walk the rest of the way.

DESCRIPTION: Old Caves Crater has been known since the first white settlers came into Flagstaff, but it has not received much publicity. This is hard to understand, because it is a fascinating site.
        It is located in a zone where there are many cinder hills, most of which were active volcanoes eons ago. The famous Sunset Crater is nearby. Old Caves Crater has their familiar rounded shape but also something different.
        You will walk up a road that has been closed to vehicular travel to the

top of the hill. It is on the southerly face of the crater. On top you will find a number of caves that appear to have been formed by gas bubbles passing through red lava. These bubbles formed caves and then burst in such a way that openings to the caves were created. The caves are not large but they are big enough for shelter, and to people without tools would have provided welcome habitations.

The site has been thoroughly pothunted and rockfalls have closed the entrances to several of the caves. In other spots it appears that pit houses were dug next to the caves. Counting the caves and the pits, this was a fairly sizeable pueblo. As one looks around at the surrounding countryside, one wonders where these people got their water, as there is none visible. Pueblo sites were always located near water, so maybe conditions have changed over the centuries or there is a hidden spring or natural tank nearby.

You will find a footpath over to the higher north face of the crater. It is an easy walk and worth doing in order to enjoy the views.

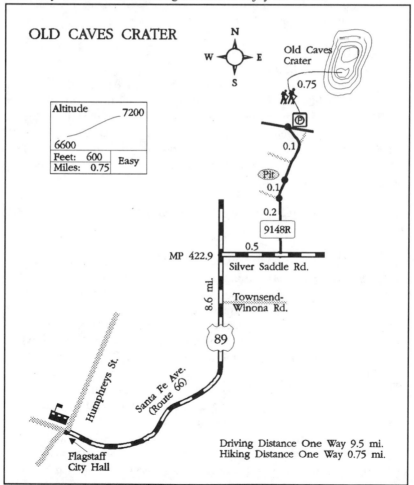

OLDHAM TRAIL NO. 1

General Information
Location Map E3
Flagstaff East and Flagstaff West USGS Maps
Coconino Forest Service Map

Driving Distance One Way: 2.3 miles (Time 10 minutes)
Access Road: All cars, All paved
Hiking Distance One Way: 3.3 miles (Time 1 hour 45 minutes)
How Strenuous: Moderate
Features: Views

NUTSHELL: This trail is part of a trail system developed by the Forest Service around Mt. Elden. Located just north of Flagstaff, this moderate hike takes you through a beautiful forest.

DIRECTIONS:
From Flagstaff City Hall Go:
          North on Humphreys Street to the stoplight at 0.60 miles. Turn right here onto Columbus Avenue and go one block east to the next stop sign, which is at Beaver Street. Turn left onto Beaver Street and go up the hill. At the 1.0 mile point you will reach Forest Avenue. Turn right on Forest and follow it over a hill. On top of the hill, at 1.9 miles, you will find Gemini Drive. Turn left onto it and at 2.3 miles you will come to Buffalo Park. Park in the parking lot at Buffalo Park.

TRAILHEAD: There are trail signs and a map at the gate in the parking lot fence.

DESCRIPTION: The Forest Service has developed a trail system around the Mt. Elden\Dry Lake Hills areas in Flagstaff and this trail connects with others in that system. You will find trail information at the trailhead.
          Buffalo Park is an open plain extending back about a half mile from the gate. In the 1960s it was run as a sort of living zoo but failed due to lack of funds. You can see some vestiges of this operation near the entrance, where a welcoming arch and buffalo statue survive. Lately the City of Flagstaff has turned the area into a public park for joggers and walkers.
          Oldham Trail No. 1 starts at the fence at the rear of the park. To reach it, stay on the main footpath from the gate, which is wide and gravelled, until you reach the natural gas substation and the back fence, at 0.60 miles. Here the footpath goes through the fence, narrows and becomes The Oldham Trail.
          The trail was originally developed by an old timer named Earl Oldham, who worked as a ranger for the Forest Service, was a member of the

Coconino County Board of Supervisors and did some sheep ranching on the side. Busy fellow.

At 1.25 miles you will reach the junction of the Oldham Trail and the **Pipeline Trail**. The two trails are marked. If you just want a simple leisurely stroll, this is a good place to turn back. Up to this point the trail is gentle with little change in altitude. Beyond this point the trail begins to climb.

After you have passed through Buffalo Park, you will be in a pine forest, which is very nice. Later the forest becomes more interesting as you hike through stands of oak, aspen, fir and spruce. Lava cliffs and groups of large boulders big as boxcars that have tumbled down from the cliffs are also interesting.

At 2.25 miles you will intersect a trail taking off to the left. This is the **Rocky Ridge Trail**. The Oldham Trail ends at 3.3 miles, where it intersects the Elden Lookout Road, FR 557. Just before the road you will pass a spectacular basalt cliff loved by rock climbers.

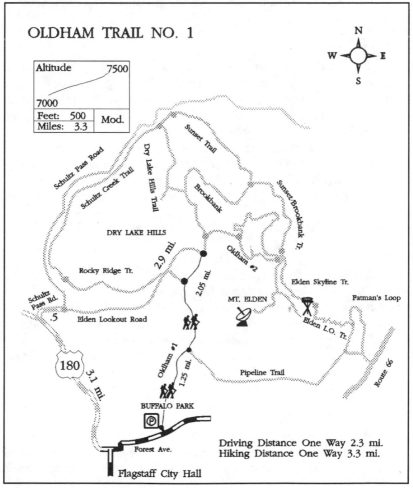

OLDHAM TRAIL NO. 2 (UPPER)

General Information
Location Map E3
Humphreys Pk. & Sunset Crater W. USGS Maps
Coconino Forest Service Map

Driving Distance One Way: 7.1 miles (Time 30 minutes)
Access Road: All cars, Last 3.5 miles medium gravel mountain road
Hiking Distance One Way: 1.75 miles (Time 1 hour)
How Strenuous: Hard
Features: Views, Forests

NUTSHELL: This is a marked and maintained trail that starts at a point on the Elden Lookout Road near the top of Mt. Elden north of Flagstaff and climbs to Sunset Park.

DIRECTIONS:
From Flagstaff City Hall Go:
          North on Humphreys Street for 0.60 miles. Turn left at the stoplight onto Columbus Avenue and follow it around a big curve to the north. You will see the street signs call this road Columbus Avenue at first, then Ft. Valley Road and then Highway 180. Stay on Highway 180 to the 3.1 miles point (MP 218.6), where the Schultz Pass Road, FR 420, goes to the right. Follow this road. At the 3.6 miles point it curves left where you will see the unpaved Elden Lookout Road (FR 557) going straight. Take the right fork and follow FR 557 to the 7.1 mile point, where you will park in an area off the left shoulder.

TRAILHEAD: Across the road you will see a signboard marking the trailhead.

DESCRIPTION: This trail is part of the Dry Lake Hills\Mt. Elden trail system, so it is marked and maintained. You will follow an old road for the first three quarters of a mile. The climb on this stretch of the trail is gradual and doesn't really prepare you for the steep climb that is to follow. This part of the trail takes you through a dense spruce forest. Some of the trees have so much moss on their north sides that you would think you were in a rain forest.
          The old road ends where it bumps up against the flank of Mt. Elden. From there a footpath climbs the mountain. This second part of the trail is very steep, really a hard climb. It also passes through a heavy forest. The trees are so thick that you don't get many views even though you are climbing high enough to have excellent vantage points.
          Near the end of the trail you will come out into an open meadow called Oldham Park. You will cross it and reach the Elden Lookout Road at a place

that is 2.3 miles up the road from where you parked. This is officially the end of the trail, but you will miss a splendid view if you stop here. Go across the road up to the skyline where you will see two trail signs. This place is Sunset Park. You can walk along the crest in either direction to enjoy the views.

The views from the top are excellent due to a forest fire called the Radio Fire that burned away many acres of timber in 1978. This was a terrible fire and we remember it well. Started by a teenager's campfire on a dry, windy June day, the fire roared up a canyon, burst over the top and raged out of control for days. At night Mt. Elden looked like a huge heap of glowing embers.

The above description follows the trail as planned by the Forest Service. However, we think that this is a much better hike if you use two cars. Park one at the 7.1 mile point and take the other one to the top and park it at the 9.4 miles point. Then you start the hike from the top.

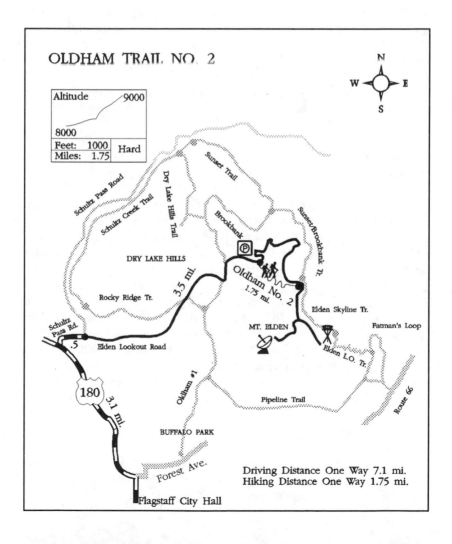

OLDHAM TRAIL NO. 2

Driving Distance One Way 7.1 mi.
Hiking Distance One Way 1.75 mi.

OLD LOWELL OBSERVATORY ROAD

General Information
Location Map F3
Flagstaff West USGS Map
Coconino Forest Service Map

Driving Distance One Way: 1.0 mile (Time 5 minutes)
Access Road: All cars, All paved
Hiking Distance One Way: 1.25 miles (Time 45 minutes)
How Strenuous: Moderate
Features: Beautiful forest, Extremely easy access

NUTSHELL: This urban trail located in west Flagstaff is a short, pleasant walk to the top of Mars Hill, which forms the western boundary of the town.

DIRECTIONS:
From Flagstaff City Hall Go:
    West on Route 66 (Santa Fe) for a distance of 0.50 miles. Turn right on Toltec Avenue. At the 1.0 mile point you will reach the driveway to your left which is the entry to the trail.

TRAILHEAD: The trail is unmistakable. It is a graded and gravelled path marked by boulders.

DESCRIPTION: This trail is part of the City of Flagstaff Urban Trail System. The first phase of its development as a trail occurred in 1991.
    As you walk the trail, look to your left at the last line of boulders just before you start up a small side canyon. The dirt road that you will see there is the original road. The little canyon is pleasant and peaceful with a nice stand of big old pine trees. How did the pioneers' axes miss these beauties?
    At 0.50 miles you will reach a fence where the improved trail stopped in 1991. The old road turns left at the fence and goes up the shoulder of Mars Hill, topping out at 1.25 miles, at the boundary of the Lowell Observatory. The city has an easement from Lowell to extend the path across its land, for a total trail length of 2.0 miles when complete (target date 1992), where it will tie in to the extensive network of roads on Observatory Mesa. Once on the mesa you can follow old roads that go all the way to **A-1 Mountain**. For the purposes of making this a short, easy hike, however, it makes sense to stop at the observatory fence. If you have never seen Lowell Observatory, this hike up the back way might make an interesting way to go there.
    This road was built by the Town of Flagstaff about 1894 as part of the town's inducements to get Dr. Percival Lowell to locate his observatory in Flagstaff. Lowell was checking out several sites and had narrowed the list to

a few contenders. Tucson was another hot prospect. Lowell sent a scientist named A. E. Douglass, who later was famed for developing the science of dendrochronology (tree ring dating), to investigate Flagstaff. The town fathers wined and dined Douglass and made such a favorable impression on him that he told Lowell Flagstaff was the place. The boosters promised Lowell that he could have his choice of ten acres of land free anywhere in the town and that the town would also build a road to the site for him. Lowell picked land at the top of the hill and the town obligingly built this road. The road has been relocated twice since then.

Lowell Observatory has been a magnificent asset for Flagstaff, crowned by the discovery there of the planet Pluto in 1932 by Clyde Tombaugh, who was working out some of Lowell's old theories. Lowell died in 1916 in his Flagstaff mansion (since torn down).

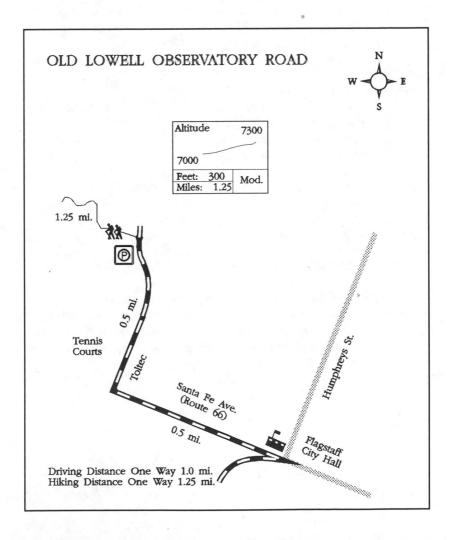

O'LEARY PEAK

General Information
Location Map E3
O'Leary Pk. & Sunset Crater W. USGS Maps
Coconino Forest Service Map

Driving Distance One Way: 22 miles (Time 30 minutes)
Access Road: All cars, Last 4 miles medium condition dirt road
Hiking Distance One Way: 1.5 miles (Time 1 hour)
How Strenuous: Hard
Features: Views, Volcanic field

NUTSHELL: This trail takes you to the top of a peak located about 20 miles northeast of Flagstaff. The peak dominates the Sunset Crater area and gives great views as a reward for a fairly strenuous climb.

DIRECTIONS:
From Flagstaff City Hall Go:
　　　　East, curving to north on Route 66 (Santa Fe). As you leave the city limits you will see that Route 66 (Santa Fe) is also Highway 89. Follow Highway 89 north out into the country. At 16.4 miles (MP 430.3) you will reach the entrance to Sunset Crater National Monument. Turn right on the road into Sunset Crater. This road is also known as FR 545. At 18.1 miles you will reach a dirt road going to your left marked FR 545A. Turn onto FR 545A and follow it. You will soon come to O'Leary Peak and begin to climb it. The road was built to service a fire lookout tower located on the top, so it is wide and in good condition. At the 22.0 miles point you will reach a gate. Park there.

TRAILHEAD: You will not see any trail signs. Walk up the road to the top.

DESCRIPTION: The gate is located at a saddle and is a good place to stop and begin this hike. You could drive all the way to the top if the gate is open, but what's the fun of that? The gate is open when a fire ranger is in the lookout tower. This means, roughly speaking, during the summer when fire danger is high. Except in bad weather the road may be driveable any time of year.
　　　　As you walk up the road you will find that it winds around the mountain. Because of this you get to see out in all directions as you go. You will have great views. At first you will see into the Sunset Crater National Monument and then into the Bonito Lava Flow, which is part of the monument. Both of these are very interesting.
　　　　At the top you will find the fire lookout tower. If the ranger is present, ask to go up. Most of these people are very cordial and enjoy a bit of company as a break from their lonely vigils, though there are times when they cannot

admit visitors for security reasons. The views from the tower are truly splendid. If you are interested in volcanos, this is a must. O'Leary Peak itself is an extinct volcano. You will see out over a huge volcanic field running for many miles north and east of the San Francisco Peaks. You will also have grand views of the Painted Desert.

The walkway to the fire tower is a strange one. Corrugated metal sections looking something like treads for a giant Caterpillar tractor have been joined together to make a deckway. This gives good footing when it is dry but we wouldn't want to walk it while it is wet. We certainly wouldn't want to be on it when lightning was flashing. The metal plates would be a powerful attractor of thunderbolts. Fire towers themselves are well grounded and you need not fear being struck while you are in one, though their metal skin will glow and sizzle and scare the hell out of you.

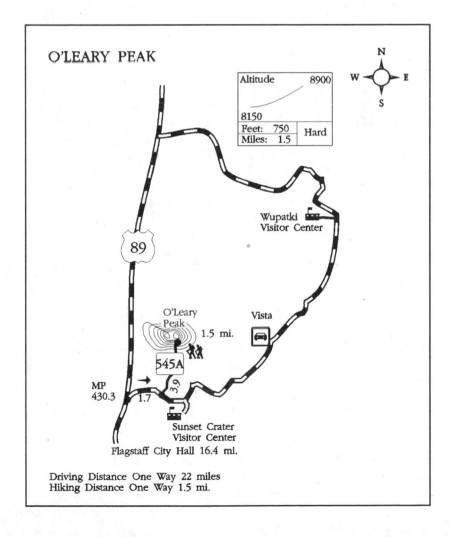

OVERLAND ROAD

General Information
Location Map E2
Bill Williams Mountain USGS Map
Kaibab (Williams District) Forest Service Map

Driving Distance One Way: 42.4 miles (Time 60 minutes)
Access Road: All cars, Last 0.4 miles good gravel road
Hiking Distance One Way: 6.0 miles (Time 3.0 hours)
How Strenuous: Moderate
Features: Historic road, Cabin ruins

NUTSHELL: This hike takes you over a portion of the 1863 Overland Road, south of Williams.

DIRECTIONS:
From Flagstaff City Hall Go:
     West on Route 66 (Santa Fe) a block, then follow the curve left on Sitgreaves Street under the railroad overpass. The street name will change to Milton Road at the first stoplight. Keep going south on Milton until you are out of town, headed toward Phoenix on I-17. At 2.0 miles you will reach Exit 340B, which is an access ramp onto I-40 West. The sign will say "Williams and Los Angeles." Get onto I-40 West and stay on it for 31.6 miles, where you will see the Williams Exit, #165. Take that exit and at the stop sign go left to Williams. Go into downtown Williams and turn left at Fourth Street, 34.5 miles, where you will see a sign reading, "Ski Area, White Horse Lake." Follow Fourth Street, which will take you out of town into a valley. Here the road is still paved and is designated FR 173. At 42.0 miles turn left onto FR 139. Take FR 139 to the 42.4 mile point, where you will see a 4 x 4 post on the right side of the road with the burro symbol burned into it. Park there.

TRAILHEAD: The burro post is at the mouth of an old road. Hike the road.

DESCRIPTION: For many years north central Arizona was unexplored and was indicated on maps of the day as *tierra incognita*, land unknown. After the United States acquired the territory in 1848, the government began to explore it, leading to the establishment of the **Beale Road**, which ran across the land from east to west. Gold was discovered in Prescott in 1863 and with the ensuing gold rush there came a clamor for a north-south road. The sensible way to approach this was to use the Beale Road as far as possible and then branch off of it to the south. This was done and the resulting road was called the Overland Road. The gold boom was short-lived and the road soon fell into disuse.
     For the first 0.85 miles of this hike you will walk along a newer road

that was laid on top of the Overland Trail. You will find that the path is marked with posts, cairns and blazes. Every quarter of a mile there is a brass cap. You will pass Deadhorse Tank and go across a meadow and up the shoulder of a hill. The increase in elevation is gradual and most of the time thereafter the trail hugs the 7000 foot contour line.

At 3.1 miles you will come to a clearing where you will find the ruins of a cabin. This was a way station called Big Spring. The spring forms a pool in the canyon behind the cabin. The trail swerves to the head of the canyon, crosses it and then comes back and begins a gradual descent.

At 4.75 miles you will come upon a big meadow with an old barn, a cabin made of railroad ties and a pond. This place is the historic Whiting Ranch. There is a modern camp called Boys' Ranch nearby. From the Whiting Ranch you walk to the end of the meadow, where the trail intersects FR 109. We stop the trail here because this makes a nice day hike. We recommend doing this as a two-car hike, parking one at the beginning and one at the end.

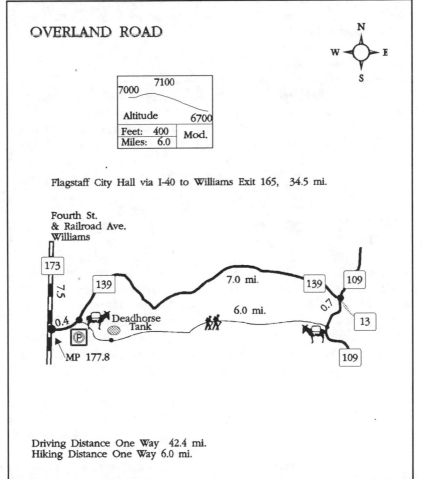

OVERLAND ROAD

N
W — E
S

7100
7000
Altitude   6700
Feet: 400   Mod.
Miles: 6.0

Flagstaff City Hall via I-40 to Williams Exit 165,   34.5 mi.

Fourth St.
& Railroad Ave.
Williams

173

7.5

139   7.0 mi.   139   109

6.0 mi.   0.7

0.4   Deadhorse Tank   13

MP 177.8   109

Driving Distance One Way   42.4 mi.
Hiking Distance One Way 6.0 mi.

PIPELINE TRAIL

General Information
Location Map F3
Flagstaff East and Flagstaff West USGS Maps
Coconino Forest Service Map

Driving Distance One Way: 2.3 miles (Time 10 minutes)
Access Road: All cars, All paved
Hiking Distance One Way: 4.0 miles (Time 2 hours)
How Strenuous: Moderate
Features: Views

NUTSHELL: This trail is part of a trail system developed by the Forest Service around Mt. Elden. Located just north of Flagstaff, this moderate hike takes you around the base of Mt. Elden to connect with the Elden Lookout trailhead in East Flagstaff.

DIRECTIONS:
From Flagstaff City Hall Go:
North on Humphreys Street to the stoplight at 0.60 miles. Turn right here onto Columbus Avenue and go one block east to the next stop sign, which is at Beaver Street. Turn left onto Beaver Street and go up the hill. At the 1.0 mile point you will reach Forest Avenue. Turn right on Forest and follow it over a hill. On top of the hill, at 1.9 miles, you will find Gemini Drive. Turn left onto it and at 2.3 miles you will come to Buffalo Park. Park in the parking lot at the park.

TRAILHEAD: There are trail signs and a map at the gate in the parking lot fence.

DESCRIPTION: The Forest Service has developed a trail system around the Dry Lake Hills\Mt. Elden areas in Flagstaff and this trail connects with others in that system. You will find trail information at the trailhead.
Buffalo Park is an open plain extending back about a half mile from the gate. In the 1960s it was run as a sort of living zoo but failed due to lack of funds. You can see some vestiges of this operation near the entrance, where a welcoming arch and buffalo statue survive. Lately the City of Flagstaff has turned the area into a public park for joggers and walkers.
Start by taking the main jogging path which goes straight back to the fence at the rear of the park. It is wide and gravelled, until you reach the natural gas substation and the rear fence, at 0.60 miles. Here the trail goes through the fence, narrows and becomes **The Oldham Trail No. 1**.
Hike the Oldham Trail No. 1 to the 1.25 miles point where you will

reach the junction of the Oldham Trail and the **Pipeline Trail**. The two trails are marked. Turn right here onto the Pipeline Trail.

Although the trail comes very close to some houses as you get into East Flagstaff, it feels quite remote in places. At about the 1.75 mile point there is a side trail going to the left. Someone has painted "Satan's Cave" on a boulder there. It is a short jaunt over to the cave and worth taking a look.

The Pipeline Trail comes close to many interesting boulder formations, with intriguing caves and crannies. Mt. Elden is essentially a giant lava pile and the lava did some interesting things as it settled and cooled.

The trail terminates at a place where it links with the **Elden Lookout Trail** in East Flagstaff. A good way to do this hike is to use a two-car shuttle. Park one car at Buffalo Park and the other at the Elden Lookout trailhead parking lot in East Flagstaff.

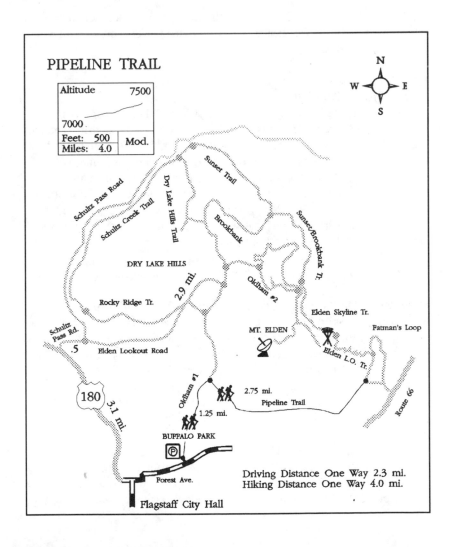

PUMPKIN TRAIL

General Information
Location Map E2
Kendrick Peak, Moritz Ridge and Wing Mt. USGS Maps
Coconino Forest Service Map

Driving Distance One Way: 25.7 miles (Time 1 hour)
Access Road: All cars, Last 11.2 miles good gravel road
Hiking Distance One Way: 5.5 miles (Time 4.0 hours)
How Strenuous: Hard
Features: Ten thousand foot peak, Views

NUTSHELL: Located 25.7 miles north of Flagstaff, Kendrick Peak is next tallest to the San Francisco Peaks. This trail switchbacks to the summit where you get great views.

DIRECTIONS:
From Flagstaff City Hall Go:
    North on Humphreys Street for 0.60 miles. Turn left at the stoplight onto Columbus Avenue and follow it around a big curve to the north. You will see the street signs call this road Columbus at first, then Ft. Valley Road and then Highway 180. Stay on Highway 180 to the 14.5 miles point (MP 230), where an unpaved road takes off to the left. Turn left onto this road, FR 245, and follow it to the 17.6 mile point where it intersects FR 171. Turn right on FR 171 and follow it to the 24.8 mile point, where you will see a sign for the Pumpkin Trail. Turn right on the drive to the trailhead, which you will reach at 25.7 miles. Park in the parking area.

TRAILHEAD: Well marked with a sign at the parking area.

DESCRIPTION: Unlike the nearby **Kendrick Mt. Trail**, which was made to provide access to a fire lookout tower by the Forest Service and was consequently engineered and built with an eye to making best use of the terrain, the Pumpkin Trail seems to have been built by and for sheepherders and just grew like topsy. It is rough and has some very sharp grades.
    From the parking lot you will climb along the side of a canyon for a mile to a fence. Here you will turn right and begin going up a ridge. At 1.4 miles you will meet the **Connector Trail** coming over from the **Bull Basin Trail.**
    Not far from this intersection you will climb into a more interesting forest, with many varieties of conifers and lots of aspens. The trail gets very rocky and rough in this stretch. At about 3.0 miles you will find breaks in the forests punctuated by meadows. The meadows provide good viewpoints,

though the footing can be hard due to the fact that the grass in the meadows hides the rocks along the trail.

From the 4.0 mile point the trail gets really steep and is hard going. You will reach the ruins of a log cabin at 5.0 miles located at the edge of the biggest meadow. The slope of this meadow falls away so steeply that they must have issued spiked shoes to the sheep.

Beyond this meadow the trail becomes primitive and even harder, clawing its way to the top just below the base of the lookout tower at 5.5 miles. Go on up to the tower for its superlative views.

This is a much harder trail than the Kendrick Mt. Trail or Bull Basin Trail. We think Bull Basin is the best of the three trails to the top, with the Kendrick Mountain Trail being next best.

You may wonder about the name. A ranch near the trailhead is named Pumpkin Center, and —yes—there was a time when pumpkins were grown at the ranch, but farming at this altitude, a dicey proposition, was discontinued.

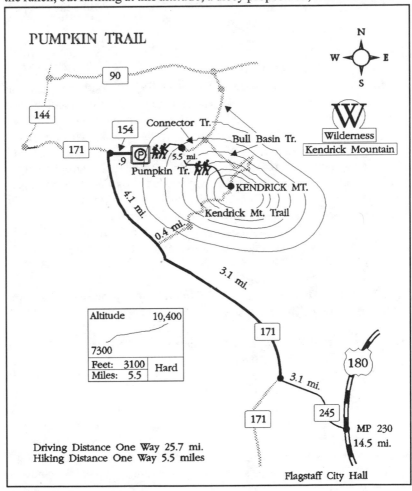

PURTYMUN TRAIL

General Information
Location Map F3
Munds Park and Wilson Mt. USGS Maps
Coconino Forest Service Map

Drive Distance One Way: 21.4 miles (Time 35 minutes)
Access Road: All cars, All paved
Hiking Distance One Way: 1.0 miles (Time 1 hour)
How Strenuous: Hard
Features: Views

NUTSHELL: This hike climbs the east wall of Oak Creek Canyon from a point directly across Highway 89A from the Junipine Resort in the upper canyon, 21.4 miles south of Flagstaff.

DIRECTIONS:
From Flagstaff City Hall Go:

West one block on Route 66 (Santa Fe) then left (south) on Sitgreaves Street under the railroad overpass. As you continue south you will see the street signs calling the street Milton Road, as Sitgreaves Street blends into Milton. At 1.7 miles you reach the intersection of Forest Meadows, where there is a traffic light. Here you turn right. You will see a sign for Highway 89A, which is the road you want. At the next corner turn left on Beulah and follow it out of town. Beulah will connect onto Highway 89A which is the road to Oak Creek Canyon and Sedona. At 13.8 miles (MP 390) you will reach the canyon rim and begin the winding descent. After you have completed the switchbacks and are on the canyon floor, drive to the 21.4 mile point (MP 382.6), the Junipine Resort. There is a public lot on the north end of the property next to the highway.

TRAILHEAD: There are no markings for this trail. Go across the highway to the Fire Station. The trail starts there.

DESCRIPTION: The people at Junipine have created a parking lot at the north end of their property that has space for several cars. If it is full then park along the road shoulder nearby. The trailhead is not conspicuous. You will see a Fire Station across the highway from the resort. The trail starts at the south side of the Fire Station where there is a yellow fire plug.

This trail was made by the Purtymun family, which homesteaded the Junipine property in the late 1800s. Like other families in the canyon they needed a way to get to the rim so that they could go to Flagstaff, so they built this trail. They did not have sophisticated equipment, just picks, shovels, crowbars and maybe a little dynamite. Their practice was to leave a wagon at the top. When they wanted to go to town they would walk a horse to the top, hitch it to the wagon and then drive to Flagstaff. In town they would load the wagon with goods, perhaps bartering some of the vegetables and fruits they had grown for flour and coffee. They would then drive the wagon back to Oak Creek Canyon and chain it to a tree at the top of the trail. After that they would carry the goods down in saddlebags. Such a trip could take three or four days.

In spite of the hardships of using the trail, the alternative was worse. There was no convenient wagon road from Sedona to Flagstaff until the Schnebly Hill Road was built in 1902. Before that the only wagon road was the rough old Beaverhead route several miles farther south. Highway 89A did not come onto the scene until much later. It was built in phases starting in the early 1920s, and it took a decade to complete.

This trail is so steep and so rough that we don't see how the Purtymuns could ever have gotten a horse up and down it. We rate this a very poor trail.

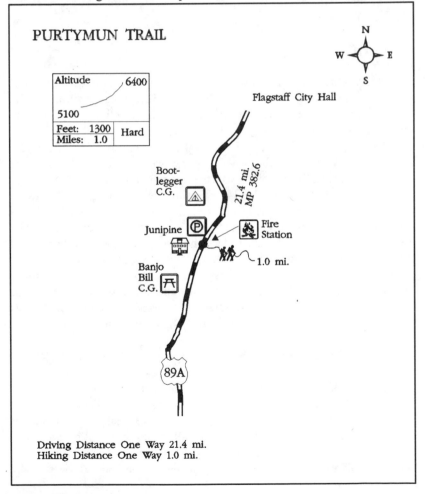

PURTYMUN TRAIL

Altitude 6400
5100
Feet: 1300 Hard
Miles: 1.0

Flagstaff City Hall

Boot-legger C.G.

Junipine

Banjo Bill C.G.

21.4 mi.
MP 382.6

Fire Station

1.0 mi.

89A

Driving Distance One Way 21.4 mi.
Hiking Distance One Way 1.0 mi.

RAIN TANK HILL

General Information
Location Map E2
Parks USGS Map
Kaibab (Williams) Forest Service Map

Driving Distance One Way: 24:3 miles (Time 40 minutes)
Access Road: All cars, Last 11 miles medium gravel road
Hiking Distance One Way: 0.5 miles (Time 30 minutes))
How Strenuous: Moderate
Features: Views

NUTSHELL: This bare hill is located almost in the center of Government Prairie some 20 miles west of Flagstaff. it is easy to climb and provides fine views from its top.

DIRECTIONS:
From Flagstaff City Hall Go:
West a block on Route 66 (Santa Fe), then south, beneath the railroad overpass on Sitgreaves Street. The street name will change to Milton Road as you go farther. At 0.50 miles you will reach a Y intersection. The right fork is named West Old US Highway 66. Take it. You will soon leave town, driving on a stretch of fabled Highway 66. At the 4.8 mile point you will merge onto Interstate-40 West. Look for Exit 185, "Transwestern Rd., Bellemont" and take it. It is at the 10.8 mile point. From the exit turn right and go to the frontage road, where you turn left onto FR 146. You are now following another stretch of U.S. 66. Stay on this to the 18 mile point, where you will see FR 107 fork right. Take FR 107 and follow it to the 23.2 mile point, just beyond the hill. Here you will find FR 793 to the right. It has no sign at its entrance and looks more like a jeep track than a real road, but it is okay for travel except when it is wet. Take FR 793 to the 23.75 miles point where you will see a sign marked 793 and 81. Turn right on FR 81 and take it to the 24.05 mile point. Here you will see a track going over to a metal tank at the back side of the hill. Follow this track to the tank and park there at the 24.3 mile point.

TRAILHEAD: No trail, no signs. Walk uphill any place that suits you.

DESCRIPTION: Government Prairie is a clear grassy plain surrounded by hills. These hills are either forested, semi-forested or bare. This hill is one of the bare ones except for one lonely little copse of aspens located on a knob above the water tank. On the official maps this hill has no name. We have called it Rain Tank Hill because of the water catching device located on its north face. A 60 foot square tract on a slope of the hill has been smoothed and covered with tarpaper. Rain hitting this surface runs to its bottom and is carried by a three-foot diameter pipe into a big storage tank. It is an adaptation of the old-fashioned rainbarrel catching water from a roof. We first saw this big black square from **Wild Bill Hill** (located to the north) and could not imagine what it was.

The north side of the hill slopes gradually up to the top, making a natural walkway. You don't need a trail. Just walk to the top. Because the hill is bare you can see clearly where you want to go. We walked first to the little knob with the aspens just to check them out and found that they are strange: they are dwarfs. Nearby **Klostermeyer Hill** has nice stands of full sized aspens, so we can't account for the dwarfing except that the soil looks different.

Rain Tank Hill is located near the center of Government Prairie and is totally bald on top so it is a superior viewpoint from which to see the prairie. We love the views to the north, so smooth, sinuous and restful.

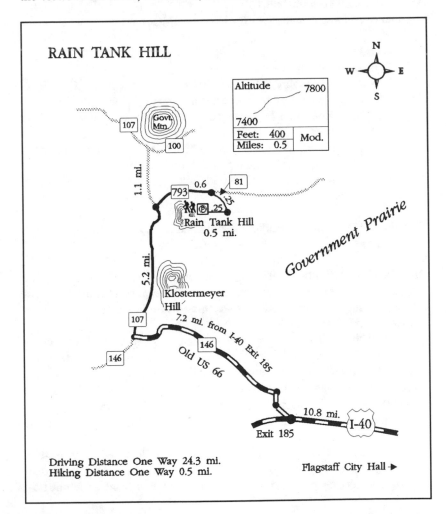

RAIN TANK HILL

Driving Distance One Way 24.3 mi.
Hiking Distance One Way 0.5 mi.

Flagstaff City Hall ➤

RED BUTTE

General Information
Location Map C2
Red Butte USGS Map
Kaibab (Tusayan) Forest Service Map

Driving Distance One Way: 63.6 miles (Time 90 minutes)
Access Road: All cars, Last 2.7 miles good dirt road
Hiking Distance One Way: 1.2 miles (Time 45 minutes)
How Strenuous: Moderate
Features: Unusual formation, Views of Grand Canyon country

NUTSHELL: This mountain stands alone near the Grand Canyon. A good trail makes a moderate climb worthwhile to enjoy the view.

DIRECTIONS:
From Flagstaff City Hall, Go:

North on Humphreys Street 0.60 miles to a stoplight. Go left on Columbus Avenue and follow the curve north. Street signs will show the street first as Ft. Valley Road, then Highway 180. This is a major road to the Grand Canyon. At 50.4 miles (MP 265.8), you will intersect Highway 64, coming out of Williams, at a place called Valle. Go right at this junction. At 60.9 miles (MP 224), you will see a road sign for Red Butte. Turn right here and follow signs. At 62.3 miles, you turn left. At 63.2 miles, you go right. At 63.6 miles you will be at the parking lot.

TRAILHEAD: This is a marked, maintained trail. There are signs at the parking area.

DESCRIPTION: Although it is a small mountain for Northern Arizona, Red Butte dominates its area. Geologists speculate that because it had a thicker lava cap than the surrounding lands had, everything else eroded away, leaving Red Butte at the original ground level.

On the south side of Red Butte you can see some red cliffs with white cliffs above them, capped by gray lava rock. These strata form interesting layers. The red stone is the Moenkopi formation, which abounds in Flagstaff. The county courthouse in Flagstaff was built of the stone in the 1890s, as were many other landmark Flagstaff buildings of that era. There was even a lively turn-of-the-century sandstone quarrying industry in Flagstaff to exploit the stone.

The trail was built in 1976-77 and is well designed. Rather than trying to go straight up the mountain, it zigzags. The climb is fairly gradual at first, then gets steep going to the top. One disappointment is that the trail takes you to the edge of the red cliffs and then veers away from them. Too bad. Hikers would like to see more of the red cliffs and get next to them.

The area at the top is small, about four acres, and bald, so that there are good views all around. Unfortunately, you can't see into the Grand Canyon. You can only see the cliffs of the North Rim and the line of the South Rim. The best views are to the East, where you see the San Francisco Peaks and a long line of lesser mountains and hills. The land around Red Butte is a flat plain and the vegetation on it is sparse. You can see signs of cattle ranching activity. Decades ago when the sheepraising business was at its zenith, there would be many hundreds of sheep quartered on this plateau.

There is a fire lookout on top, and you can climb it and walk along its deck for the best views. Twenty minutes spent looking at the landscape from there is a better geology lesson than many hours in the classroom.

There is a helicopter landing pad at the top if you are a member of the jet set.

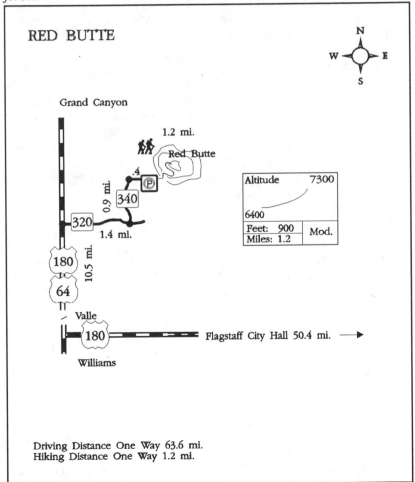

RED MOUNTAIN

General Information
Location Map D2
Ebert Mountain USGS Map
Coconino Forest Service Map

Personal
Favorite

Driving Distance One Way: 31.7 miles (Time 40 minutes)
Access Road: All cars, Last 0.33 miles good gravel road
Hiking Distance One Way: 1.25 miles (Time 40 minutes)
How Strenuous: Moderate
Features: Unique experience allows you to go into the heart of a cutaway volcano

NUTSHELL: Located 31.7 miles north of Flagstaff, this moderate hike takes you into the heart of Red Mountain to enjoy its otherwordly sculptures and formations. **A personal favorite.**

DIRECTIONS:
From Flagstaff City Hall Go:
North on Humphreys Street for 0.60 miles. Turn left at the stoplight onto Columbus Avenue and follow it around a big curve to the north. You will see the street signs call this road Columbus at first, then Ft. Valley Road and then Highway 180. Stay on Highway 180 to the 31.4 miles point (MP 247), where an unpaved road, FR 9023V, takes off to the left. You will see a sign reading, "Red Mountain Geological Area." Turn left onto FR 9032V and follow it to the 31.7 mile point, where there is a parking lot.

TRAILHEAD: The trailhead is the gate at the parking lot.

DESCRIPTION: The Forest Service has done some nice work on this trail. When we first did this hike in 1985 there was no trail and hikers had to thread their way through a maze of bad roads. The trail is now well maintained and easy to follow. Look for white plastic diamonds nailed to trees; these mark the path.

Your objective will have been in sight for miles. Red Mountain looks just like hundreds of other cinder hills in the area north of Flagstaff except for one thing: its east face is sheared off cleanly, as if someone had done a cross-section of it to expose its innards. These insides appear red. Geologists tell us that all red cinder hills are like this in their interior.

This is juniper country and the land is pretty flat. It is an easy walk though the trail rises constantly. At 0.75 miles the trail leaves the old road it has been following and goes into the bed of a wash. This makes for fine walking as the bed is hard sand, and it makes a perfect entrance into Red Mountain. As you come nearer, the streambed becomes the bottom of a V flanked by high black cinder shoulders. Then you see some strange black lava formations forming a sort of gate at the entrance to the insides of the mountain. The area has an Easter Island appearance of mystery.

At the 1.2 mile point, you will see a dam made of rock. It is silted full. You can climb up the dam (our preferred route) or go up the black cinders to your right. Once you top out, you are in a basin surrounded by weird hoodoos. You don't see black lava on the inside. The prevailing color is red there. You will also see an unexpected mustard colored rock in the lower formations. The place reminds us of Bryce Canyon, Utah, on a smaller scale.

Once on the inside, the trail disappears. No worries. You can explore all around, enjoying the colors, shapes, play of light and all the other features that make this place so special. You feel cut off from the world in Red Mountain. Everywhere you look there is something to delight your eye. Spend as much time as you like and then return to the normal world refreshed.

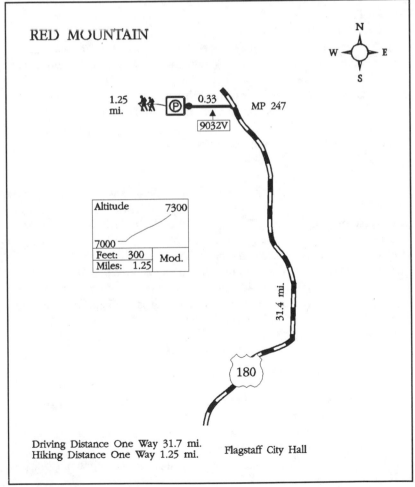

RED MOUNTAIN

1.25 mi.

0.33

MP 247

9032V

Altitude 7300
7000
Feet: 300
Miles: 1.25   Mod.

31.4 mi.

180

Driving Distance One Way 31.7 mi.
Hiking Distance One Way 1.25 mi.   Flagstaff City Hall

RIO DE FLAG TRAIL

General Information
Location Map F3
Flagstaff West USGS Map
Coconino Forest Service Map

Driving Distance One Way: 1.2 mile (Time 5 minutes)
Access Road: All cars, All paved
Hiking Distance One Way: 1.2 miles (Time 30 minutes)
How Strenuous: Easy
Features: Urban trail

NUTSHELL: This urban trail in south Flagstaff is a pleasant 1.2 mile walk.

DIRECTIONS:
From Flagstaff City Hall Go:
    East on Route 66 (Santa Fe) for one block. Turn right on Beaver Street and go south four blocks to Butler Avenue, where there is a stoplight. Turn left on Butler Avenue and follow it east for four blocks to O'Leary Street. Turn right on O'Leary Street and follow it four blocks south, where you will see the parking area to your left as you come to the bottom of a long hill.

TRAILHEAD: This is a marked and maintained trail. You will see a sign at the parking lot.

DESCRIPTION: Flagstaff is developing an ambitious system of urban trails. This trail shares a common trailhead with the **Sinclair Wash Trail**, which goes west from the parking lot, toward the Northern Arizona University campus, while the Rio de Flag Trail goes east toward a shallow canyon. The Rio de Flag trail was opened in the fall of 1989. The Sinclair Wash Trail was added to the trail system in the fall of 1990 and extended in 1991.
    The trail follows an old road. A row of boulders across the entrance now keeps vehicles from the road, as this path is for pedestrian use (and bicycles) only. The trail follows along the course of the whimsically named Rio de Flag as it curves and recurves along a canyon. The rio's streambed is usually dry, containing water only after the spring snowmelt in April or May or after a summer cloudburst of rain.
    The trail is built mostly above the bottom and the riverbed (riobed?) has been banked and channeled so that the trail should stay dry except in the time of a truly major flood.
    The trail is the width of a single lane road and has been graded and surfaced so that the footing is very good.
    After the first two hundred yards, you pass out of sight of habitation.

Although you are surrounded by industry on the north and residences on the south, the canyon is deep enough so that you don't see any of this and it feels as if you are out in the country.

The walls of the canyon are mostly a buff colored limestone, some of which was crushed to make the surface for the trail. This sedimentary rock is a fairly soft stone that formed in layers. As these layers have eroded they have made ledges. Here and there you will find some interesting formations in the stone.

At the end of the hike you are jarred when you come out of the canyon to find that you are under the roaring traffic of Interstate 40 on bridges high overhead. This is an unwelcome return to "civilization" after a rustic respite.

The beauty of this trail is that it is very easy and quick to reach. Five minutes' driving time and you are on your way, able to stretch your legs in a pretty setting. You may have to share this trail with bicyclers and joggers but that is not difficult because the path is wide enough.

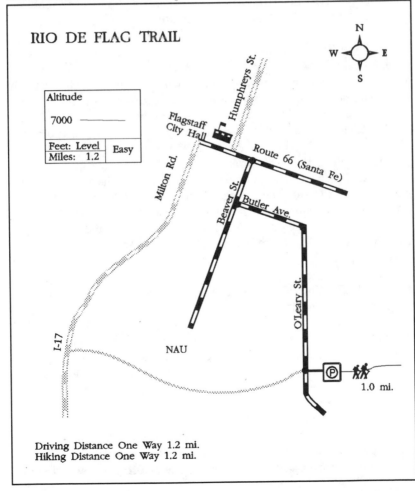

ROCKY RIDGE TRAIL

General Information
Location Map E3
Humphreys Peak & Flagstaff West USGS Maps
Coconino Forest Service Map

Driving Distance One Way: 3.9 miles (Time 20 minutes)
Access Road: All cars, Last .25 miles medium gravel road
Hiking Distance One Way: 3.0 miles (Time 1.5 hours)
How Strenuous: Moderate
Features: Shady forest in the hills

NUTSHELL: This is a marked and maintained trail that hugs the base of the south face of the Dry Lake Hills about 4 miles north of Flagstaff and goes from the Schultz Pass Road to the Elden Lookout Road.

DIRECTIONS:
From Flagstaff City Hall Go:
      North on Humphreys Street for 0.60 miles. Turn left at the stoplight onto Columbus Avenue and follow it around a big curve to the north. You will see the street signs call this road Columbus Avenue at first, then Ft. Valley Road and then Highway 180. Stay on Highway 180 to the 3.1 miles point (MP 218.6), where the Schultz Pass Road, FR 420, goes to the right. Follow the Schultz Pass Road. As it starts around a curve to the left, at the 3.6 miles point, you will see the unpaved Elden Lookout Road going straight. Eschew this and stay on the paved road. The paving will end soon and the road will become gravel. At the 3.9 miles point, you will see a gate, which closes the road in winter. Just beyond the gate is FR 9128Y which goes downhill to your right. Take this. At the bottom turn left and follow the road a few yards to a fence, where you park.

TRAILHEAD: You will see a wooden sign for the Rocky Ridge Trail in the fence opening to your right.

DESCRIPTION: This trail starts at the same place that the **Schultz Creek Trail** ends. There are two distinct openings in the fence for the respective trails. The Rocky Ridge Trail has a sign whereas the Schultz Creek Trail does not.
      The trail climbs gradually until it reaches a point about three hundred feet higher than the beginning and then pretty well holds that contour. You will walk through a pine forest which is so thick that you are able to get only a few views through the trees. You will see Buffalo Park and the NAU campus clearly, but most of Flagstaff is below a mesa that cuts off your view of the town.

The trail takes you around the west toe of the Dry Lake Hills and then follows along their south face. From the one mile point onward you will be aware that the Elden Lookout Road is nearby on your right. Sometimes you can only hear sounds coming from it, while in other places you can see the road and will be a stone's throw from it. Mountain bikers love the road and many of them use the Rocky Ridge Trail as well.

The best way to do this hike is to use two cars. Park one at the trailhead. The other car should be parked at a point that is 2.7 miles up the Elden Lookout Road from its beginning. There is a cattle guard and fence at this point and there are spaces to park several cars there and up the road a bit.

We find this trail not to be so interesting as some others in the area. It doesn't go high enough to provide the alpine vegetation of other trails and doesn't rise above the tree line so as to provide good views. Call it mediocre, vanilla pudding.

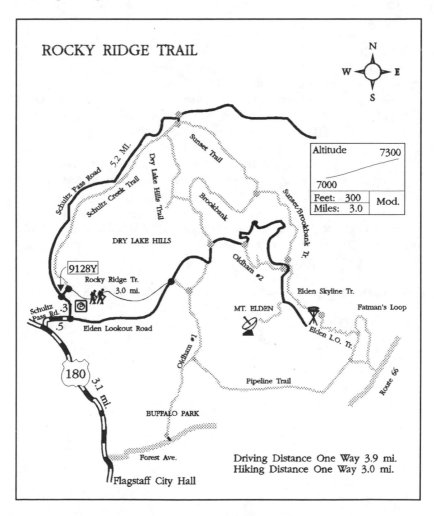

RS HILL

General Information
Location Map E2
Parks USGS Map
Coconino Forest Service Map

Driving Distance One Way: 24.5 miles (Time 40 minutes)
Access Road: All cars, Last 1.2 miles good gravel road
Hiking Distance, Complete Loop: 6.0 miles (Time 3 hours)
How Strenuous: Moderate
Features: Pine forest, Beautiful meadows with views

NUTSHELL: This hike circles RS Hill in the Government Prairie area west of Flagstaff.

DIRECTIONS:
From Flagstaff City Hall Go:
    West a block on Route 66 (Santa Fe), then south, beneath the railroad overpass on Sitgreaves Street. The street name will change to Milton Road as you go farther. At 0.50 miles you will reach a Y intersection. The right fork is named West Old US Highway 66. Take it. You will soon leave town, driving on a stretch of fabled Highway 66. At the 4.8 mile point you will merge onto Interstate-40 West. Look for Exit 178 at the 18.0 mile point, and take it. Turn right at the stop sign and travel to the 18.2 mile point, where there is a second stop sign. Turn left here and go to the 18.8 mile point, where you will see the Parks Store to your right. Turn right here, on the Spring Valley Road (FR 141). It is paved to the 23.2 mile point, and is a good gravel road beyond. At 24.5 miles you will see a sign for the Cross Country Ski Trail. Turn left here into the parking lot and park.

TRAILHEAD: You will see a large wooden signboard with a trail map.

DESCRIPTION: The Forest Service has created three cross-country ski trails in this area. The trails are marked in the trees. For the RS Hill Trail you will be guided by blue triangles.
    You will start on a road after going through a gate. Be sure to watch for the place at about 0.40 miles where the trail veers off to the left, away from the road. You will at times be on roads and at other times will be offroad all through this hike. Be sure to follow the triangles. It becomes a game.
    At 0.75 miles you will reach a beautiful meadow beyond an aspen grove. In the middle of the meadow is Shoot-Em-Up-Dick Tank. We'd love to know how this tank got its name. To your right you will look at a big mountain, Kendrick Peak.

Beyond the meadow you will come onto FR 76 and walk it for a short distance until you reach the place where the **Eagle Rock Trail** forks to the left. Beyond is the junction of FR 76 and FR 104. Here you turn onto FR 104 but soon veer to the right, going into aspen groves and through a gate.

From this point onward you come close to the base of RS Hill and begin to circle it clockwise. You will go down a steep path and then hit an old road which you follow to RS Tank. Just past the tank the trail leaves the road and goes uphill on a shoulder. This area is very rich in obsidian and you will find hunks of it everywhere. It looks like small pieces of coal with a dull side and a shiny side. This obsidian was prized by the ancient Indians for its quality and is found in ruins throughout the area, indicating it was a valued trade item for arrowheads, knives and axes.

At about the four mile point you will see Spring Valley to your left. From this point you walk a road back to the junction of FR 76 and FR 104, then retrace your steps to the parking lot. You never do climb RS Hill.

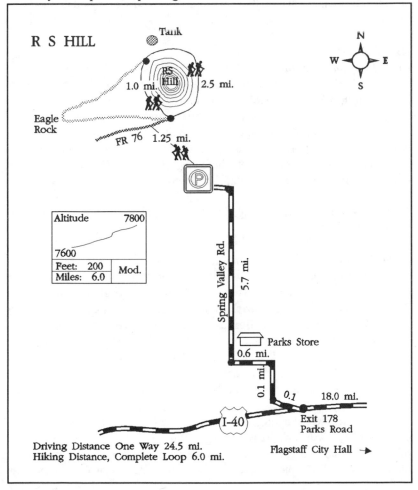

SADDLE MOUNTAIN

General Information
Location Map E2
Kendrick Pk. & White Horse Hills USGS Maps
Coconino Forest Service Map

Driving Distance One Way: 25.3 miles (Time 50 minutes)
Access Road: All cars, Last 4.5 miles good dirt road
Hiking Distance One Way: 2.9 miles (Time 90 minutes)
How Strenuous: Moderate
Features: Views, Volcanic field

NUTSHELL: Located 25 miles north of Flagstaff, this hike takes you up an abandoned fire lookout road that corkscrews around a bare mountain, giving 360 degree views.

DIRECTIONS:
From Flagstaff City Hall Go:
North on Humphreys Street for 0.60 miles. Turn left at the stoplight onto Columbus Avenue and follow it around a big curve to the north. You will see the street signs call this road Columbus at first, then Ft. Valley Road and then Highway 180. Stay on Highway 180 to the 20.8 miles point (MP 236.5), where the unpaved road FR 514 takes off to the right. Turn right onto FR 514 and drive it to the 23.4 mile point where you will see FR 550 to the left. Turn left on FR 550 and take it to the 25.3 mile point and park there.

TRAILHEAD: There are no signs, but the road up the mountain is obvious. Hike up the road.

DESCRIPTION: Saddle Mountain is located in an ancient volcanic field. The views from the top will show you the scope of the field. The mountains that you see in the region are all extinct volcanos. Some of them, such as the San Francisco Peaks and Kendrick Mountain are high enough to catch clouds and get a lot of rain and snow. Because of this moisture they support abundant vegetation. In time soil forms on these favored mountains, covering with topsoil the cinders and lava that formed the mountains. On the lesser mountains, hills and cinder cones such as Saddle Mountain, there are only a few areas where soil has formed and most of the mountainsides are still bare cinders.

A fire swept Saddle Mountain years ago and burned away most of its scant timber growth. The fire was a tragedy but it had its good side. As a result of it you are able to get unobstructed views. The road circles around the mountain as it climbs the mountain, so you are able to see in every direction.

From the 1920s to the 1960s there was a fire lookout tower on the top of Saddle Mountain and the Forest Service built a decent road to the top of the mountain for access to the tower. The tower was replaced with a transmitter after the fire tower was removed. The road is still maintained so that the transmitter can be serviced. You could drive the road if you are a lazy bones, but this is a book of hikes.

At the top you can see all the way to the Grand Canyon when you look north. To the east you can see Sunset Crater and the Painted Desert. To the south you see the north face of the San Francisco Peaks. To the west you can see Kendrick Peak. This is an excellent viewpoint.

The Forest Service would not have located a lookout tower here if the views were restricted. Today fewer fire towers are needed because inter-tower and tower-to-base communication is greatly improved, so there is virtually no new tower construction and many of the old ones have been torn down.

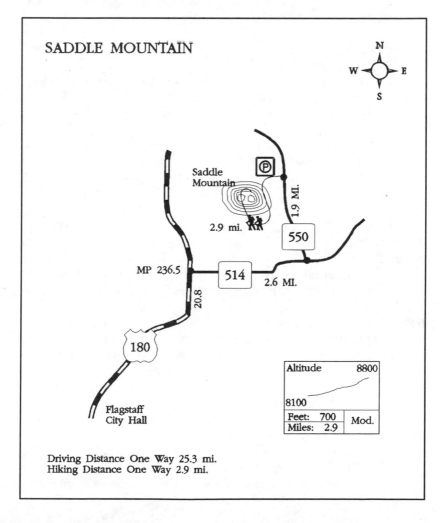

SADDLE MOUNTAIN

N
W — E
S

Saddle Mountain

1.9 MI.

2.9 mi.

550

MP 236.5   514   2.6 MI.

20.8

180

Altitude   8800

8100

| Feet: | 700 | Mod. |
| Miles: | 2.9 | |

Flagstaff
City Hall

Driving Distance One Way 25.3 mi.
Hiking Distance One Way 2.9 mi.

SANDY SEEP

General Information
Location Map E3
Flagstaff E. & Sunset Crater W. USGS Maps
Coconino Forest Service Map

Driving Distance One Way: 7.0 miles (Time 15 minutes)
Access Road: All cars, Last 0.1 mile good dirt road
Hiking Distance, Complete Loop: 2.8 miles (Time 1.5 hours)
How Strenuous: Easy
Features: Strange white hills, Views

NUTSHELL: This trail takes you from a point on Highway 89 in East
Flagstaff to an unusual hill made of crumbling white sandstone.

DIRECTIONS:
From Flagstaff City Hall Go:
　　　　East on Route 66 (Santa Fe). Highway 89 runs concurrently with
Route 66 (Santa Fe) as the highway goes through Flagstaff, so you will see road
signs with both designations. At 6.4 miles (MP 420.7), as you are leaving town
and starting to get out into the country, you will see the stoplight at the junction
of Highway 89 and the Townsend-Winona Road. Look for a dirt road (FR
9129) going into the trees to your left one half mile beyond the stoplight, at 6.9
miles (MP 421.1). Take this dirt road to the parking area at the fence, total 7.0
miles.

TRAILHEAD: There are lath-type trail signs. You will also see a sign
through the fence saying , "Sandy Seep Vehicle Closure. This area closed to
motor vehicles to protect the critical Sandy Seep deer winter range and to offer
non-motorized recreation opportunities." Go through the opening and walk
a few yards to your left, where you will pick up an old road. Follow the road.

DESCRIPTION: The road is easy to walk and makes a good hiking path
because it has been closed to motor vehicles. At about one third of a mile you
will come to the back fence. The road turns right here. Keep following it. The
road will wind through the forest and at about one mile you will come to a green
water trough at the base of a hill. The hill is not visible from the starting point,
and is a peculiar hill as you will see. The road curves around it. At 1.4 miles
you will see that the hill is composed of white sandstone, an anomaly in this
area. Walk to the 1.5 mile point, where you see a trail sign leave the road to
the left for the **Elden Red Hills Trail**. Go right here to the saddle between the
two white hills. The area in front of the saddle is Sandy Seep.
　　　　You will find that the area feels just as if you were walking on a loose

sandy beach. The white sandstone of which the hill is composed has broken down into a deep bed of sand here, a most unusual land feature in the area.

You will see a few scooped out hollows. These are intended to create water holes and will contain water during wet times. At the saddle you will see a plastic pipeline going down the crease between the two hills. Follow this down. There is a good footpath here. There are a couple of places where the line has been pierced to create drinking pools along the way.

The woods in this cleft between the hills are heavy and attractive with a few spruces and firs mixed in with the prevailing pines. You will come out at the bottom of the hill at the place where the green water trough is located. From there you simply retrace your steps back to the parking area.

Sandy Seep is a good place to see deer coming in for water.

This is a short hike, easy to reach. A good leg stretcher.

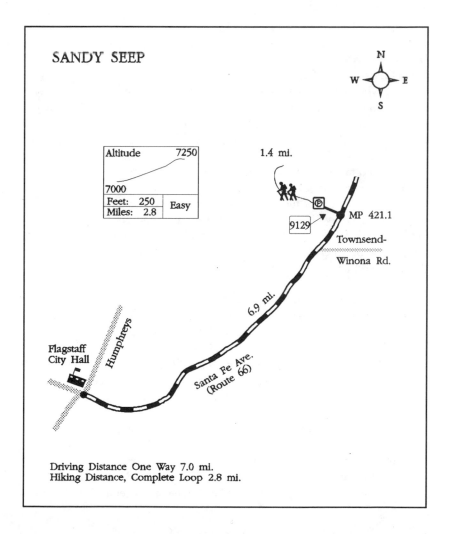

SANDY SEEP

Altitude 7250
7000
Feet: 250   Easy
Miles: 2.8

1.4 mi.

9129

MP 421.1

Townsend-
Winona Rd.

6.9 mi.

Humphreys

Flagstaff
City Hall

Santa Fe Ave.
(Route 66)

Driving Distance One Way 7.0 mi.
Hiking Distance, Complete Loop 2.8 mi.

SCHULTZ CREEK TRAIL

General Information
Location Map E3
Humphreys Peak USGS Map
Coconino Forest Service Map

Driving Distance One Way: 8.5 miles (Time 30 minutes)
Access Road: All cars, Last 4.5 miles medium gravel road
Hiking Distance One Way: 4.25 miles (Time 2.25 hours)
How Strenuous: Moderate
Features: Scenic creekside trail is easy to reach

NUTSHELL: This is a marked and maintained trail that starts high on the Schultz Pass Road north of Flagstaff and follows a creekside downward.

DIRECTIONS:
From Flagstaff City Hall Go:
    North on Humphreys Street for 0.60 miles. Turn left at the stoplight onto Columbus Avenue and follow it around a big curve to the north. You will see the street signs call this road Columbus Avenue at first, then Ft. Valley Road and then Highway 180. Stay on Highway 180 to the 3.1 miles point (MP 218.6), where the Schultz Pass Road, FR 420, goes to the right. Follow this road. At 3.6 miles it curves to the left and you will see the unpaved Elden Lookout Road going straight. Eschew this and stay on the paved road. The paving will end soon and the road will become gravel. As you drive, look down into the canyon to your right and you will see a trail running along the canyon parallel to the road. This is the Schultz Creek Trail. Follow the road to the 8.3 mile point, where you will see a sign for the Sunset Trail. Turn right on this access and park in the parking area, by the sign board, at 8.5 miles.

TRAILHEAD: You will see a wooden sign for the Sunset Trail. The Schultz Creek Trail runs in the opposite direction and is marked with a lath showing it to be a trail closed to motor travel but giving no name.

DESCRIPTION: The Schultz Creek Trail follows the course of the old Schultz Pass Road. That road was so near the bottom of the creek that it often flooded, so in the 1930s the present road was built higher up the shoulder, requiring much blasting and earth removal.
    Down at creekside you will have a delightful ramble. The path is easy to walk, made of soft soil with few rocks. You will see many wildflowers growing in the upper reaches of the trail where the forest is an interesting mixture of pine, aspen, fir and spruce, with willows in the creek.
    The trail has a constant downward slope that is gentle and not taxing

on the knees.

This is a multiple use trail, maintained by a coalition of motorcycle clubs, mountain bikers, hikers and horse riders.

The trail is always just a stone's throw from the road, which is to your right, and you will see and hear cars pass. This and the presence of bikes mar the natural feeling of this otherwise fine trail.

Near the bottom you will encounter several concrete slabs. This is the site of a 1930s CCC camp. The workers who lived there built the present road.

Forest Service maps measure this hike at 3.5 miles, which would be right only if you started at FR 789 at the top and were able to park beyond the fence at the bottom.

The best way to do this hike is as a two car shuttle, parking one at Sunset and the other at the low end on FR 9128Y as shown on the map.

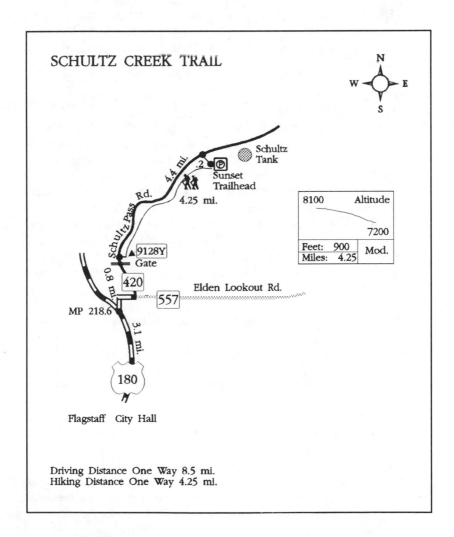

SCHULTZ CREEK TRAIL

Schultz Tank

Sunset Trailhead

4.4 mi.

4.25 mi.

Schultz Pass Rd.

9128Y
Gate

420

8100   Altitude

7200

Feet: 900
Miles: 4.25   Mod.

Elden Lookout Rd.

557

MP 218.6

3.1 mi.

180

Flagstaff   City Hall

Driving Distance One Way 8.5 mi.
Hiking Distance One Way 4.25 mi.

SECRET MOUNTAIN

General Information
Location Map F2
Loy Butte, Sycamore Point USGS Maps
Coconino Forest Service Map

Personal Favorite

Driving Distance One Way: 28.65 miles (Time 60 minutes)
Access Road: All cars, Last 26.0 miles dirt road, rough spots
Hiking Distance One Way: 1.6 miles (Time 1 hour)
How Strenuous: Moderate
Features: Historic cabin, Pristine first growth forest, Views

NUTSHELL: Located 28.65 miles southwest of Flagstaff, this hike takes you from a scenic lookout on the Mogollon Rim across a ridge to Secret Mountain where you will find an historic cabin and another lookout. **A personal favorite.**

DIRECTIONS:
From Flagstaff City Hall Go:
        West a block on Route 66 (Santa Fe), then south, beneath the railroad overpass on Sitgreaves Street. The street name will change to Milton Road as you go farther. At 0.50 miles you will reach a Y intersection. The right fork is named West Old US Highway 66. Take it. You will soon leave town. At 2.6 miles you will reach a road going to the left. This is the Woody Mountain Road, FR 231. Take it. It is paved about a mile and then turns into a cinder road. At 16.6 miles you will intersect FR 538. Turn right onto FR 538 and follow it to the 25.85 mile point, where FR 538B branches off to the right. Take FR 538 to the left. At 27.45 miles you will come to the intersection of 538K. Go left here, staying on 538. At 28.65 miles you will come out onto a ridge. Park by the sign at the end of the road.

TRAILHEAD: The trail is not marked. Head east out on the toe of the ridge.

DESCRIPTION: Before you start the hike, take a while and enjoy the views from the rim where you have parked. They are fine. Then take the trail. It is maintained and is easy to follow even though it is not posted. You will also find blazes on trees along the route.
        At 0.4 miles, you come off a knob onto a saddle where there is a gate. Here the trail splits. The fork to the right is the Loy Canyon Trail and the fit hiker can follow it about five miles, descending 2,000 feet. Instead, turn left and go uphill. You will reach the top of a knob at 0.6 miles then go downhill.
        At 1.0 miles you will enter a fold between three hills. On a small bench of land here you will find an old log corral and a dam. Beyond the corral

you will at all times have a ravine to your right as you hike. Enjoy this forest. It has never been logged. Imagine what northern Arizona would look like if it were all like this. It is breathtaking.

At 1.5 miles you will come to another shelf of land, the site of Secret Cabin and another corral. There is also a spring pond in a rock basin. The cabin is about 20 by 12 feet and only 5 feet high. This remote place was homesteaded by a family in the 1870s but they couldn't make a go of it. It was then taken over by Mormons seeking a hideout from polygamy prosecution. After that it was used by horse thieves, who would steal horses around Sedona, lead them to this hideout via the Loy Canyon Trail and eventually take them to Flagstaff and points north.

From the cabin you go west into the ravine and across it. You will walk up about 0.1 mile to a lookout point on the rim of Secret Mountain where you will have sensational views. There is a satellite trail there going south and east about 0.75 miles to another viewpoint.

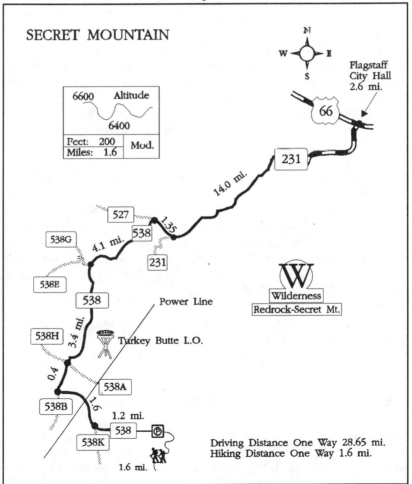

SECRET MOUNTAIN

6600 Altitude
6400
Feet: 200 Mod.
Miles: 1.6

Flagstaff City Hall 2.6 mi.

66

231

14.0 mi.

527
538 1.35
538G
4.1 mi.
231
538E
538
Power Line
538H
3.4 mi.
0.4
Turkey Butte L.O.
538A
538B
1.6
1.2 mi.
538
538K
1.6 mi.

W
Wilderness
Redrock-Secret Mt.

Driving Distance One Way 28.65 mi.
Hiking Distance One Way 1.6 mi.

SINCLAIR WASH TRAIL

General Information
Location Map F3
Flagstaff West USGS Map
Coconino Forest Service Map

Driving Distance One Way: 1.2 miles (Time 5 minutes)
Access Road: All cars, All paved
Hiking Distance One Way: 3.2 miles (Time 1.5 hours)
How Strenuous: Easy
Features: Urban trail

NUTSHELL: This urban trail in south Flagstaff is a pleasant 3.2 mile walk near the southern edge of the Northern Arizona University campus.

DIRECTIONS:
From Flagstaff City Hall Go:
East on Route 66 (Santa Fe) Avenue for one block. Turn right on Beaver Street and go south four blocks to Butler Avenue, where there is a stoplight. Turn left on Butler Avenue and follow it east for four blocks to O'Leary Street. Turn right on O'Leary Street and follow it four blocks south, where you will see the parking area to your left as you come to the bottom of a hill.

TRAILHEAD: This is a marked and maintained trail. You will see a sign at the parking lot.

DESCRIPTION: Flagstaff is developing an ambitious system of urban trails. This trail shares a common trailhead with the **Rio de Flag** trail, which goes east from the parking lot, while the Sinclair Wash Trail goes west, toward the Northern Arizona University campus. The Rio de Flag trail was opened in the fall of 1989. The Sinclair Wash Trail was added to the trail system in the fall of 1990 and extended in 1991.

This trail is not a scenic trail. It goes past Brannen Homes, a low-cost housing project, and then parallels the major road through the south campus of Northern Arizona University. In the university area the trail goes through a forest of jack pines. It is marked by a pole fence.

The trail crosses under I-17, (where its name officially changes to the University Heights to Ft. Tuthill Trail), then goes to Forest Meadows Street, where you cross at a stoplight. From there you turn south in front of WalMart and head toward Ft. Tuthill, the trail's ultimate destination. At the time this was written (December 1991) the trail goes past University Heights subdivision and then on to Mt. Dell subdivision, after which it follows an old road toward Ft. Tuthill. The trail ended in December, 1991 on an old railroad bed 1.2 miles short of Ft. Tuthill. When finished, it will be 2.2 miles long from I-17. A branch of the University Heights Trail will go west to Woody Mt. and The Arboretum sometime in the 90s.

The City of Flagstaff seems to be doing a first class job on this project, grading the trail, importing topsoil in some areas and defining the trail with a pole fence. If the City takes this much care with all its proposed routes the result will be a system of marvelous urban trails.

Sinclair Wash starts its life in the Woody Mountain country. You pass over it when you drive to the Arboretum (a visit to which is recommended) on the Woody Mountain Road, FR 231. The wash used to be a significant land feature that one saw when driving into Flagstaff from the south. The development of shopping centers has now all but obliterated Sinclair Wash in town.

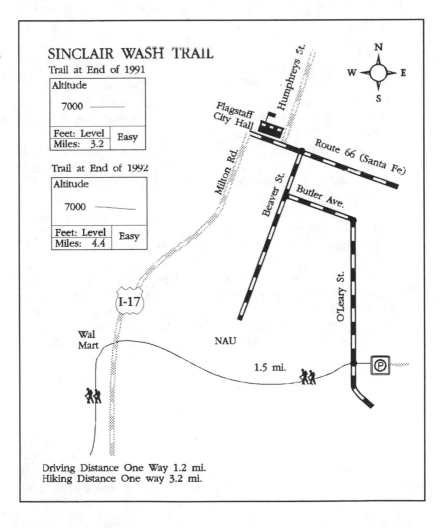

SLATE LAKE LAVA CAVE

General Information
Location Map E2
Kendrick Peak USGS Map
Coconino Forest Service Map

Driving Distance One Way: 28.5 miles (Time 45 minutes)
Access Road: All cars, Last 2.1 miles rough dirt road
Hiking Distance One Way: 0.50 miles (Time 1 hour)
How Strenuous: Moderate
Features: Unusual underground lava tube

NUTSHELL: This underground lava tube located 28.5 miles northwest of Flagstaff is a unique experience.

DIRECTIONS:
From Flagstaff City Hall Go:
North on Humphreys Street for 0.60 miles. Turn left at the stoplight onto Columbus Avenue and follow it around a big curve to the north. You will see the street signs call this road Columbus at first, then Ft. Valley Road and then Highway 180. Stay on Highway 180 to the 26.4 miles point (MP 241.9), where an unpaved road takes off to the left. Turn left onto this road, FR 9002H, and follow it to the 28.3 mile point where you will see an unmarked dirt road taking off to the left. Turn left onto this road and follow it about 0.20 miles, the 28.5 mile point, where it ends at a crudely defined loop. Park there.

TRAILHEAD: Look for a hole in the ground to the left of the parking place. There was one small sign when we visited in September, 1991.

DESCRIPTION: There is nothing about the topography to alert you to the fact that you are in the presence of the Slate Lake Lava Cave. When you turn off of Highway 180, you enter some flat land between the north side of Kendrick Peak and the south side of Slate Mountain. The road goes in a generally southwesterly direction toward Kendrick Peak but never comes very close to Kendrick.

The country is rangeland at first and then you enter into a forest consisting of young pines. You will see three rusted out junked pickup trucks off the road along the way. The road is a primitive one with patches where exposed rocks make you nervous about your undercarriage, but we got through in our trusty Toyota Tercel all right. The majority of the road surface is dirt. Don't try this road when it is wet.

When you think of a cave, you usually picture an opening in a cliff face, but that is not the case here. Even after you turn off onto the driveway to the cave, the last 0.20 miles, there are no cliffs in sight. Instead what you will see is literally a hole in the ground. The exposed rim of lava rock around its opening will attract your attention first. There is no line of stones around it as there is for its nearby cousin, the **Lava River Cave**.

The entrance has not been improved. Rock has fallen from the ceiling of the cave and you have to thread your way around it. A short distance from the entrance you will find a Register in an ammo can. We were surprised to find quite a number of names in it, as this place is little known.

Typical of such caves, it is very cool. Once you walk beyond the point where light from the opening goes, the cave is pitch black. You must have reliable lights. Each member of your party should have a good flashlight with fresh batteries and a backup light as well. The floor is very rough, so good shoes are needed. You also need warm clothes. A hard hat is recommended.

See the entry for Lava River Cave for more information about how these lava tubes are created. Read *Rules of the Trail* at page 224 about caves.

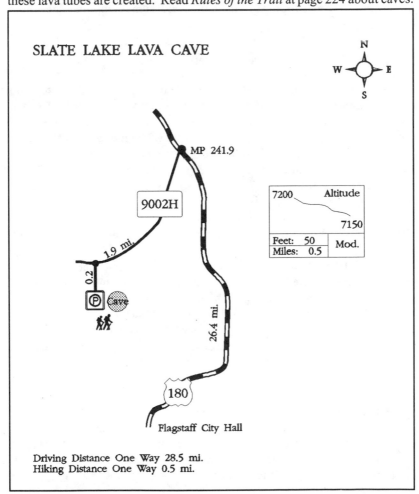

SLATE MOUNTAIN

General Information
Location Map D2
Kendrick Peak USGS Map
Coconino Forest Service Map

Driving Distance One Way: 29.1 miles (Time 40 minutes)
Access Road: All cars, Last 2 miles good gravel road
Hiking Distance One Way: 2.1 miles (Time 80 minutes)
How Strenuous: Moderate
Features: Excellent views, Nature trail with explanatory signs

NUTSHELL: Located 29.1 miles north of Flagstaff, this moderate hike follows an old road to the top of a mountain, with signs identifying local flora posted along the way.

DIRECTIONS:
From Flagstaff City Hall Go:
North on Humphreys Street for 0.60 miles. Turn left at the stoplight onto Columbus Avenue and follow it around a big curve to the north. You will see the street signs call this road Columbus at first, then Ft. Valley Road and then Highway 180. Stay on Highway 180 to the 26.9 miles point (MP 242.4), where an unpaved road, FR 191, takes off to the left. Turn left onto FR 191 and follow it to the 28.8 mile point. There you will see a road to your right that is marked as the trail access. Turn right onto this road and drive it to the 29.1 mile point, where you will park.

TRAILHEAD: You will see a road going up the mountain. Hike up this road.

DESCRIPTION: Like some other hikes in the book, this road was built to provide access to a fire lookout tower that was later dismantled. The road is now closed for vehicular traffic and makes a fine hiking trail.
Slate Mountain is an extinct volcano, like so many other mountains and hills north of Flagstaff. Enough soil has formed on its slopes to support a decent amount of vegetation, but there are also many areas where the black cinders of which the mountain is composed are on the surface.
As you climb the mountain you wind around the two knobs that form a saddle, so that you are able to see in all directions. You will have some great views as you go and will have even better views at the top.
One thing you can count on when you take one of these hikes to a spot where there was (or presently is) a fire lookout tower is that you will have great views, because the Forest Service located the towers in places where you can see forever. At the top of Slate Mountain there are just a few low-growing

pines, so you can see freely to the north, south and west.

Immediately to the north you will see **Red Mountain**. Just a few years ago there was a bit of a stir in Flagstaff when a mining company indicated that it thought that there was gold in the red cinders of Red Mountain and it was going to set up a gold mining operation. Red cinders do contain minuscule quantities of gold, but you have literally to move mountains of it to recover any of the precious metal.

Kendrick Peak is nearby, and an active fire lookout is maintained on its summit during the fire season.

The identified plants we saw (starting from the top of the mountain and working down) were: Oregon Grape, Fremont Holly-berry, Rabbit Brush, Currant, Douglas Fir, Mountain Mahogany, Limber Pine, Ponderosa Pine, Juniper, Alligator Juniper, Prickly Pear, Yucca, Pinyon Pine, Cliff Rose and Dwarf Mistletoe.

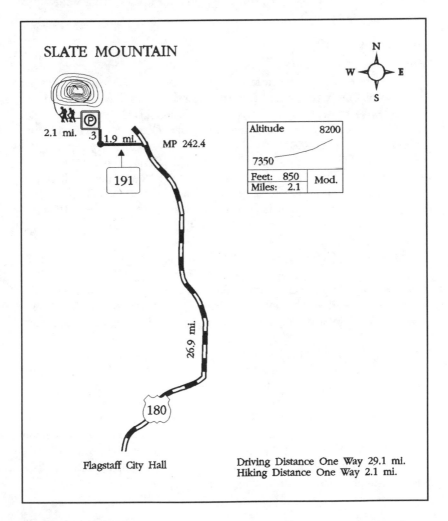

SLATE MOUNTAIN

2.1 mi.   .3   1.9 mi.   MP 242.4

191

Altitude   8200

7350

Feet: 850   Mod.
Miles: 2.1

26.9 mi.

180

Flagstaff City Hall

Driving Distance One Way 29.1 mi.
Hiking Distance One Way 2.1 mi.

SPRING VALLEY CROSS COUNTRY TRAIL

General Information
Location Map E2
Parks USGS Map
Coconino Forest Service Map

Driving Distance One Way: 24.5 miles (Time 40 minutes)
Access Road: All cars, Last 1.2 miles good gravel
Hiking Distance, Complete Loop: 8.0 miles (Time 4.5 hours)
How Strenuous: Moderate
Features: Fine forest, Beautiful meadows with views

NUTSHELL: This hike takes you on a loop route in the Spring Valley area west of Flagstaff.

DIRECTIONS:
From Flagstaff City Hall Go:
        West a block on Route 66 (Santa Fe), then south, beneath the railroad overpass on Sitgreaves Street. The street name changes to Milton Road. At 0.50 miles is a Y intersection. The right fork is West Old US Highway 66. Take it. You will soon leave town, driving on a stretch of Route 66. At the 4.8 mile point you merge onto I-40 West. Look for Exit 178 at the 18.0 mile point, and take it. Turn right at the stop sign and travel to the 18.2 mile point, where there is a second stop sign. Turn left here and go to the 18.8 mile point, where you find the Parks Store. Turn right, on the Spring Valley Road (FR 141). It is paved to the 23.2 mile point, and is a good gravel road beyond. At 24.5 miles is a sign for the Cross Country Ski Trail. Turn left into the parking lot.

TRAILHEAD: You will see a large wooden signboard with a trail map.

DESCRIPTION: The Forest Service has created three cross-country ski trails in this area marked with triangles. The **RS Hill Trail** is the easiest. The **Eagle Rock Trail** is harder and a bit longer. The Spring Valley Trail combines both trails.
        You start on a road, then at 0.40 miles veer off into the woods. You will at times be on roads and at other times will be offroad on this hike. Be sure to follow the triangles. It becomes a game: red for Eagle Rock, blue for RS Hill.
        At 0.75 miles you will reach a beautiful meadow beyond an aspen grove in the middle of which is Shoot-Em-Up-Dick Tank. At the other side you will come onto FR 76 and walk it for a short distance until you reach the place where the **Eagle Rock Trail** forks to the left. Go left. The trail will soon come out of the woods and join FR 104, which you will hike to Eagle Rock Pass. Look for Eagle Rock to your left just before the pass.

From the gate at the pass you will descend steeply on a footpath to join another road, where you will turn to the right. At 3.8 miles you will reach a sign showing where the RS Hill Trail comes in from the right. You do not turn here, but go straight.

From this point onward you hike close to the base of RS Hill and begin to circle it clockwise. Just beyond the trail junction is RS Tank. Then the trail leaves the road and goes uphill on a shoulder through an area very rich in obsidian and you will find hunks of it everywhere. This obsidian was prized by the ancient Indians for its quality and was a valued trade item for arrowheads, knives and axes. It can hold an edge the thinness of one micron.

As you round the hill you will see Spring Valley to your left. From here you walk a road back to the junction of FR 76 and FR 104, then retrace your steps to the parking lot. You never do climb Eagle Rock or RS Hill.

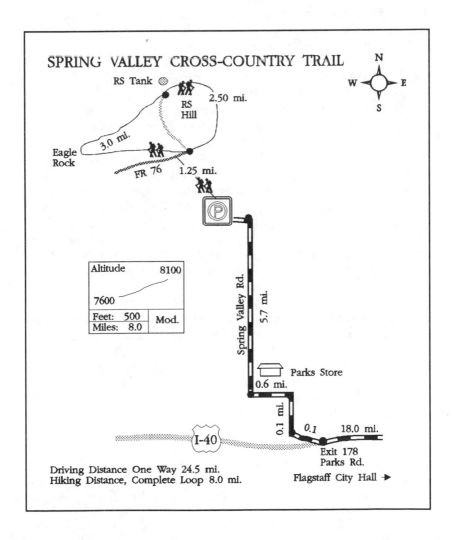

SPRING VALLEY CROSS-COUNTRY TRAIL

RS Tank

RS Hill

2.50 mi.

N
W — E
S

Eagle Rock

3.0 mi.

FR 76   1.25 mi.

Altitude   8100

7600

| Feet: 500 | Mod. |
| Miles: 8.0 | |

Spring Valley Rd.

5.7 mi.

Parks Store
0.6 mi.

0.1 mi.

0.1   18.0 mi.

I-40

Exit 178
Parks Rd.

Driving Distance One Way 24.5 mi.
Hiking Distance, Complete Loop 8.0 mi.

Flagstaff City Hall →

STERLING PASS

General Information
Location Map F3
Munds Park and Wilson Mt. USGS Maps
Coconino Forest Service Map

Drive Distance One Way: 23.5 miles (Time 30 minutes)
Access Road: All cars, All paved
Hiking Distance One Way: 2.4 miles (Time 90 minutes)
How Strenuous: Hard
Features: Views, Great rock formations

NUTSHELL: Located 23.5 miles south of Flagstaff, just above the north end of Manzanita Campground, and just below Slide Rock Lodge, this steep hike goes through a heavy forest to a mountain pass.

DIRECTIONS:
From Flagstaff City Hall Go:
West one block on Route 66 (Santa Fe) then left (south) on Sitgreaves Street under the railroad overpass. As you continue south you will see the street signs calling the street Milton Road, as Sitgreaves Street blends into Milton. At 1.7 miles you reach the intersection of Forest Meadows, where there is a traffic light. Here you turn right. You will see a sign for Highway 89A, which is the road you want. At the next corner turn left on Beulah and follow it out of town. Beulah will connect onto Highway 89A which is the road to Oak Creek Canyon and Sedona. At 13.8 miles (MP 390) you will reach the canyon rim and begin the winding descent. After you have completed the switchbacks and are on the canyon floor, drive to the 23.5 mile point (MP 380.5), the north end of the Manzanita Campground. There is no parking lot and the shoulders are narrow. Do what you can to park close.

TRAILHEAD: There is a rusty sign marking this maintained trail on the west side of the road. The sign reads, "Sterling Pass #46."

DESCRIPTION: This trail rises steeply, climbing all the way. For the first portion you parallel a little side canyon, which may contain running water during spring thaw. When it does, it creates a charming waterfall near the highway. The trail wanders back and forth over the streambed four times.
For those who think of the Oak Creek area as sunswept expanses of redrock dotted with cactus, this trail will be an eye-opener. It goes through a cool pine forest. While you will cross over a bit of red slickrock at the beginning and will see some gorgeous red cliffs and buttes as you progress, the soil underfoot is a rich brown loam. In addition to the familiar ponderosa pine you

will see some Douglas fir and a few spruces. After about the first quarter mile the area feels primeval and is truly delightful.

Because the forest is so heavy, you can't see much until you have gone about 1.25 miles. Until then you get glimpses of giant white cliffs ahead of you (west) and red cliffs on your right and left. Then you rise above the trees and get great views across Oak Creek Canyon and nearby. The cliffs here are a treat to the eye, highly sculptured, with many interesting lines and angles. You will find a viewpoint at a bend of the trail where you can look over into an adjacent canyon to your left for views of soaring white cliffs.

The crest is at 1.65 miles, at a saddle. There is a heavy stand of trees here with oaks on the east and oaks and maples on the west. Because of the trees the views are not as good at the top as they are below. This is a true mountain pass, there being a decided gap in the cliffs here.

The trail continues down the other side, another 0.75 miles, to intersect the Vultee Arch Trail almost at its terminus.

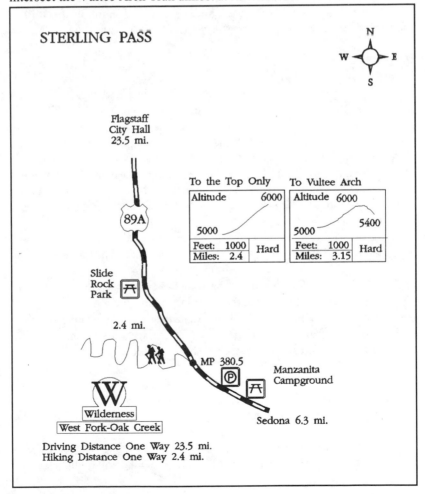

STERLING PASS

N
W — E
S

Flagstaff
City Hall
23.5 mi.

89A

To the Top Only

Altitude	6000
5000	
Feet: 1000	Hard
Miles: 2.4	

To Vultee Arch

Altitude 6000	
5000	5400
Feet: 1000	Hard
Miles: 3.15	

Slide
Rock
Park

2.4 mi.

MP 380.5

Manzanita
Campground

Wilderness
West Fork-Oak Creek

Sedona 6.3 mi.

Driving Distance One Way 23.5 mi.
Hiking Distance One Way 2.4 mi.

STRAWBERRY CRATER

General Information
Location Map E3
Strawberry Crater USGS Map
Coconino Forest Service Map

Driving Distance, One Way: 26 miles (Time 40 minutes)
Access Road: All cars, Last 9 miles gravel, in medium condition
Hiking Distance, One Way: 1 mile (Time 45 minutes)
How Strenuous: Moderate
Features: Volcano, Indian Ruins, Painted Desert Views

NUTSHELL: This hike takes you to an extinct volcano located 26 miles north of Flagstaff. There is a marked and maintained trail. You follow this trail up the face of the crater to enjoy great views and Indian ruins.

DIRECTIONS:
From Flagstaff City Hall, Go:
 East, then North on Route 66 (Santa Fe), which becomes Highway 89 in East Flagstaff. Follow Highway 89 North out of town. At 20.4 miles (MP 434.4), nearly at the bottom of a long downgrade, take FR 546 (unpaved) to the right. Follow FR 546 easterly to the 24.0 mile point, where it meets FR 779. Here FR 546 veers to the right. Go straight on FR 779, which will take you directly to Strawberry Crater. You will soon see the crater ahead. At 26.0 miles, you will reach a huge powerline. Just beyond it, roads go left, right and straight ahead. Go straight. You will hit a cable fence in 0.10 miles, and see a Wilderness sign. Park there.

TRAILHEAD: Look for trail signs at the parking place. The trail goes north.

DESCRIPTION: There seems to be something special about Strawberry Crater. It will loom into view at the 24 mile point as you are driving toward it and from that point forward, it will dominate the landscape. There are many extinct volcanoes in the area, and most of them are smooth and rounded. Strawberry Crater is an exception, It is sharp, jagged and broken at the rim of the side that is facing you.

 Psychic friends tell us that this was a sacred place to the ancients and that they get spiritual feelings here akin to those experienced in the Sedona Vortex centers. Our own feeling was that there is something special about this place.

 Strawberry Crater was recently incorporated into a federally pro-tected Wilderness Area. There is an official trail to take you to the top of the crater.

The trail goes around to the north face of the crater and makes the ascent from there. This is an addition made since the first printing of this book.

When you get to the top you will want to enjoy the views and then do some exploring. Around the inside rim at the top, you will find vestigial Indian ruins. These are nothing much, just lines of cinder clods, none of them piled very high. It is hard to imagine that they ever made a habitation. Perhaps they were just a shelter or windbreak.

You can see that the crater has a open end to the east through which lava flowed and created a lava field. It is very interesting to go down to the lava field and do some exploring there. You will find some additional ruins in that area.

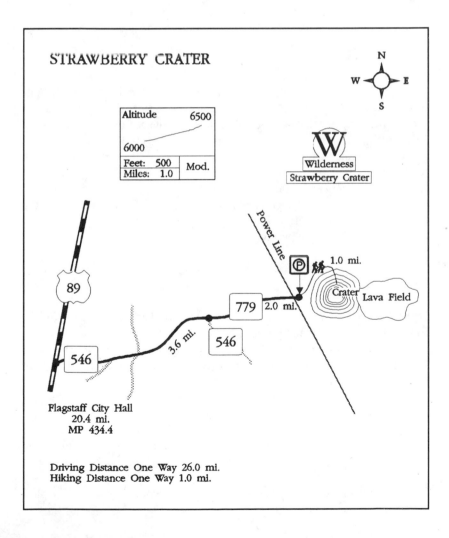

STRAWBERRY CRATER

Altitude 6500
6000
Feet: 500 | Mod.
Miles: 1.0

Wilderness
Strawberry Crater

Power Line

1.0 mi.
Crater Lava Field

89

779 | 2.0 mi.

3.6 mi.
546

546

Flagstaff City Hall
20.4 mi.
MP 434.4

Driving Distance One Way 26.0 mi.
Hiking Distance One Way 1.0 mi.

SUNSET TRAIL

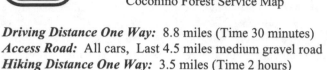

General Information
Location Map E3
Flagstaff East and Flagstaff West USGS Maps
Coconino Forest Service Map

Personal
Favorite

Driving Distance One Way: 8.8 miles (Time 30 minutes)
Access Road: All cars, Last 4.5 miles medium gravel road
Hiking Distance One Way: 3.5 miles (Time 2 hours)
How Strenuous: Hard
Features: Views, Variety of scenery, Excellent forests

NUTSHELL: This is a marked and maintained trail that starts high on the Schultz Pass Road north of Flagstaff and winds to the top of Mt. Elden.

DIRECTIONS:
From Flagstaff City Hall Go:
North on Humphreys Street for 0.60 miles. Turn left at the stoplight onto Columbus Avenue and follow it around a big curve to the north. You will see the street signs call this road Columbus Avenue at first, then Ft. Valley Road and then Highway 180. Stay on Highway 180 to the 3.1 miles point (MP 218.6), where the Schultz Pass Road, FR 420, goes to the right. Follow this road. At 3.6 miles where it curves to the left you will see the unpaved Elden Lookout Road going straight. Eschew this and stay on the paved road. The paving will end soon and the road will become gravel. Follow the road to the 8.7 mile point, where you will see a sign for the Sunset Trail. Turn right on this road and park in the parking area, by the sign board.

TRAILHEAD: You will see a wooden sign for the Sunset Trail at the parking area.

DESCRIPTION: The Sunset Trail goes to Sunset Park, near the top of Mt. Elden. It is a part of the Dry Lake Hills\Mt. Elden Trail system.
You will skirt Schultz Tank which is a sizeable body of water and then go up a side canyon. Since the canyon faces north and gets lots of water, it is lush and supports a nice forest.
At the 1.0 mile point you will cross a road and break into a clearing from where you will have good views of the San Francisco Peaks. At the 1.33 mile point you will go over the crest of a hill and from that point onward will be unable to see the Peaks. You will follow a shoulder of the Dry Lake Hills to the 1.6 mile point, where there is a trail junction. Take the fork to the left, downhill. The trail signs here are confusing. They omit the Sunset Trail.
The trail will take you down a fold between the Dry Lake Hills and

Mt. Elden and then you will climb steeply up to the top of a ridge on Mt. Elden. On the way up you will pass through a very attractive alpine forest. Once you reach the ridge line you will drop over the other side slightly and walk along the shoulder to a trail junction at 3.5 miles just above the Elden Lookout Road. We have the trail stop here, though officially it goes on for another mile to the lookout tower.

At the top of the ridge you enter an area that was badly burned in the catastrophic Radio Fire in 1978. The area is starting to heal and you will see stands of young aspen thriving in favored spots. The only good thing about the fire was that with the tree cover burned away you can now get superior views to the east.

This is a hard hike if you go back the way you came. We love it as a two-car shuttle, parking one at the Sunset Trailhead and the other at a point 5.75 miles up the Elden Lookout Road. We prefer to start at the top. Done this way, the hike is **A Personal Favorite**.

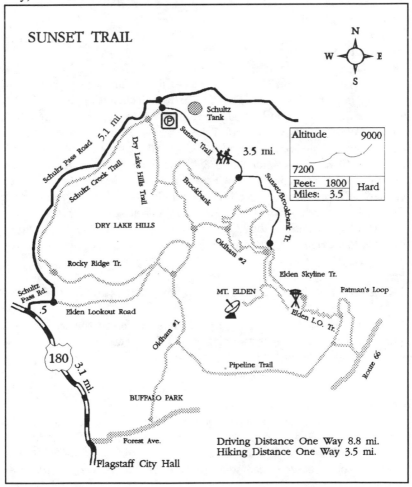

SYCAMORE RIM TRAIL

General Information
Location Map F2
Bill Williams Mountain and Garland Prairie USGS Maps
Kaibab (Williams District) Forest Service Map

Driving Distance One Way: 28.2 miles (Time 45 minutes)
Access Road: All cars, Last 12.4 miles good gravel road
Hiking Distance, Complete Loop: 12.0 miles (Time 7.0 hours)
How Strenuous: Hard due to extremely rocky trail
Features: Cabin ruins, Canyon springs, Views, Waterfall

NUTSHELL: This hike displays the features of the terrain southwest of Flagstaff including spring-fed canyon pools, a waterfall, a huge canyon, a prairie and a hill climb.

DIRECTIONS:
From Flagstaff City Hall Go:
West a block on Route 66 (Santa Fe), then south, beneath the railroad overpass on Sitgreaves Street. The street name will change to Milton Road as you go farther. At 0.50 miles you will reach a Y intersection. The right fork is named West Old US Highway 66. Take it. You will soon leave town, driving on a stretch of fabled Highway 66. At the 4.8 mile point you will merge onto Interstate-40 West. Look for Exit 178, "Parks Road" and take it. It is at the 18.0 mile point. From the exit turn left and go toward Garland Prairie. When you cross the railroad tracks you will be on FR 141, the main road through Garland Prairie. Stay on it to the 27.6 miles point, where it meets FR 131. Turn left on FR 131 and take it to the 28.0 mile point, where you will see an unmarked jeep trail to the right. Take this and follow it to the 28.2 mile point where you will find a parking area. Park.

TRAILHEAD: There is a large sign with map at the parking area.

DESCRIPTION: The Sycamore Rim Trail is a loop and you can start it at various places, but we suggest starting at Dow Spring and working clockwise from there. Dow Spring has been captured and flows through a metal pipe into a small canyon. It is a dependable perennial spring. Take note of the little canyon into which it flows. You will see this develop into one of the biggest canyons in Arizona, Sycamore, as you hike.
You will hike right along the rim of this canyon. At 1.0 miles the canyon has deepened. Look into it and you will see a series of beautiful rock pools in which grow an unusual lily pad. These pools are fed by LO Spring. From this point as you head south the canyon begins to get *significant*,

deepening as you go.

At 3.65 miles you will reach the Sycamore Vista point on the trail, where Sycamore Canyon is at full size. From here you hike a fairly bare area with canyon views often in sight until you come downhill and into another canyon. You will follow this canyon for some time, first to Sycamore Falls at 5.65 miles and then to Pomeroy Tanks at 6.9 miles. These tanks are delightful copies of the LO Springs pools. As you begin to leave this canyon you will cross the **Overland Road**, which is well marked, at 7.35 miles. You will cross FR 13 at 7.65 miles where there is a sign showing you are headed for KA Hill. The ascent of KA Hill is fairly gradual and you will reach its top at 9.52 miles, where there is an altitude marker. Heavy trees at the top provide few views. Then you descend the hill, crossing FR 13 at 10.7 miles.

At 11.07 miles you will cross the Overland Road again. At 11.25 miles you will come to the signed site of a sawmill operated from 1910-1920. From here it is 0.75 miles back to Dow Spring.

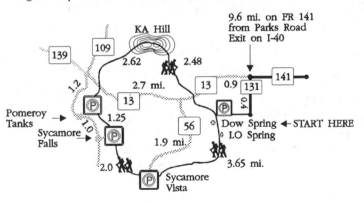

SYCAMORE RIM TRAIL

Altitude	7287
6600	KA Hill
Feet: 687	Hard
Miles: 12.0	

Flagstaff City Hall via I-40 to Parks Rd. Exit 178 is 18.0 mi.

9.6 mi. on FR 141 from Parks Road Exit on I-40

KA Hill

139 109

2.62 2.48

2.7 mi. 13 0.9 131 141

13 0.4

Pomeroy Tanks 1.25

Sycamore Falls 1.0 56 Dow Spring ◄ START HERE

1.9 mi. LO Spring

2.0 3.65 mi.

Sycamore Vista

Driving Distance One Way 28.2 mi.
Hiking Distance, Complete Loop 12.0 mi.

TEN-X NATURE TRAIL

Driving Distance One Way: 71.1 miles (Time 90 minutes)
Access Road: All cars
Hiking Distance One Way: 0.75 miles (Time 30 minutes)
How Strenuous: Easy
Features: Nature trail near the Grand Canyon

NUTSHELL: This nature trail adjacent to the Ten-X Campground gives a good introduction to plants of the Grand Canyon rim.

DIRECTIONS:
From Flagstaff City Hall, Go:
North on Humphreys Street 0.60 miles to a stoplight. Go left on Columbus Avenue and follow the curve north. Street signs will show the street first as Ft. Valley Road, then Highway 180. This is a major road to the Grand Canyon. At 50.4 miles (MP 265.8), you will intersect Highway 64, coming out of Williams, at a place called Valle. Go right at this junction and follow the highway to the 70.2 miles point (MP 233.5). Turn right on the road into the Ten-X Campground. Keep following the main road through the campground. You will first encounter Loop A, then Loop B, then Loop C. Your destination is Loop C. Park between camping spaces 57 and 58 on Loop C at the 71.1 mile point.

TRAILHEAD: You will find the trailhead clearly marked and posted at the parking place. The trail heads off to the northeast from there.

DESCRIPTION: There is a maze-type opening in the fence where you enter the trail. At this place a dispenser has been set up, from which you can take free leaflets describing the plants that you will see along the trail. Numbered posts are set out along the way and these posts identify the plants by number. Without the guide, the trail is not very interesting.
The trail winds through the woods behind the campground in a counterclockwise arc, but it does not form a loop that returns to the starting point. You will end the trail at a place on the road that is about 0.8 miles from where you park; so you will probably prefer to walk back to the trailhead on the trail rather than the road.
Twenty-nine plants are identified for the hiker, and some comments about their uses by the native Indians is made. One of our favorites is the

cliffrose, plant number two on the trail, which is found abundantly all through the northern Arizona high country. When we took this hike in late September, the cliffroses were blooming. They emitted a sweet aroma. At this time of year they also bear their seeds, which have an interesting curved plumy tail.

You will also find considerable sagebrush, a plant that is not common around Flagstaff, but is found in huge numbers from the Grand Canyon northward, literally covering many of the high deserts of the Colorado Plateau.

The woods through which the trail goes are nice and open, furnishing a good example of the pine woodlands of the area.

The campground is open only during the summer season, roughly from Easter to Halloween, so don't count on using it during the off season. There is a charge for staying at the campground, but there is none for merely using the trail.

This hike would not be worth the long travel distance for its own sake, but if you are in the area, it is like a lovely living botany lesson.

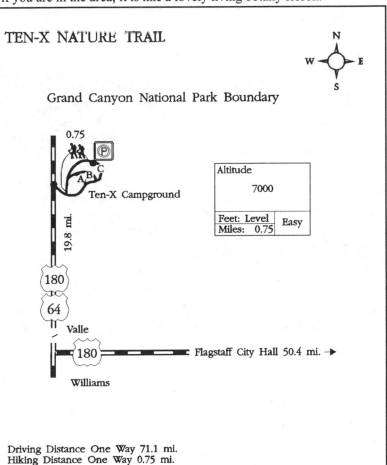

THOMAS POINT

Drive Distance One Way: 19.5 miles (Time 30 minutes)
Access Road: All cars, All paved
Hiking Distance One Way: 1.00 miles (Time 60 minutes)
How Strenuous: Hard
Features: Views

NUTSHELL: This is a marked and posted trail that climbs the east wall of upper Oak Creek Canyon from a point directly across Highway 89A from the West Fork trailhead, 19.5 miles south of Flagstaff.

DIRECTIONS:
From Flagstaff City Hall Go:
　　　West one block on Route 66 (Santa Fe) then left (south) on Sitgreaves Street under the railroad overpass. As you continue south you will see the street signs calling the street Milton Road, as Sitgreaves Street blends into Milton. At 1.7 miles you reach the intersection of Forest Meadows, where there is a traffic light. Here you turn right. You will see a sign for Highway 89A, which is the road you want. At the next corner turn left on Beulah and follow it out of town. Beulah will connect onto Highway 89A which is the road to Oak Creek Canyon and Sedona. At 13.8 miles (MP 390) you will reach the canyon rim and begin the winding descent. After you have completed the switchbacks and are on the canyon floor, drive to the 19.5 mile point (MP 384.5). Park on the shoulder of the road.

TRAILHEAD: On the east side of the road twenty yards up Highway 89A from the entrance to the West Fork Trail you will see a rusty sign reading, "Thomas Point #142." The sign is set back about 20 feet from the highway.

DESCRIPTION: There is no official parking area for this hike. Cars park all along the shoulder of the highway here, mostly for the **West Fork** hike. You can go up the highway about a quarter of a mile and park off the road at the Call of the Canyon. It will be downhill to your left.

　　　You will probably see a multitude of people hiking the West Fork trail. Instead of following the horde, walk up the road on the right side of the highway about 20 yards north of the West Fork entrance. There you will see a groove worn into the soil bank and the trailhead sign at the head of the groove. Look sharp, for the sign is hard to see.

After hiking a short distance you will climb high enough to get good views of the sheer white cliffs of the West Fork and East Pocket areas across the canyon. You can see the path of Oak Creek and glimpse bits of the highway.

At about the half mile point you wind around onto an unshaded south face of the canyon wall. Here the pines disappear and you are in the chaparral and juniper life zone. These plants are small compared to the pines so you have better views along this part of the trail. Near the top you come back into the pine and spruce forest again.

At the top pine needles may cover the trail and make it indistinct, so look for cairns. They mark an extension of the trail to a viewpoint to the north, where Thomas Point is located. Thomas Point is well named, for it is a peninsula or tongue pointing west. Standing at the tip of the point you will have good views.

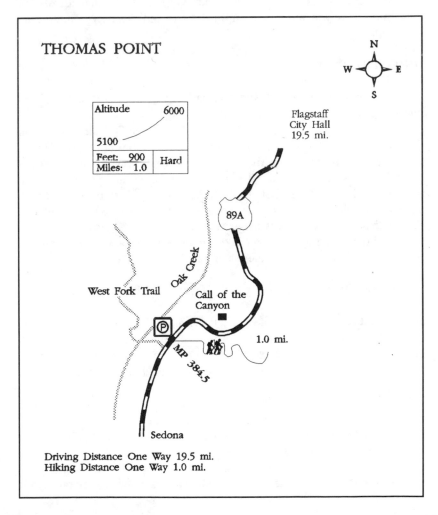

THOMAS POINT

Altitude 6000
5100
Feet: 900
Miles: 1.0   Hard

Flagstaff
City Hall
19.5 mi.

89A

Oak Creek

West Fork Trail

Call of the
Canyon

MP 384.5

1.0 mi.

Sedona

Driving Distance One Way 19.5 mi.
Hiking Distance One Way 1.0 mi.

TUNNEL (WATERSHED) ROAD

General Information
Location Map E3
Humphreys Peak USGS Map
Coconino Forest Service Map

Driving Distance One Way: 9.4 miles (Time 30 minutes)
Access Road: All cars, Last 5.8 miles good gravel road
Hiking Distance One Way: 8.5 miles (Time 4.5 hours)
How Strenuous: Hard if you go full distance
Features: High mountains, Interesting tunnel, Excellent views

NUTSHELL: Located about 10 miles north of Flagstaff, this moderate but long hike takes you through beautiful forests and meadows on the San Francisco Peaks.

DIRECTIONS:
From Flagstaff City Hall Go:
    North on Humphreys Street for 0.60 miles. Turn left at the stoplight onto Columbus Avenue and follow it around a big curve to the north. You will see the street signs call this road Columbus at first, then Ft. Valley Road and then Highway 180. Stay on Highway 180 to the 3.1 miles point (MP 218.6), where a paved road goes to the right. This is the Schultz Pass Road. Turn right and follow this road. At 3.6 miles it curves to the left and you will see an unpaved road going straight. Stay on the paved road. The paving will end soon and the road will become gravel surfaced. Follow it to the 8.8 mile point, just beyond the **Weatherford Trail** sign, where FR 146 intersects the road from the left. Turn left onto FR 146 and take it to the 9.4 mile point where you will reach a locked gate. Park off the road by the gate.

TRAILHEAD: Not a marked trail. You walk FR 146 beyond the gate.

DESCRIPTION: The City of Flagstaff maintains FR 146 for access to the city's watershed, particularly the works at Jack Smith Spring, so it is kept in good condition. The only vehicle travel allowed is for city maintenance trucks. Mountain bikers love this road and you are very likely to find them there on weekends.
    The grade of this road is gentle, running along the 8000 foot contour of the mountain for the first couple of miles, then beginning a climb that terminates at about 9400 feet at Jack Smith Spring. When you take the **Inner Basin Trail** hike, you will visit Jack Smith Spring.
    You will reach the tunnel for which the hike is named at 2.0 miles. At that point the road builders hit a lava dike and decided to bore through it

rather than blast it away. The tunnel is about 25 feet long, 10 feet wide and 12 feet high, and adds a pleasing note of interest. Hikers who want a mild but rewarding hike might want to turn back at the tunnel.

There are many fine views from the road, especially off to the hiker's right, into the Sunset Crater area. The volcanic nature of the terrain is plainly displayed and you will see a myriad of cinder cones, which are the remains of small volcanos.

You can hike all the way to Jack Smith Spring, 8.5 miles, if you are hardy and quick, but this requires a 17 mile round-trip hike at high altitudes, which may be too arduous for many readers. So, pick your spot anywhere and turn back at your own comfort point.

The road doesn't really end at Jack Smith Spring. It continues climbing 5.50 miles farther to the north face of the San Francisco Peaks. The **Bear Jaw** and **Abineau Canyon** trails terminate on the far reaches of FR 146. The leg of FR 146 from Jack Smith to the end is the Abineau Pipeline Trail.

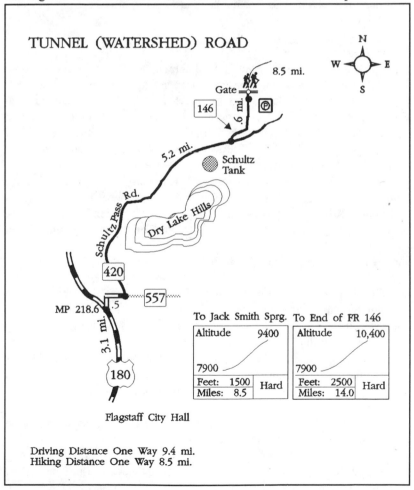

TUNNEL (WATERSHED) ROAD

8.5 mi.

Gate

146   .6 mi.

5.2 mi.

Schultz Tank

Schultz Pass Rd.

Dry Lake Hills

420

557

MP 218.6   .5

3.1 mi.

180

Flagstaff City Hall

To Jack Smith Sprg.		To End of FR 146	
Altitude	9400	Altitude	10,400
7900		7900	
Feet: 1500	Hard	Feet: 2500	Hard
Miles: 8.5		Miles: 14.0	

Driving Distance One Way 9.4 mi.
Hiking Distance One Way 8.5 mi.

TURKEY HILL

General Information
Location Map F3
Flagstaff East USGS Map
Coconino Forest Map

Driving Distance One Way: 8.75 miles (Time 20 minutes)
Access Road: All cars, Last 0.35 miles rough cinder road
Hiking Distance One Way: 1.0 miles (Time 30 minutes)
How Strenuous: Moderate
Features: Easy access, Views

NUTSHELL: This cinder hill is located so as to give good views. You hike an abandoned road that goes around and around the hill to the top.

DIRECTIONS:
From Flagstaff City Hall Go:
        East on Route 66 (Santa Fe). Highway 89 runs concurrently with Route 66 (Santa Fe) as the highway goes through Flagstaff, so you will see road signs with both designations. At 3.8 miles (MP 418.2/200) you will come to a fork, where East Old U.S. 66 goes to the right. Turn right onto Old 66 and follow it to the 7.7 mile point, where there is a cinder road to the left. Turn left onto this road, FR 791, and follow it to the 8.4 mile point, where the road splits. Both the left and right forks are marked FR 510B. Take the left fork. Up to this point the road has been good, but it now turns pretty bad. There are ruts and exposed rocks. If you are not in a high clearance vehicle you should park at the 510B fork. If you can make it, go up to the 8.75 miles point, where there is an unmarked road going to the left. Park on the right shoulder here.

TRAILHEAD: There are no trail signs. You hike the road.

DESCRIPTION: At one time there was a cinder pit operation on this hill. The road you will hike was built to service the pit. You will see a number of side roads as you walk along. At every junction take the right fork, always staying on the outside of the hill and moving upward.
        You will soon come to the pit. There you will see that a road keeps going up the hill to the right of the pit. Stay on it and continue the ascent. From this point onwards it is easy to tell what the roads are doing and to follow the correct one.
        The road literally winds completely around the hill as it climbs. The vegetation is mostly low so that you can see clearly. The views are good. You are looking at some interesting landscapes: volcano fields, and beyond them, the Painted Desert. You can get a good look at Anderson Mesa. To the west

you can see parts of Flagstaff.

The top of Turkey Hill is a true top. There are no false tops or benches. You suddenly pop up onto a small flat summit from which you can see out on all sides.

On the maps, you will see references to Turkey Hills. The other hill is quite a bit smaller and is to the north of the one you can hike.

You will also see the Turkey Hills Pueblo on maps. This is located north of the hiking hill also. The best way to reach it is by going east on the Townsend-Winona Road for 3.0 miles from the stoplight, then turning right on an unmarked gravel road and following it for 0.15 miles. There you will see a burglar-proof chain-link fence surrounding about a half acre of ground to your right. Unfortunately there isn't much to see: just low lines of rubble marking pit houses and you can't get inside for a closer look.

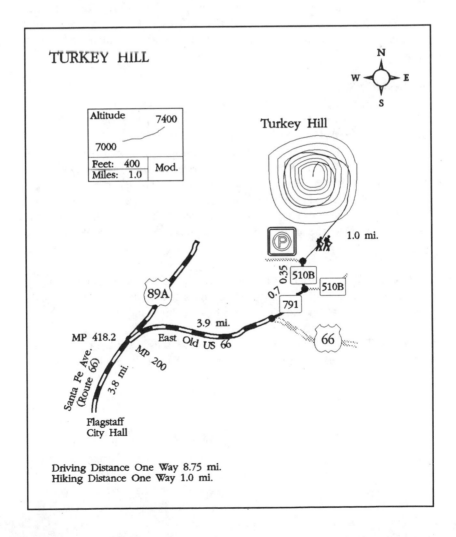

TURKEY TANKS–COSNINO CAVES

General Information
Location Map E3
Sunset Crater East, Winona USGS Maps
Coconino Forest Service Map

Driving Distance One Way: 18.6 miles (Time 30 minutes)
Access Road: All cars, Last 0.2 miles good gravel road
Hiking Distance One Way: 0.6 miles (Time 45 minutes)
How Strenuous: Easy
Features: Caves with ruins, Historic site

NUTSHELL: Located 18.6 miles east of Flagstaff, this easy hike takes you along a portion of San Francisco Wash to visit Turkey Tanks (natural ponds) and Cosnino Caves (Indian ruins). You will also see a fragment of the historic Beale Road.

DIRECTIONS:
From Flagstaff City Hall Go:
      East, curving to north on Route 66 (Santa Fe). As you leave the city limits you will see that Route 66 is also Highway 89. Follow Highway 89 north. At 6.5 miles (MP 420.5) you will reach the last stoplight in town at the junction of the Townsend-Winona Road. Turn right here onto the Townsend-Winona Road and follow it to the 14.7 miles point (MP 428.7) where it intersects Leupp Road. Turn left on the Leupp Road and go to the 18.4 mile point (MP 432.4). Turn right on an unmarked black gravel road and follow it to the 18.6 mile point, where you will be on the rim of the canyon at San Francisco Wash. Park there.

TRAILHEAD: Look for trees marked with white diamonds about two inches square. Park by the diamond-marked tree closest to the canyon, where you will see an old road cut down to the canyon floor. This is the trailhead.

DESCRIPTION: The white diamonds on the trees mark the route of the historic Beale Road. This road was built in 1858 by the U.S. Government to open up the recently acquired Arizona territory. It ran from Ft. Wingate, New Mexico to the Colorado River. The road came through this point to take advantage of the water at Turkey Tanks. You can follow the diamonds east about a mile to Cochrane Hill if you want a little side trip.
      The place where you parked was once a ranch operated by the Sykes brothers who had a post office in the ranch house in 1881. Now you can see nothing of the dwelling except a small pile of stones, the remains of the chimney. Godfrey Sykes's autobiography called *A Westerly Trend*, University

of Arizona Press, 1984, describes this place, and is a good read.

Walk down onto the canyon floor (it's easy) and then turn right, following the canyon bottom. At 0.4 miles you will come to a bend where the highway is just above your head. On the bank under the road you will encounter the Cosnino Caves. These are lava blowouts. The entire bank is honeycombed with them. Early archaeologists made significant finds of museum quality artifacts in these caves but by the 1950s they were disregarded to the extent that the present road was run right over the top of them, doing extensive damage. Early travellers using the Beale Road were fascinated with these caves and all the diarists commented on them.

From the caves go back to where you started and walk upstream. In 0.2 miles you will come to a stone dam located at the last tank in the chain of Turkey Tanks. It is easy to skirt the dam on the right and come up on top of it. The dam seems almost comically deep. It was built in the 1930s. Before that, travellers relied on the natural ponding effects of the native rock basins.

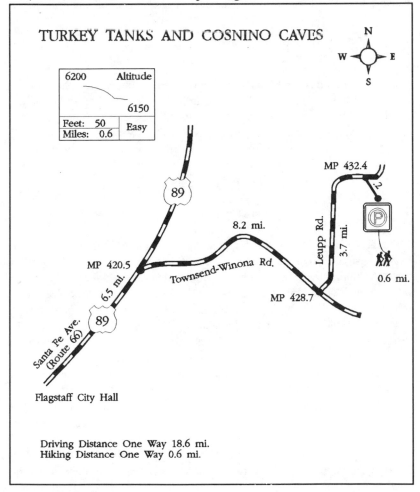

TURKEY TANKS AND COSNINO CAVES

6200   Altitude
                     6150
Feet: 50   Easy
Miles: 0.6

MP 432.4

8.2 mi.

Leupp Rd.   3.7 mi.

MP 420.5

Townsend-Winona Rd.

6.5 mi.

0.6 mi.

MP 428.7

Santa Fe Ave. (Route 66)   89

Flagstaff City Hall

Driving Distance One Way 18.6 mi.
Hiking Distance One Way 0.6 mi.

VEIT SPRINGS

General Information
Location Map E3
Humphreys Peak USGS Map
Coconino Forest Service Map

Driving Distance One Way: 11.8 miles (Time 30 minutes)
Access Road: All cars, All paved
Hiking Distance One Way: 1.0 miles (Time 30 minutes)
How Strenuous: Easy
Features: Alpine forests, Historical cabin, Rock art

NUTSHELL: The hike takes you to an old cabin site on the San Francisco Peaks about 12 miles north of Flagstaff, a lush, peaceful Shangri-La. **A personal favorite.**

DIRECTIONS:
From Flagstaff City Hall Go:
        North on Humphreys Street for 0.60 miles. Turn left at the stoplight onto Columbus Avenue and follow it around a big curve to the north. You will see the street signs call this road Columbus at first, then Ft. Valley Road and then Highway 180. Stay on Highway 180 to the 7.3 miles point (MP 223), where the road to the Snow Bowl branches off to the right. It is well posted. Follow the Snow Bowl road to the 11.8 miles point. There you will see a driveway to your right. Pull in and park there.

TRAILHEAD: Posted at the gate.

DESCRIPTION: At the parking area there is a gate. Go through it. There is a large sign beyond the gate telling about the area. The trail goes uphill to the right behind the sign, not straight ahead along the old jeep road.
        Although a lot of snow falls on the San Francisco Peaks, very little of the water produced by the snow appears there in streams, ponds or springs. Due to their volcanic origin, the Peaks are quite porous and most of the water produced by snowmelt sinks in and goes into underground rivers. Here and there you will find a spring. This hike takes you to such a site.
        The early settlers in the area looked carefully for springs and used most of them as sites for sheep or cattle operations. One such settler was Ludwig Veit, who homesteaded the area reached by this hike in 1892. If you look carefully you will see his name chiseled into the face of a lava boulder near the cabin.
        As you walk the trail you will come to a fork at about 0.20 miles. Take the right fork here. You will follow an old wagon road to the cabin from this

point. At 0.90 miles the road winds around to a plaque set into a boulder. The plaque honors Lamar Haines, a Flagstaff outdoorsman.

There is a basalt ridge running through the area of the cabin site, furnishing a sort of wall or backdrop to it. One of the richest stands of aspens on the Peaks is located to the east of the plaque.

Follow the road from the plaque up to the old log cabin. The cabin is very low. Veit was either a midget or the cabin was used only for sleeping. Adults can't stand up in it. Above the cabin is a pond formed by the water from the main spring. Between the pond and the cliff is a small stone shed. In the face of the cliff a frame has been built around the opening to the spring.

If you walk the face of the cliff to your left (as you face the spring), you will go around a bend and find a secondary spring. There are pictographs on the rock walls surrounding it.

This is a terrific place to enjoy changing aspen leaves in October.

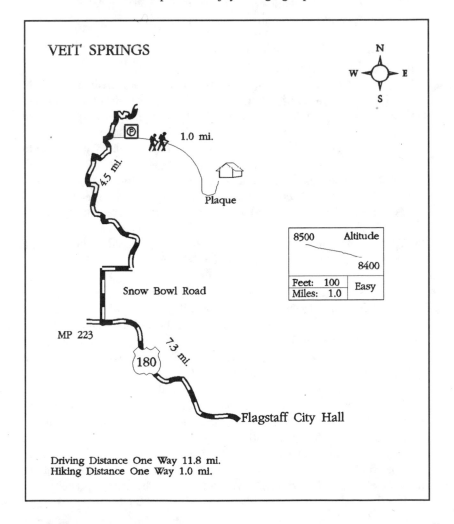

VEIT SPRINGS

N
W — E
S

1.0 mi.

4.5 mi.

Plaque

8500	Altitude
	8400
Feet: 100	Easy
Miles: 1.0	

Snow Bowl Road

MP 223

180 7.3 mi.

Flagstaff City Hall

Driving Distance One Way 11.8 mi.
Hiking Distance One Way 1.0 mi.

WALKER LAKE

General Information
Location Map E3
Humphreys Peak and Wing Mt. USGS Maps
Coconino Forest Service Map

Driving Distance One Way: 21.8 miles (Time 40 minutes)
Access Road: All cars, Last 2.2 miles good dirt road
Hiking Distance One Way: 0.50 miles (Time 1 hour)
How Strenuous: Easy
Features: Views

NUTSHELL: This is a gentle hike to the crater of an ancient volcano located about 20 miles north of Flagstaff.

DIRECTIONS:
From Flagstaff City Hall Go:
North on Humphreys Street for 0.60 miles. Turn left at the stoplight onto Columbus Avenue and follow it around a big curve to the north. You will see the street signs call this road Columbus at first, then Ft. Valley Road and then Highway 180. Stay on Highway 180 to the 19.6 miles point (MP 235.1), where the unpaved Hart Prairie Road branches off to the right. Turn right onto this road, which is also identified as FR 151 and follow it to the 21.2 miles point. There FR 418 branches to the left. Take FR 418 and follow it just 0.10 miles, to the 21.3 mile point. There you will reach an unmarked dirt road to the left. Turn left onto it and follow it to the 21.8 miles point, where you will park.

TRAILHEAD: There are no trail signs. You will see a blocked road going up to the top of a cinder cone. You hike this road.

DESCRIPTION: The road is easy walking, being broad with a gradual grade. It is about 0.20 miles to the top, where you will find yourself on the rim of a volcanic crater. This was a small volcano so the crater is fairly shallow. Walker Lake is in the center of the crater. The lake, never very big, often dries up completely in the summer. The best time of year to find water in it is in the spring, after the snow melts, which is usually in April or May.
The road forks at the top and you can walk either left or right on it. The left fork goes directly down to the lake, while the right fork sweeps around through a stand of aspen and firs and is more scenic. It is only about 0.10 miles to the lake by the left fork, slightly longer than that by the right fork.
The north rim of the crater is rather bare due to a forest fire. It is higher than the south rim. It is worth a climb up the north rim if you are willing to make the effort, for fine views from the top unimpeded by trees. There is no

trail to the north rim but it is easy to bushwhack your way there. You can't get lost.

We saw lots of elk sign at Walker Lake.

This is a pretty and little known spot. The San Francisco Peaks area is dotted with over one hundred volcanic craters. This is one of the most accessible and scenic of them, with the bonus of a lake. Most craters are pretty bare, but this one has lots of vegetation and a nice friendly feel.

There is a strange pit lined with steel panels near the pond. Our guess is that it is an old well site. Take a look and see what you think.

The cinders in most Northern Arizona volcanic craters are black or red, but at Walker Lake they are brown. This gives the place more of an earthy, less moonlike appearance and is less stark, more inviting.

This is an easy, charming hike, well worth the modest effort it requires.

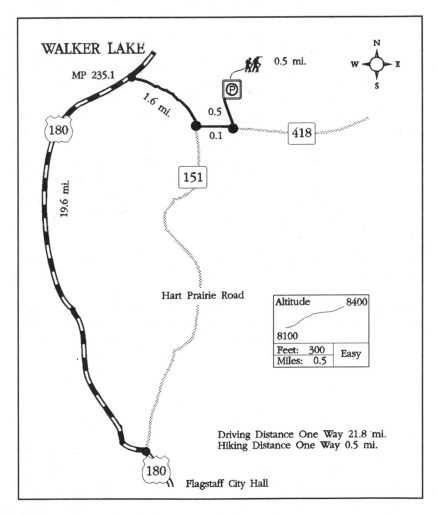

WALNUT CANYON ISLAND TRAIL

Driving Distance One Way: 17.3 miles (Time 25 minutes)
Access Road: All cars, All paved
Hiking Distance, Complete Loop: 0.8 miles (Time 45 minutes)
How Strenuous: Moderate
Features: Indian ruins, Scenic canyon

NUTSHELL: This is the main trail in the Walnut Canyon National Monument, located just a few miles east of Flagstaff. The trail is paved, has steps and handrails and takes you to a series of cave dwellings in a scenic canyon.

DIRECTIONS:
From Flagstaff City Hall Go:
East on Route 66 (Santa Fe). Highway 89 runs concurrently with Route 66 (Santa Fe) as the highway goes through Flagstaff, so you will see road signs with both designations. At 4.1 miles you will see a sign to your right marking the entrance to Interstate-40. Take this entrance and at 4.3 miles turn left on the Interstate-40 East Exit. This will place you on I-40 headed east. At 14.3 miles (MP 204) you will reach the Walnut Canyon turn, Exit 204. Turn right on this and follow the paved road to Walnut Canyon. You will reach the parking lot at the Visitor Center at 17.3 miles.

TRAILHEAD: You must go through the Visitor Center to gain access to this trail.

DESCRIPTION: You have to pay a fee for this hike and the trail has posted hours. It is quite popular and definitely not a wilderness experience. The trail has been tamed so that everyone can use and enjoy it. Walnut Canyon and **Wupatki** are the finest Indian ruins in the Flagstaff area and are definitely worth seeing. So lay your craving for wilderness aside and enjoy this domesticated hike.

To get to the trail, you have to go right through the Visitor Center, from which you emerge onto the rim of Walnut Canyon. The canyon itself at this point is a very impressive sight.

Then you begin the hike by going down a ridge that connects to the "Island" after which the trail is named. It isn't really an island, but is a peninsula. The trail winds around the peninsula.

All along the trail there is an undercut ledge that in many spots was cut deep enough to form caves suitable for cliff dwellings. The walls of many dwellings remain or have been restored and you will walk right along beside them. In addition to these ruins that have been made accessible by the trail you can see others on the opposite walls of the canyon. Some of them are up so high that you wonder how any human being could have used them. They either had a series of tremendous ladders or they could climb like mountain goats. Where did the children play? How did they get water? It is a marvel and a mystery.

The trail is paved for its entire length and signs are posted here and there giving information about the natural history and the history of the Sinagua Indians, who built the dwellings.

One of the main features of the trail is a series of innumerable stairsteps. We counted 232 of them on the main drop from the Visitor Center to the sign that says it is one hundred and eighty-five feet to the top.

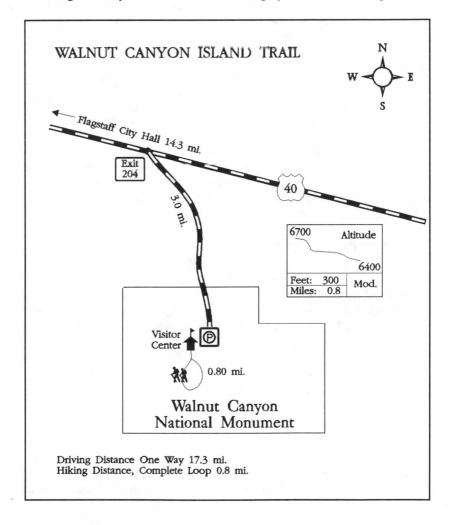

WALNUT CANYON RIM TRAIL

General Information
Location Map F3
Flagstaff East USGS Map
Coconino Forest Service Map

Driving Distance One Way: 17.3 miles (Time 25 minutes)
Access Road: All cars, All paved
Hiking Distance One Way: 0.42 miles (Time 30 minutes)
How Strenuous: Easy
Features: Indian ruins, Scenic canyon

NUTSHELL: This is a paved easy trail in the Walnut Canyon National Monument, located just a few miles east of Flagstaff. It features Indian ruins, a nature trail and fine views of an impressive canyon.

DIRECTIONS:
From Flagstaff City Hall Go:
     East on Route 66 (Santa Fe). Highway 89 runs concurrent with Route 66 (Santa Fe) as the highway goes through Flagstaff, so you will see road signs with both designations. At 4.1 miles you will see a sign to your right marking the entrance to Interstate-40. Take this entrance and at 4.3 miles turn left on the Interstate-40 East Exit. This will place you on I-40 headed east. At 14.3 miles (MP 204) you will reach the Walnut Canyon turn, Exit 204. Turn right on this and follow the paved road to Walnut Canyon. You will reach the parking lot at the Visitor Center at 17.3 miles.

TRAILHEAD: The trail starts to the left of the door entering the Visitor Center. It is posted.

DESCRIPTION: You are supposed to go into the Visitor Center and pay a fee for this hike. The Visitor Center is also the trailhead for the **Walnut Canyon Island Trail**. It is possible to do both hikes on the same trip. There are posted hours for the use of the trail.

     To get to the trail, walk right up to the door of the Visitor Center and you will see the sign for the Rim Trail pointing to your left.

     The trail is paved all the way and signs are posted here and there along the trail giving information about the plants and animals of the area and the history of the Sinagua Indians, who inhabited the area centuries ago. The signs are nicely done. There are several good viewpoints along the trail. Walnut Canyon is deep and twisting and cliff dwellings are scattered along its walls. Some of them seem to be located in absolutely inaccessible places and you are forced to wonder how humans could have used them. Some of these dwellings are hard to see because they are all built out of the native rock and blend right in with the canyon walls.

The walls of Walnut Canyon are a buff colored limestone hundreds of feet thick. In many places in the Flagstaff area the primary layers of rock have been covered by lava from all the volcanos that erupted in the region. When the earth's crust has been cracked as it has here, you can see the limestone underneath the lava. Fossils are found in the limestone, causing scientists to believe that the whole region was once covered by a sea. This is mightily impressive when you consider that the plateau around Flagstaff is seven thousand feet high. This suggests that there must have been huge upthrusts to force the ocean floor above sea level. Geologists love this place.

The trail ends at a viewpoint on the rim. On the way back, you will veer off to the right to see the ruins of a pit house and pueblo. The trail then exits into the parking lot. Although it is touristy, Walnut Canyon is a special place and this is a worthwhile hike.

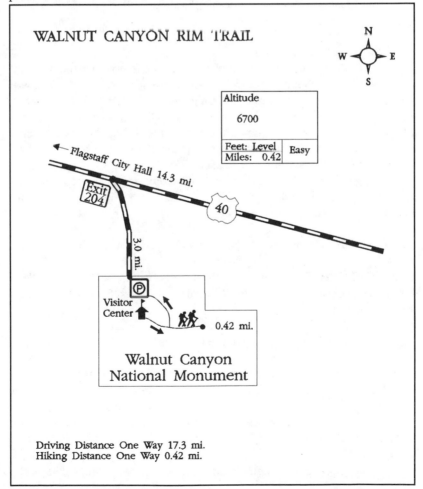

WALNUT CANYON RIM TRAIL

Altitude	
6700	
Feet: Level	Easy
Miles: 0.42	

← Flagstaff City Hall 14.3 mi.

Exit 204

40

3.0 mi.

Visitor Center

0.42 mi.

Walnut Canyon
National Monument

Driving Distance One Way 17.3 mi.
Hiking Distance One Way 0.42 mi.

WEATHERFORD CANYON

General Information
Location Map E3
Humphreys Peak USGS Map
Coconino Forest Service Map

Driving Distance One Way: 8.8 miles (Time 30 minutes)
Access Road: All cars, Last 4.0 miles medium gravel road
Hiking Distance One Way: 2.0 miles (Time 1 hour)
How Strenuous: Moderate
Features: High mountains, Aspen groves

NUTSHELL: This trail climbs through a scenic canyon on the southeast face of the San Francisco Peaks 8.8 miles north of Flagstaff.

DIRECTIONS:
From Flagstaff City Hall Go:
North on Humphreys Street for 0.60 miles. Turn left at the stoplight onto Columbus Avenue and follow it around a big curve to the north. You will see the street signs call this road Columbus Avenue at first, then Ft. Valley Road and then Highway 180. Stay on Highway 180 to the 3.1 miles point (MP 218.6), where a paved road goes to the right. This is the Schultz Pass Road, FR 420. Turn right and follow this road. At 3.6 miles you reach a curve to the left where you will see an unpaved road going straight. Stay on the paved road. The paving will end soon and the road will become gravel surfaced. Follow it to the 8.8 mile point, where you will see a sign for the **Weatherford Trail**. Park anywhere near the Weatherford trailhead.

TRAILHEAD: Begin this hike by taking The Weatherford Trail.

DESCRIPTION: The trailhead for this hike is also the "official" trailhead for the Weatherford Trail, the one indicated by the Forest Service on its maps and guides.
You will hike the closed road for about 0.75 miles, just beyond the place where a newly built logging road takes off to the left. This area was being logged in November, 1990, when we hiked this trail.
You will see another blocked road to your right going down into a canyon at this point. Follow it. The canyon is Weatherford Canyon. Soon after you begin this new trail you will see a road forking to the right. Do not take it. Go straight up the canyon, walking along the canyon floor. The trail seems to have been an old wagon road, as it is broader than a footpath. Higher up it does turn into a footpath.
You will pass through incredible aspen groves on this hike. In the

lower reaches of the canyon there is a stand of aspen saplings thick as hair that all seem to be the same height and age. This would indicate that they are the product of some bumper year, and from their age we would speculate that they are the result of the huge snowfall that hit the Flagstaff area in December, 1967. This dumped over twenty feet of snow on the San Francisco Peaks and caused a correspondingly wet spring in 1968.

Just before the trail ends you come to Aspen Spring, where a pond has been created. In a wet year this pond holds water year around and is a great place to spot animals.

The trail ends where it comes out into an open park and intersects the Weatherford Trail. The Weatherford Canyon Trail can be used as an interesting approach to or return from the Weatherford Trail.

The Forest Service may close the portion of the canyon beyond Meadow Tank to protect the habitat.

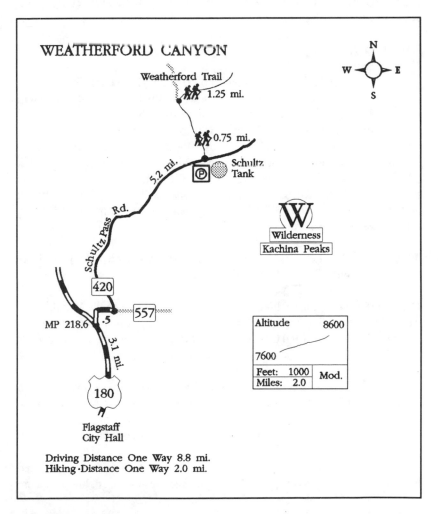

WEATHERFORD TRAIL

General Information
Location Map E3
Humphreys Peak USGS Map
Coconino Forest Service Map

Driving Distance One Way: 13.7 miles (Time 40 minutes)
Access Road: All cars, Last 4 miles medium cinder road
Hiking Distance One Way: 6.0 miles (Time 3.5 hours)
How Strenuous: Hard
Features: Highest mountains, Alpine forests, Excellent views

NUTSHELL: This is the easiest trail to the top of the San Francisco Peaks, some 14 miles north of Flagstaff.

DIRECTIONS:
From Flagstaff City Hall Go:
North on Humphreys Street for 0.60 miles. Turn left at the stoplight onto Columbus Avenue and follow it around a big curve to the north. You will see the street signs call this road Columbus at first, then Ft. Valley Road and then Highway 180. Stay on Highway 180 to the 7.3 miles point (MP 223), where the road to the Snow Bowl branches to the right. It is well posted. Follow the Snow Bowl road to 9.7 mile point, where you will see an unpaved road, FR 522, branching to the right. Turn right onto FR 522, which is also known as the Friedlein Prairie Road. At 9.8 miles this road will fork. Take the left fork and drive FR 522 to the 13.7 mile point. There you will find that a parking lot has been created. Park in the lot.

TRAILHEAD: You will see a blocked road just beyond the parking lot. Hike the blocked road. There are no trail signs.

DESCRIPTION: These directions are for our easy way to the Weatherford Trail. For the "official" Forest Service way, which is longer and harder, see the entry for **Weatherford Canyon**. The parking area is at a place where roads converge. There are indications that the Forest Service may block the road, forcing use of the official trailhead.

In about 0.30 miles up the Weatherford Road, take note of a trail coming onto the road from your left. This is the end of the **Kachina Trail**, a favorite hike. You will then see a big meadow. There are several roads branching off the main road. Follow the road that takes you across the meadow and moves uphill.

At the end of the meadow the road will enter a shaded area framed by aspens and marked by a sign. When you see these you will know you are on the Weatherford Trail. Up the trail from here about 0.20 miles you will find a trail logbook in an ammunition can chained to a log. Please make an entry for yourself in this book. It is fun to read it and see who has been here.

The Weatherford Trail was built as a private toll road, construction lasting from 1920 to 1928. The Great Depression wiped out any chances of success the road might have had. It fell into disuse and was incorporated into the Kachina Wilderness Area in 1984. The trail tops out at 6.0 miles at Doyle Saddle (formerly called Fremont Saddle) where you get great views out over the countryside and down into the **Inner Basin** of the Peaks.

The trail goes another 3.0 miles to meet the **Humphreys Trail,** from where you can go another half mile to the highest point in Arizona. If you are hardy enough to handle the distance you can set up a long hike for a two-car shuttle, parking one car at the Snow Bowl and the other at the Weatherford Trail parking area, a total of 12.0 hard miles. If the Forest Service shuts off the Friedlein Prairie Road, the trip would be 13.5 miles.

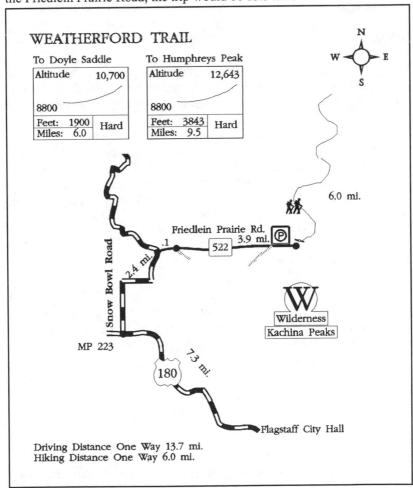

WEATHERFORD TRAIL

N
W—E
S

To Doyle Saddle	To Humphreys Peak
Altitude 10,700	Altitude 12,643
8800	8800
Feet: 1900 Hard	Feet: 3843 Hard
Miles: 6.0	Miles: 9.5

6.0 mi.

Friedlein Prairie Rd. 3.9 mi.

.1 522

2.4 mi.

Snow Bowl Road

Wilderness
Kachina Peaks

MP 223

7.3 mi.

180

Flagstaff City Hall

Driving Distance One Way 13.7 mi.
Hiking Distance One Way 6.0 mi.

WEST FORK

General Information
Location Map F3
Dutton Hill and Munds Park USGS Maps
Coconino Forest Service Map

Drive Distance One Way: 19.5 miles (Time 30 minutes)
Access Road: All cars, All paved
Hiking Distance One Way: 3.00 miles (Time 90 minutes)
How Strenuous: Moderate
Features: Gorgeous canyon with perennial stream

NUTSHELL: One of the best and most popular hikes in Arizona. The trailhead is located 19.5 miles south of Flagstaff. **A personal favorite**.

DIRECTIONS:
From Flagstaff City Hall Go:
West one block on Route 66 (Santa Fe) then left (south) on Sitgreaves Street under the railroad overpass. As you continue south you will see the street signs calling the street Milton Road, as Sitgreaves Street blends into Milton. At 1.7 miles you reach the intersection of Forest Meadows, where there is a traffic light. Here you turn right. You will see a sign for Highway 89A, which is the road you want. At the next corner turn left on Beulah and follow it out of town. Beulah will connect onto Highway 89A which is the road to Oak Creek Canyon and Sedona. At 13.8 miles (MP 390) you will reach the canyon rim and begin the winding descent. After you have completed the switchbacks and are on the canyon floor, drive to the 19.5 mile point (MP 384.5) and park on the side of the road.

TRAILHEAD: On the west (right) side of the road you will see a rusty sign reading, "West Fork #108." The trail goes downhill.

DESCRIPTION: There is no official parking area for this hike. Cars park all along the shoulders of the highway nearby. You can stop about a quarter of a mile above the trailhead and park off the road at the Call of the Canyon. It will be downhill, branching to the west of the highway.
You will probably see a multitude of people hiking the West Fork trail. There are several homes in the trailhead area and some of their driveways look like the entry to the trail. You will see a wooden barricade marking the West Fork Trail.
You walk down an old driveway that was built to provide access to Mayhews Lodge. You cross the creek, which usually has a makeshift bridge. This is a good time to check conditions. If the water is high, then you should

take this hike another day unless you are prepared to do a lot of wading, because the West Fork Trail meanders across the stream a dozen times.

Once across the creek, you come upon the site of Mayhews Lodge, built as a hunting and fishing lodge in the early 1900s. The path forks at the entrance to the lodge. The left fork goes around the ruins, while the right fork goes through them, under an ivy covered arch. The Forest Service bought the lodge in the 1960s only to have it burn shortly afterward.

As you enter the West Fork canyon you become immediately aware of the charm of this place, with the gentle stream flowing through a lush habitat framed by tremendous and colorful canyon walls.

The path follows along and over the streambed. At the crossings you will usually find stepping stones that allow you to get across without getting wet. Some people prefer to wear old tennies and wade. You will find distance markers every half mile. The canyon is 12 miles long, but we recommend doing 3.0 miles for a day hike.

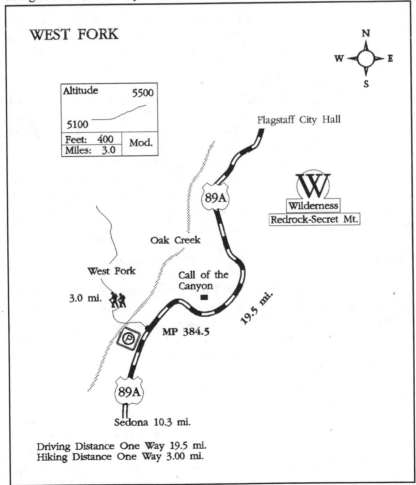

WEST FORK

N
W — E
S

Altitude   5500

5100

Feet:	400	Mod.
Miles:	3.0	

Flagstaff City Hall

89A

W
Wilderness
Redrock-Secret Mt.

Oak Creek

West Fork

Call of the Canyon
■

3.0 mi.

19.5 mi.

MP 384.5

89A

Sedona 10.3 mi.

Driving Distance One Way 19.5 mi.
Hiking Distance One Way 3.00 mi.

WEST FORK HEAD

General Information
Location Map F2
Bellemont, Dutton Hill, Flagstaff West, Wilson Mt. USGS Maps
Coconino Forest Service Map

Driving Distance One Way: 21.1 miles (Time 40 minutes)
Access Road: All cars, Last 18.5 miles good gravel road
Hiking Distance One Way: 1.0 miles (Time 40 minutes)
How Strenuous: Moderate
Features: Extremely attractive canyon, Lush vegetation

NUTSHELL: The West Fork of Oak Creek is a beautiful canyon. The hike at its end, where it meets Highway 89A is famous. This hike is at the beginning of the canyon, about 21 miles south of Flagstaff and has its own considerable attractions.

DIRECTIONS:
From Flagstaff City Hall Go:
　　　　West a block on Route 66 (Santa Fe), then south, beneath the railroad overpass on Sitgreaves Street. The street name will change to Milton Road as you go farther. At 0.50 miles you will reach a Y intersection. The right fork is named West Old US Highway 66. Take it. You will soon leave town. At 2.6 miles you will reach a road going to the left. This is the Woody Mountain Road, FR 231. Take it. It is paved about a mile and then turns into a cinder road. Stay on FR 231 to the 21.1 mile point, where the road crosses a bridge. You will see a sign there showing that the bridge spans West Fork. Go just past the bridge and park on the right shoulder.

TRAILHEAD: Not marked. Go down into the canyon.

DESCRIPTION: As you travel FR 231 you will encounter many side roads. The best way to describe the route is to tell you to stay on FR 231 at all times. It winds around in a bewildering way, but generally is the main travelled road everywhere. It is well posted.
　　　　When you get to the bridge over West Fork you will see a canyon to your left which is fairly shallow right at the bridge. This is the head or beginning of West Fork. Those who are familiar with West Fork at its mouth where it meets Oak Creek will be surprised by the beginning of West Fork as it seems to be just another ravine in country full of ravines. Go down into the canyon and start walking along the right hand bank of the streambed. You will pick up the trail there.
　　　　At 0.2 miles you will come to a large sign that reads, *"WEST FORK*

OF OAK CREEK. You are entering a very remote canyon. There is no developed hiking trail. Only experienced hiking parties should attempt this hike. DO NOT go alone." Don't worry. The first mile of the canyon does have a trail and is plenty safe. We feel that the warning on the sign is appropriate only if you go beyond the first mile. After the first mile the trail disappears and you have to hop the rocks in the streambed as the canyon narrows and the shoulders and shelves disappear.

This is the place to stop. The canyon is about 12.0 miles long, and beyond the safe first mile can be dangerous. The heart of the canyon is also a sensitive environmental area in which overuse by humans is discouraged.

This canyon is incredibly lush. You will think you are in a Pacific Northwest rain forest. Many of the trees are festooned with Spanish moss. The variety of plantlife is mind boggling (including poison ivy). This is a special place and a magic hike.

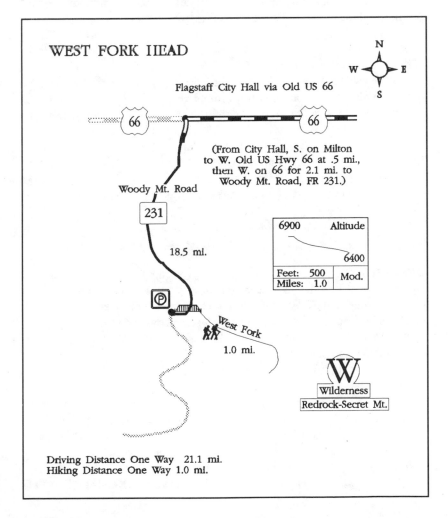

WEST FORK HEAD

Flagstaff City Hall via Old US 66

66   66

(From City Hall, S. on Milton to W. Old US Hwy 66 at .5 mi., then W. on 66 for 2.1 mi. to Woody Mt. Road, FR 231.)

Woody Mt. Road

231

18.5 mi.

6900	Altitude
	6400
Feet: 500	Mod.
Miles: 1.0	

West Fork

1.0 mi.

W

Wilderness
Redrock-Secret Mt.

Driving Distance One Way 21.1 mi.
Hiking Distance One Way 1.0 mi.

WHITE HORSE HILLS

General Information
Location Map E3
White Horse Hills USGS Map
Coconino Forest Service Map

Driving Distance One Way: 23.4 miles (Time 45 minutes)
Access Road: All cars, Last 3.75 miles good gravel road
Hiking Distance One Way: 1.0 miles (Time 45 minutes)
How Strenuous: Moderate
Features: Views

NUTSHELL: This moderately strenuous hike to the top of a mountain located just north of the San Francisco Peaks gives great views.

DIRECTIONS:
From Flagstaff City Hall Go:
    North on Humphreys Street for 0.60 miles. Turn left at the stoplight onto Columbus Avenue and follow it around a big curve to the north. You will see the street signs call this road Columbus at first, then Ft. Valley Road and then Highway 180. Stay on Highway 180 to the 19.6 miles point (MP 235.1), where you will turn right onto the unpaved Hart Prairie Road, FR 151. Follow FR 151 to the 21.2 miles point, where you turn left onto FR 418. Follow FR 418 to the 23.4 mile point, where you will see a trail sign and the entrance to the trailhead on your left. Pull into the driveway and park.

TRAILHEAD: You will see a large sign announcing the trail at the parking place.

DESCRIPTION: The trail climbs gradually except for one steep haul from about 0.50 to 0.70 miles. It is easy to follow. You are on one mountain that has four knobs on it. The trail forks to go to the two highest knobs. You will reach the first fork at 0.50 miles. Take the left hand trail there. It climbs steeply up the mountain. At 1.0 miles you will reach another fork at a saddle. From that point you can go left for about 0.10 miles to the top of an 8700 foot high knob or right for 0.20 miles to the top of a 9000 foot high knob. We recommend that you do both.

    From either of the tops you are treated to magnificent views of the north face of the San Francisco Peaks. Mt. Humphreys, the tallest peak, really shows its stuff from here and is very imposing. The lower top of White Horse is a splendid viewpoint from which to see the changing aspen leaves in October. Visibility is not so good on the higher top because of trees growing there.

    From the lower top you can enjoy views into Kendrick Park, the

Hochderffer Hills, **Saddle Mountain,** the Grand Canyon Plateau, the Vermil-ion Cliffs and countless cinder cones. To the east you can see sweeping views of Deadman Flat and **O'Leary Peak.**

While the soil, terrain and vegetation look typical of the area when you start climbing on this trail, you become aware about half way up the trail that the earth beneath your feet has turned red. It looks like the soil in southern Utah or Sedona. In fact, the Flagstaff area would be part of an unbroken belt of red stone had it not been for the volcanic eruptions that covered it with lava and cinders and wrenched things askew with violent uplifts.

Near the top of White Horse you will find a white limestone layer. This limestone seems identical to the stone found around Walnut Canyon and Lake Mary many miles to the south.

On the 9000 foot knob is a cairn of stones containing a metal box with a register for hikers to sign.

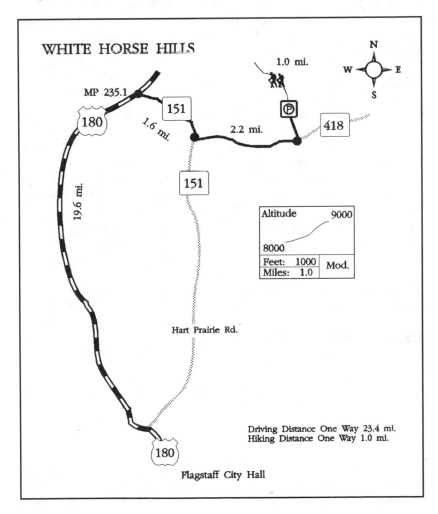

WILD BILL HILL

General Information
Location Map E2
Wing Mountain USGS Map
Coconino Forest Service Map

Personal
Favorite

Driving Distance One Way: 21.85 miles (Time 40 minutes)
Access Road: High clearance only, Last 2.0 miles rough dirt road
Hiking Distance One Way: 1.5 miles (Time 1 hour)
How Strenuous: Moderate
Features: Hoodoos in volcano's center, Views

NUTSHELL: This mountain 21.85 miles west of Flagstaff is located at the east edge of Government Prairie and is an extinct volcano. It is easily climbed to enjoy a look into the heart of the volcano and views over the prairie. **A personal favorite**.

DIRECTIONS:
From Flagstaff City Hall Go:
North on Humphreys Street for 0.60 miles. Turn left at the stoplight onto Columbus Avenue and follow it around a big curve to the north. You will see the street signs call this road Columbus at first, then Ft. Valley Road and then Highway 180. Stay on Highway 180 to the 14.5 miles point (MP 230), where an unpaved road takes off to the left. Turn left onto this road, FR 245, and follow it to the 17.6 mile point where it intersects FR 171. Turn left onto FR 171 and follow it to the 19.75 mile point, where FR 156 goes off to the right. Turn right on FR 156 and take it to the 21.35 mile point. Turn left on a primitive unmarked road and follow it to the 21.85 miles point, where you park. You will be 0.25 miles away from the hill.

TRAILHEAD: You will see Wild Bill Hill to your left. There is no trail. Just walk across country to the hill and climb it to the saddle.

DESCRIPTION: Wild Bill Hill is one of many hills that form a ring around Government Prairie. Several of them provide good hikes and are listed in this book.
This hill is shaped like a three-leaf clover. When you reach the top of the saddle, at an aspen grove, about 0.75 miles from where you parked, you will see a bare knob to your right, a wooded knob (the highest) to your left, and the smallest knob to the north. We suggest that you climb the bare knob first. The views from there are great. You have good lines of sight in all directions except to the north, where the lowest knob blocks your view. Out over Government Prairie you can see for miles. If you know where to look, you can

see the Beale Road coming across from Government Mountain. In fact, you can see it here better than you can as you walk the old road. See **Beale Road on Government Prairie**.

Then come back to the saddle. You will see a game trail there headed to the west. Follow it about 0.15 miles and you will come to a place where you look down into the core of the volcano. Here is a wonderful moonlike landscape of hoodoos. You can walk to the north knob on a game trail from there, though the views are not so good because of the timber,

If you want to climb the highest knob, don't do it from the hoodoos even though you see a game trail going west, because it is very steep there. . Come back to the first saddle and ascend it from there.

These three knobs are fascinating. The soil of which each is composed is quite different. The highest wooded knob is made of loose red cinders. The lowest knob is of brown cinders. The bare knob is of hard packed red cinders with many loose rocks on the surface.

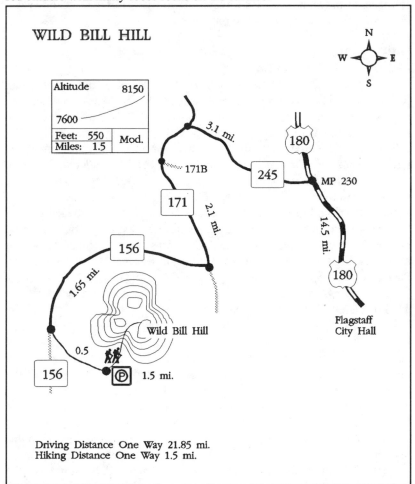

WILDCAT HILL

General Information
Location Map F3
Flagstaff East USGS Map
Coconino Forest Map

Driving Distance One Way: 7.0 miles (Time 20 minutes)
Access Road: All cars, Last 0.20 miles rough cinder road
Hiking Distance One Way: 0.1 miles (Time 30 minutes)
How Strenuous: Moderate
Features: Cave, Pit house ruins, Rock Art, Scenic canyon

NUTSHELL: Located on the fringe of town, this canyon suddenly appears as a deep slash. On its steep lava walls are several panels of rock art and a cave. On top are the remains of several pit houses.

DIRECTIONS:
From Flagstaff City Hall Go:
     East on Route 66 (Santa Fe). Highway 89 runs concurrently with Route 66 (Santa Fe) as the highway goes through Flagstaff, so you will see road signs with both designations. At 3.8 miles (MP 418.2/200) you will come to a fork, where East Old U.S. 66 goes to the right. Turn right onto Old 66 and follow it to the 5.8 mile point (MP 202), where you will see a street sign to your left marked *El Paso Flagstaff* and beyond that a sign for the *Wildcat Hill Waste Water Treatment Plant.* Turn left onto this good gravel road. At 5.95 miles you will see a road going left. Ignore it. At 6.4 miles you will see the turnoff to the El Paso Station. Ignore it. The road will curve around the back of the El Paso property and you will reach another fork at 6.8 miles. You can see the canyon from here. Take the right fork, which runs along the rim of the canyon and follow it to the 7.0 mile point where you will see an old barbed wire fence. Park here.

TRAILHEAD: There are no trail signs.

DESCRIPTION: You have parked on a high point just off the rim of the canyon. Walk over to the canyon and take a look at it. It is a strange gash in the earth. On each end of the canyon is gentle wide country; then suddenly the earth's crust split and made this steep narrow rock-lined canyon. You will see a stream flowing in the bottom of the canyon. Beware! The water you see there is treated sewage coming out of the wastewater treatment plant.
     You do not actually walk down to the bottom of the canyon on this hike, but stay up on a bench about a third of the way down.
     Begin by walking downhill, looking to your left. You will see the

remains of pithouses on the rim of the canyon to the left of where you parked, at a place where the canyon walls are not so steep and sheer. From there come back toward the parking spot, working your way down to a lower ledge at the base of the cliffs and boulders. You will see a fairly deep cave here, its roof blackened by the smoke of countless fires. Beyond, look on every smooth boulder face for rock art. The art seems scattered without a pattern.

There are several panels. We counted at least six. The art is rather basic, not as elaborate as that encountered at other sites.

When you reach the end of the area of the sheer cliffs, walk back up to the top and return to your car. There is a bit of rock art across the canyon, but it is hardly worth the effort. The most interesting sights are on your side.

There is a major drawback to this interesting, scenic spot: the effluent pouring out of the sewage plant. To be blunt about it, it stinks. We have been here in winter and in summer and winter was better because the smell was much milder. Locals calls this place Sewer Canyon.

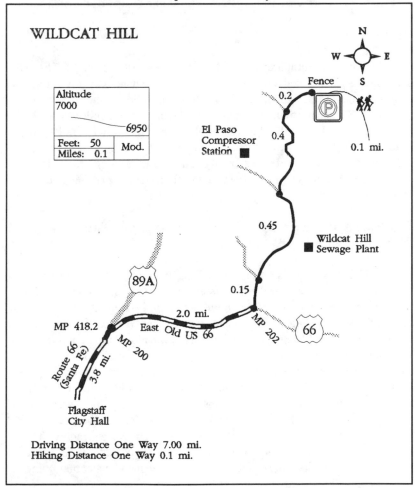

WILSON MEADOW

General Information
Location Map E3 ·
Humphreys Peak and Wing Mountain USGS Maps
Coconino Forest Service Map

Driving Distance One Way: 14.9 miles (Time 35 minutes)
Access Road: All cars, Last 4.7 miles good gravel
Hiking Distance One Way: 1.0 miles (Time 30 minutes)
How Strenuous: Easy
Features: Aspen groves, Meadow Views

NUTSHELL: Located on the San Francisco Peaks, about 15 miles north of Flagstaff, this short, easy walk displays the alpine beauty of the area.

DIRECTIONS:
From Flagstaff City Hall Go:
North on Humphreys Street for 0.60 miles, to the stoplight. Then take a left onto a street marked Columbus Avenue, which changes to Ft. Valley Road as it makes a curve to the north. Outside the city limits, the road becomes Highway 180, a major route to the Grand Canyon. At 10.2 miles (MP 225.1), turn right onto FR 151, the Hart Prairie Road, and follow it to the 14.7 miles point, where an unmarked gravel road takes off to the right. This access is rough because of exposed rocks, but it is only 0.2 miles long. Turn right and drive to the 14.9 miles point, where you will find a fenced parking place. Park there.

TRAILHEAD: You will see a "Road Closed" sign at a gate in the parking area fence. Walk up this road.

DESCRIPTION: The sign at the parking lot identifies this merely as a "Wildlife Habitat Area" and it is not named on any map that we could find. You will see a reference to the Wilson Foundation on the sign. As we made this beautiful hike, enjoying the flowers, the meadow and the views, it occurred to us that it would be fitting to call it the Wilson Meadow hike in honor of The Wilson Foundation, for it spearheaded a fight two decades ago to prevent the commercial development of Hart Prairie, under the slogan, "Save the Peaks." Had it not been for it bearing the brunt of years of costly litigation, this pristine area would now be covered with condos. Thanks, folks! This is a wonderful place and we are grateful that you saved it for nature lovers.

The hike consists of following a closed road up the meadow. This is a wet area with underground water marked by lines of water loving shrubs. After one half mile the tracks peter out near a large metal water tank lying on its side. No problem. Just keep hiking toward the top of the meadow, to the tree line.

From the half mile point you begin to get wonderful views. Turn around every so often and enjoy them. Three major mountains and an infinity of hills cover the landscape. Beginning on your right hand, the tallest mountains are Kendrick, Sitgreaves and Bill Williams. The hike ends at a fence at the top of the meadow.

We made the hike in mid-August and the meadow was full of flowers and high grass. Instead of going to the fence, we veered to the right near the top, into a grove of spruce and aspen, so cool on a hot day. The rippling of the wind in the aspen leaves sounded like water running. As we approached, we flushed a fawn out of his bed of ferns and he blinked at us sleepily before bounding away. Almost every one of the aspens in the grove shows signs of having been rubbed by antlers. At dusk several deer came out to feed. We saw abundant elk sign but no elk this day.

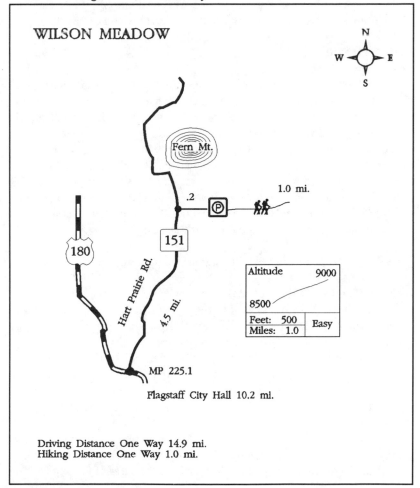

WILSON MEADOW

N
W—◯—E
S

Fern Mt.

1.0 mi.

.2

Ⓟ

151

180

Hart Prairie Rd.

4.5 mi.

Altitude	9000
8500	
Feet: 500	Easy
Miles: 1.0	

MP 225.1

Flagstaff City Hall 10.2 mi.

Driving Distance One Way 14.9 mi.
Hiking Distance One Way 1.0 mi.

WINTER CABIN TRAIL

General Information
Location Map F2
Sycamore Point USGS Map
Coconino Forest Service Map

Driving Distance One Way: 26 miles (Time 1 hour)
Access Road: All cars, Last 22.4 miles dirt road, some rough spots
Hiking Distance One Way: 1.5 miles (Time 1 hour)
How Strenuous: Moderate
Features: Views, Sycamore Canyon access, Cabin

NUTSHELL: Located about 26 miles southwest of Flagstaff, this is a scenic trail in its own right as well as being an access trail into Sycamore Canyon. There is an interesting cabin in an idyllic glade at the end of this hike.

DIRECTIONS:
From Flagstaff City Hall Go:
    West one block on Route 66 (Santa Fe), then south (left) beneath the railroad overpass on Sitgreaves Street. The street name will change to Milton Road as you go farther. At 0.50 miles you will reach a Y intersection. The right fork is named Old West US Highway 66. Take it. You will soon leave town. At 2.6 miles you will reach a paved road going to the left. This is the Woody Mountain Road, FR 231. Take it. It is paved about a mile and then turns into a cinder road. At 16.6 miles you will intersect FR 538. Turn right onto FR 538 and follow it to the 25 mile point, where it intersects FR 538H. Turn right on FR 538H and take 538H to its end at 26 miles. This road may be rather rough. You will find a parking area at the end of the road.

TRAILHEAD: You will see a big sign at the parking area.

DESCRIPTION: Take a look at Sycamore Canyon from the rim before you start down the main trail. You will find a footpath to the left of the main trail at the beginning of the main trail. This side path goes out to the rim. Sycamore Canyon is a huge wild canyon and the view from the top will take your breath away. If it doesn't, you are either insensitive or very jaded.

    The main trail is a maintained footpath which goes through an attractive mixed forest with oaks and other trees adding variety to the prevailing Ponderosa pines. Although the trail is maintained and the footing is good, it is quite steep.

    Winter Cabin is located at the 1.5 mile point, on a shelf of land. A nearby stream flows intermittently. The glade where the cabin is situated is very scenic, a remote peaceful paradise far from the cares of the world. You may not want to come back out.

The cabin is an old log relic with a corrugated metal roof. It is still in good condition. It is hard to tell how the place got its name, Winter Cabin, because you can't imagine cowboys surviving the winter here. Heavy snows fall in this area and once the snow season begins in the autumn, this place would be totally cut off from the outside world.

From the cabin the trail goes on down 1.5 miles farther to Ott Lake (a misnomer, as it is usually dry) and from there goes another 2.0 miles into the bottom of Sycamore Canyon. Don't try hiking through Sycamore Canyon from beginning to end unless you are prepared for it. Unprepared people die there.

Stopping at the cabin makes a dandy day hike that can be handled by almost anyone who is reasonably fit.

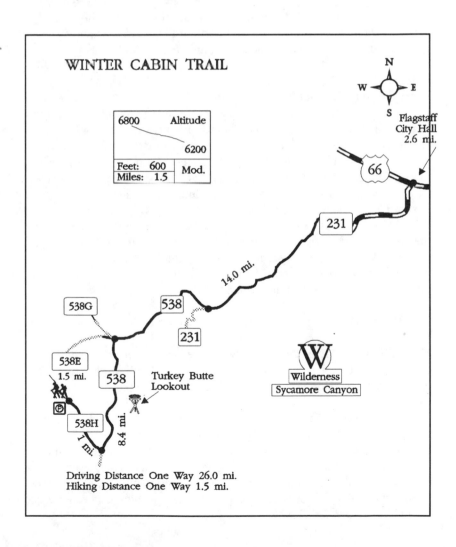

WINTER CABIN TRAIL

Altitude	
6800	
	6200
Feet: 600	Mod.
Miles: 1.5	

Flagstaff City Hall 2.6 mi.

66

231

14.0 mi.

538G

538

231

538E
1.5 mi.

538

Turkey Butte Lookout

W
Wilderness
Sycamore Canyon

538H

8.4 mi.

1 mi.

Driving Distance One Way 26.0 mi.
Hiking Distance One Way 1.5 mi.

WUPATKI RUIN TRAIL

General Information
Location Map E4
Wupatki SW USGS Map
Coconino Forest Service Map

Driving Distance One Way: 37.8 miles (Time 60 minutes)
Access Road: All cars, All paved
Hiking Distance, Complete Loop: 0.40 miles (Time 45 minutes)
How Strenuous: Easy
Features: Views, Indian ruins

NUTSHELL: This is a fascinating easy trail starting at the Visitor Center in Wupatki National Monument 37 miles north of Flagstaff. It features pueblo ruins, a ball court, an amphitheater and a unique blow hole.

DIRECTIONS:
From Flagstaff City Hall Go:
  East, curving to north on Route 66 (Santa Fe). As you leave the city limits you will see that Route 66 (Santa Fe) is also Highway 89. Follow Highway 89 north out into the country. At 16.4 miles (MP 430.3) you will reach the entrance to Sunset Crater National Monument. Turn right on the road into Sunset Crater. This road is also known as FR 545. At 18.4 miles you will reach a ticket booth where you will have to pay admission. Just beyond that is the Visitor Center, which is worth a look. At 26.0 miles you reach the Painted Desert Vista. This is a lookout point where we recommend stopping to enjoy the view. Under the right lighting conditions it is superb. At 37.8 miles you enter the Wupatki National Monument, which adjoins Sunset Crater and you will see the road to the Wupatki Visitor Center to your left. Take the road to the Visitor Center and park in the parking lot there.

TRAILHEAD: The trail starts at the right hand side of the Visitor Center.

DESCRIPTION: Even though this is a "tame" hike, being the furthest thing from a wilderness adventure, it is very interesting and well worth taking. This is a favorite excursion for visiting relatives. It will keep even the small fry happy.
  The setting is lovely. The ruins are situated on the side of a small valley, where exposed layers of Moenkopi (red) sandstone provided plentiful building materials. The Sinagua Indians, who built the pueblo, fitted their construction around some of the existing boulders in fascinating ways so that they could use the boulders as much as possible to serve as walls and buttresses. Across the valley you can see a couple of small pueblos, but you are not

permitted to visit them. Beyond the far end of the valley you can see the Painted Desert, a vast multicolored area.

From the pueblo at the top of the valley you walk downhill to an amphitheater, then to the valley floor to a ball court and a blow hole. The blow hole is wonderful. During the cool hours of the day, in the morning and evening, the blow hole draws in air. When the day is hot, during the afternoon, the blow hole expels air. It is like some giant breathing. The breaths can be quite forceful, causing a loud rushing noise.

Along the trail are posted several markers which are keyed into a trail guide. You pick up the guide at the beginning of the trail. If you want to keep it, you put fifty cents into the box at the end of the trail. If you do not want to keep it, you return it to the box.

There are other ruin sites throughout the Wupatki National Monument that you can visit. All of them are worth a look if you like ruins. Check at the Visitor Center for details.

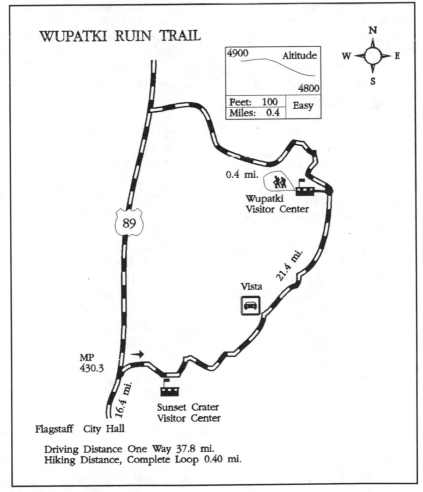

INDEX

A

A-1 Mountain 8
A(u)bineau Canyon Trail 14
AB Young Trail 10
Antelope Hills 12

B

Babe's Hole 16
Beale Road Hikes:
    Government Mt. West 18
    Government Prairie 20
    Laws Spring 22
    Turkey Tanks 188
Bear Jaw Canyon Trail 24
Benham Trail 26
Bill Williams Mt. Trail 28
Bill Williams Mountain Hikes:
    Benham Trail 26
    Bill Williams Mt. Trail 28
    Clover Spring 40
Bismarck Lake Elk Preserve 30
Brookbank Trail 32
Bull Basin Trail 34

C

Cabins and Cabin Ruins:
    Antelope Hills 12
    Babe's Hole 16
    Beale Rd. on Gvt. Prairie 20
    Bull Basin Trail 34
    Dorsey Spring Trail 54
    Dow Spr. to Pomeroy Tnk. 56
    Dry Lake Hills 58
    Hog Hill Trail 82
    Inner Basin Trail 88
    Kelsey-Winter Cabin Trail 96
    Kendrick Mountain Trail 98
    Overland Trail 136
    Pumpkin Trail 140
    Secret Mountain 162
    Sycamore Rim Trail 178
    Veit Spring 190
    Winter Cabin Trail 214

Casner Mountain Trail North 36
Chavez Pass 38
Clover Spring 40
Coconino Rim Trail 42
Connector Trail 44
Cookstove Trail 46
Cosnino Caves 188

D

Davenport Hill Trail 48
Dogtown Nature Trail 50
Doney Trail 52
Dorsey Spring Trail 54
Dow Spring to Pomeroy Tnk. 56
Dry Lake Hills 58
Dry Lake Hills/Mt. Elden Hikes:
    Brookbank Trail 32
    Dry Lake Hills 58
    Elden Lookout Trail 62
    Elden Pueblo 64
    Elden Red Hills Trail 66
    Elden Skyline Trail 68
    Fat Man's Loop 70
    Little Elden 112
    Oldham Trail #1 128
    Oldham Trail #2 130
    Pipeline Trail 138
    Rocky Ridge Trail 152
    Sandy Seep 158
    Schultz Creek Trail 160
    Sunset Trail 176

E

Eagle Rock 60
Elden Lookout Trail 62
Elden Pueblo 64
Elden Red Hills Trail 66
Elden Skyline Trail 68

F

Fat Man's Loop 70
Fisher Point 72
Flagstaff Urban Trail System:

Old Lowell Observatory 132
Rio de Flag Trail 150
Sinclair Wash Trail 164

G

Government Knoll 74
Government Prairie Hikes:
Antelope Hills 12
Beale Rd., Gvt. Prairie W. 18
Beale Rd. on Gvt. Prairie 20
Government Knoll 74
Klostermeyer Hill 102
Rain Tank Hill 144
Wild Bill Hill 208
Grand Canyon Area Hikes:
Coconino Rim Trail 42
Red Butte 146
Ten-X Nature Trail 180
Grand Falls 76
Griffiths Spring Canyon 78

H

Harding Spring 80
Hog Hill Trail 82
Humphreys Trail 84

I

I-40 Parks Nature Trail 86
Indian Ruins:
Chavez Pass 38
Doney Trail 52
Elden Pueblo 64
Keyhole Sink 100
Old Caves Crater 126
Strawberry Crater 174
Turkey Hill 186
Turkey Tanks 188
Walnut Canyon Island 194
Walnut Canyon Rim 196
Wildcat Hill 210
Wupatki Ruin 216
Inner Basin Trail 88

K

KA Hill 90
Kachina Trail 92
Kelsey Spring Trail 94
Kelsey-Winter Cabin Trail 96
Kendrick Mountain Hikes:
Bull Basin Trail 34
Connector Trail 44
Kendrick Mountain Trail 98
Pumpkin Trail 140
Kendrick Mountain Trail 98
Keyhole Sink 100
Klostermeyer Hill 102

L

Lakeview Trail 104
Lava Flow Trail 106
Lava River Cave 108
Lava Tubes:
Lava Flow Trail 106
Lava River Cave 108
Slate Lake Lava Cave 166
Ledges Trail 110
Little Elden 112
Little Round Mountain 114

M

Maxwell Trail 116
Meteor Crater 118
Mormon Lake Area Hikes:
Lakeview Trail 104
Ledges Trail 110
Mormon Lake Nature Tr. 120
Mormon Mountain 122
Mormon Lake Nature Trail 120
Mormon Mountain 122
Mountain Bike Rides 222-224

O

Oak Creek Canyon Hikes:
AB Young Trail 10
Cookstove Trail 46

Harding Spring Trail 80
Oak Creek Vista 124
Purtymun Trail 142
Sterling Pass 172
Thomas Point 182
West Fork 202
Oak Creek Vista 124
Old Caves Crater 126
Oldham Trail #1 128
Oldham Trail #2 130
Old Lowell Observatory Rd. 132
O'Leary Peak 134
Overland Road 136
Overland Road Hikes:
Dow Spr. to Pomeroy Tk. 56
KA Hill 90
Overland Road 136
Sycamore Trail 178

P

Personal Favorites:
Babe's Hole 16
Kachina Trail 92
Red Mountain 148
Secret Mountain 162
Sunset Trail 176
Veit Spring 190
West Fork 202
Wild Bill Hill 208
Pipeline Trail 138
Pumpkin Trail 140
Purtymun Trail 142

R

Rain Tank Hill 144
Red Butte 146
Red Mountain 148
Rio de Flag Trail 150
Rock Art Sites:
Beale Rd. to Laws Spring 22
Keyhole Sink 100
Veit Spring 190
Wildcat Hill 210

Rocky Ridge Trail 152
RS Hill 154

S

Saddle Mountain 156
Sandy Seep 158
San Francisco Peaks Hikes:
Abineau Canyon Trail 14
Bear Jaw Canyon Trail 24
Bismarck Lake Elk Presv. 30
Humphreys Trail 84
Inner Basin Trail 88
Kachina Trail 92
Tunnel Road 184
Veit Spring 190
Walker Lake 192
Weatherford Canyon 198
Weatherford Trail 200
Wilson Meadow 212
Schultz Creek Trail 160
Secret Mountain 162
Sinclair Wash Trail 164
Slate Lake Lava Cave 166
Slate Mountain 168
Springs, Hikes that Contain:
Babe's Hole 16
Beale Rd. to Laws Spring 22
Clover Spring 40
Cookstove Trail 46
Dorsey Spring Trail 54
Dow Spr. to Pomeroy Tk. 56
Griffiths Spring Canyon 78
Hog Hill Trail 82
Inner Basin Trail 88
Kelsey Spring Trail 94
Kelsey-Winter Cabin Trail 96
Little Elden 112
Overland Road 136
Sandy Seep 158
Secret Mountain 162
Veit Spring 190
Winter Cabin Trail 214
Spring Valley Hikes:

INDEX

Eagle Rock 60
RS Hill 154
Spring Valley X-Country 170
Spring Valley Cross-Country 170
Sterling Pass 172
Strawberry Crater 174
Sunset Crater/Wupatki Area:
Doney Trail 52
Lava Flow Trail 106
O'Leary Peak 134
Wupatki Ruin Trail 216
Sunset Trail 176
Sycamore Canyon Area Hikes:
Babe's Hole 16
Casner Mt. Trail North 36
Dorsey Spring Trail 54
Dow Spr. to Pomeroy Tk. 56
Hog Hill Trail 82
Kelsey Spring Trail 94
Kelsey-Winter Cabin Trail 96
Sycamore Rim Trail 178
Winter Cabin Trail 214
Sycamore Rim Trail 178

Watershed Rd. (*see* Tunnel) 184
Weatherford Canyon 198
Weatherford Trail 200
West Fork 202
West Fork Head 204
White Horse Hills 206
Wild Bill Hill 208
Wildcat Hill 210
Wilson Meadow 212
Winter Cabin Trail 214
Wupatki Ruin Trail 216

T
Ten-X Nature Trail 180
Thomas Point 182
Tunnel Road 184
Turkey Hill 186
Turkey Tanks 188

V
Veit Spring 190

W
Walker Lake 192
Walnut Canyon Island Trail 194
Walnut Canyon Rim Trail 196
Waterfalls, Hikes that Contain:
Dow Sp. to Pomeroy Tk. 56
Grand Falls 76
Sycamore Rim Trail 178

MOUNTAIN BIKES, TRAILS SUITABLE FOR

Beale Road, Government Mountain West: A nice ride with historical interest. Instead of riding the hike portion, bike on down to FR 115 and go right. Ride up 115 for 1.5 miles, and then go left on FR 2030 to Laws Spring and check it out.

Beale Road on Government Prairie: Once you get out onto Government Prairie, you will see all kinds of ride possibilities on the roads there. A great place for biking.

Brookbank Trail: Some steep portions, with genuine stump jumping through the woods.

Casner Mountain Trail North: Wonderful scenery. Some steep pulls. It is possible for strong riders to go down the south face of Casner Mountain and ride to Sedona. Wilderness Area on all sides. Stay on roads.

Coconino Rim: An easy trail. You can go for many miles.

Davenport Hill: A nice ride on a summer day. You'll have to carry up some of the steep parts.

Dry Lake Hills: Popular because it is so close to town. Good exploring, fairly level. Connections to other trails in Mt. Elden/Dry Lake Hills trail system.

Eagle Rock: A couple of steep parts, otherwise a good ride in pretty country.

Elden Red Hills: Do this one from the top. An excellent ride. Trail is in good condition.

Elden Skyline Trail: This is an easy ride along the ridgecrest of Elden. Don't try to go down the Elden Lookout Trail; it is too steep.

Fat Man's Loop: A couple of rough spots, one getting your rig through boulders.

Fisher Point: A local favorite. Many riders go in from Lone Tree Road. You could start as the book does, then exit onto Lone Tree.

Grand Falls: A long ride with a good payoff. Deep black cinders in spots can cause poor traction. Choking dust at times.

KA Hill: If you like to do hills, this one is about a 700 foot climb with good exploring in the vicinity.

Keyhole Sink: This is a short, fun ride from the parking space. You might want to throw in a stretch of Route 66 on this one.

Lava River Cave: Park your vehicle at Highway 180 and bike to the cave. Good roads all around this area.

Ledges Trail: Not very hard. Good viewpoint. Lots of good roads in this Mormon Lake area.

Little Elden: Good trails and roads, no major climb or drop. Interesting country.

Little Round Mountain: Wonderful scenery with great backroads. Stay on the roads and don't ride in the adjacent Wilderness Area.

Old Caves Crater: Easy to reach, fascinating to see, but deep black cinders cause traction problems in places.

Oldham Trail #1: Good trail for bikes and popular. You climb through woods to emerge onto Elden Lookout Rd., on which you can return .

Oldham Trail #2: A very steep pitch on a narrow twisting trail that winds through deep woods. Not for beginners. Go from top to bottom.

Old Lowell Observatory: Primo trail, wide and even, to the top of Mars Hill. From there go onto Observatory Mesa, a large area with good roads.

O'Leary Peak: Lots of walking for all but the strongest riders, but good views and a rocket ride coming down.

Overland Road: For stumpjumpers. Horse drawn wagons made it on this road 100 years ago. Well marked, fun to follow markers.

Pipeline Trail: Popular. You can start at Buffalo Park and exit at the Elden Lookout Trailhead by the mall in East Flagstaff.

Rain Tank Hill: Don't ride on the hill, just inspect the rain tank, scout Government Prairie and take a ride over the inviting area roads..

Rio de Flag Trail: Like riding on a road, wide, well-graded and level.

Rocky Ridge Trail: Fairly easy. Emerge onto Elden Lookout Road and come back that way.

RS Hill: Good ride. One exciting drop. Nice country. You may want to explore beautiful Spring Valley area while there. Many roads.

Saddle Mountain: Long and steep but good road. Great views.

Sandy Seep: A new (1991) trail. Easy to reach. Good for bikes.

Schultz Creek: Fine ride, but watch for branches in your teeth.

Sinclair Wash: This urban trail is in excellent shape, fairly flat. Goes from NAU area to (when complete) Ft. Tuthill.

Slate Lake Lava Cave: Park your truck just off Highway 180 and ride the roads to the cave.

Slate Mountain: A long hard climb. Great views. Uses old roads, so is wide and clear.

Spring Valley Cross-Country Trail: Good thrill drop at Eagle Pass, otherwise mostly level.

Strawberry Crater: Park just off the highway and ride to the crater, where you must stop as it is a Wilderness Area.

Sunset Trail: Very good, interesting terrain, but challenging stretches.

Tunnel Road: One of the best. The road is a corridor of land excluded from the Wilderness Area, so it is open to bikes. The Bear Jaw and Abineau trails at the end of the road are in the Wilderness, so can't be ridden.

Turkey Hill: A hard ride, requires carrying. A zipper downhill.

Walker Lake: A very pleasant ride to a scenic spot. Easy. Good road.

White Horse Hills: Hard in spots due to steepness. Old roads all the way. Great views of north sides of Peaks.

Wildcat Hill: Easy ride. From the rock art site you will see many interesting road possibilities through the area.

NOTE: We have not personally tested the bike rides, and are relying on what we have seen and heard from friends who are bikers.

RULES OF THE TRAIL

Artifacts: Leave potsherds, arrowheads and other artifacts where you find them.

Aspens: Don't carve on the white bark of these lovely trees. Cutting the bark opens them to infection and possible death.

Bikes: Stay on roads and trails. You cannot ride your bike inside a Wilderness Area. Some people will go into an area on a road and then sneak onto a wilderness trail. These scofflaws cause road closures. Abuse it and lose it.

Cabins: Northern Arizona's climate is hard on cabins and they are scarce. Treat the few remaining ones gently. Don't climb on them, pry boards off or go digging for buried treasure.

Caves: Though caves appear indestructible, they are actually quite fragile. Whatever happens in them stays, as they are not self-cleaning. No graffiti, no smoking, no fires. Don't urinate or defecate in them or leave glass that might break. No firearms or fireworks. Slate Lake Lava Cave is still semi-primitive. Stay on its marked path and don't touch its lava or mud formations.

Dogs: If you take your dog along on a hike, it should be on a leash.

Garbage: Pack it in, pack it out.

Rock Art: Don't touch it. Skin oils cause deterioration. Professionals don't even apply chalk in order to photograph rock art these days.

Ruins: Just look, don't touch. Preserve them. Don't pothunt, climb walls or do anything else that might harm them.

Springs: Springs are vital to the survival of wildlife. Camp no closer than 200 feet. Don't do anything that could pollute a spring like bathing in it or throwing objects in it. Never use one for a latrine. As for yourself, even the purest looking water may contain harmful microbes. Today, the fear of giardia makes the wise hiker cautious about drinking untreated water.

Trails: Stay on trails. They have been designed not only to provide access but also to bypass areas that can be harmed by people walking on them. Don't cut switchbacks. It is disheartening to see how fast a trail can be destroyed by careless use.

Wilderness Areas: These are special places. The goal is to leave them unimpaired for future use and enjoyment as a wilderness. Here the hiker is king. No mechanized travel is permitted within them, not even bicycles. Though they appear very rugged, they are in fact quite fragile environments. Use them lightly. Leave no trace. They are a gift.